RIDING THE RIM
To Save America's Wetlands

TERRY L. FORRETTE

authorHOUSE®

AuthorHouse™
1663 Liberty Drive
Bloomington, IN 47403
www.authorhouse.com
Phone: 1-800-839-8640

First published by AuthorHouse 8/9/2010

ISBN: 978-1-4520-6168-9 (e)
ISBN: 978-1-4520-6167-2 (sc)
ISBN: 978-1-4520-6166-5 (hc)

Library of Congress Control Number: 2010910966

Printed in the United States of America

This book is printed on acid-free paper.

Terry L. Forrette
P.O. Box 81
Mandeville, LA 70470
www.tlforrette.com

Front cover photo used with permission from America's WETLAND Foundation.

To Linda

The joy and happiness in my life

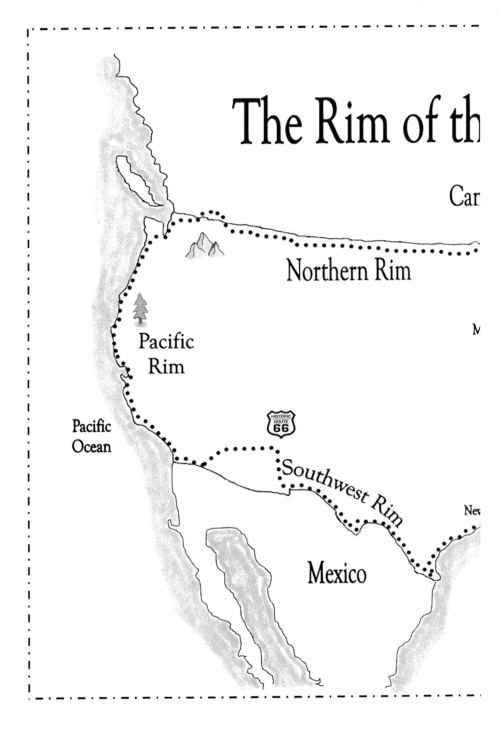

The Rim of th

Car

Northern Rim

Pacific
Rim

Pacific
Ocean

Southwest Rim

Mexico

Nev

ie United States

iada

Maritimes

Atlantic
Ocean

ladison, WI

Eastern
Rim

Charleston, SC

v Orleans, LA

Gulf Coast

N

W — *E*

S

Illustrated by Phillip Forrette

Key West, FL

Gulf of Mexico

Acknowledgement

I would like to acknowledge the contributions of my friend and collaborator George Sanchez to this book. The shape and texture of the book is due in no small part to him. He helped turn a journal into a narrative, and brought life to the feelings and thoughts that accompanied me on my journey. In the end we shared the journey and emerged on the other side, brethren of the road. JJ and Adam, thank you for your editing prowess.

I also need to recognize the many people who helped take *Riding The Rim* from an idea in my living room to a 16,500 mile motorcycle trip around the perimeter of the United States. America's WETLAND Foundation who partnered with us when no one else could see our vision, the Coast Guardians for their financial support, Aerostich for keeping me safe and warm, my family and friends who kept the kitchen light on, the generosity of Northshore H.O.G. and the riders who I met on the road, and last but not least Duke Johns and the team at Medical Specialties who shared my belief that a motorcycling environmentalist could make a difference.

Contents

Introduction

This is the story of a three month, 16,500 mile motorcycle trip around the perimeter of the lower 48 states of the United States of America. It is also about the devastation brought by Hurricane Katrina because of the loss of Louisiana's wetlands. Finally, it is about discovery— my discovery of those places, their peoples, and, in the end, of myself. This is a story of Riding the Rim— my crusade against a man-made catastrophe and my quest to educate the country about the devastating consequences of the loss of America's wetlands.

Part I:
How Could We Have
Let This Happen?

Before The Ride

O nce, well, maybe twice in a lifetime, everyone gets the chance to do something significant, I mean really significant! (I must qualify this by saying that this does not include the birth of my children, meeting my wife, nor saving a person choking on his meal in a restaurant.) The events I am talking about are those times when, with forethought and conscious direction, we set about a series of events that create change, that make a difference. In my case it was the creation of a project called Riding the Rim. In the late summer of 2005 I set into motion a series of events that I hoped would bring about, real positive change for my state and in turn for the country.

The spark of the idea that eventually turned into Riding the Rim (RTR) began in Mandeville - a sleepy small town, not 25 miles from New Orleans, Louisiana and was in direct response to the catastrophic events wrought by the failure of the levees in New Orleans, brought about, in part, by Hurricane Katrina, and, even more so by the reckless folly of Man. As has been reported in books, magazines and newspaper articles, as well as television news stories and documentaries, Hurricane Katrina caused destruction so vast that New Orleans is still recovering more than four years after it made landfall.

More specifically, however, RTR was the result of my new-found awareness of the vital role that the wetland areas play in hurricane protection. Make no mistake, the flooding of New Orleans was a man-made disaster brought about by an ill-conceived and poorly executed system of levees protecting the city. However, that would not have mattered had not the wetlands south of the city been disappearing at an ever-increasing rate over the last fifty years.

In 1965 Hurricane Betsy actually delivered a harder blow to the city than Katrina, yet the flooding was minor and due, once again to the man-made failure of a few levees. Though it was a stronger storm than Katrina when it hit New Orleans, Betsy's wrath had been mitigated on its way to the city because of the existence of the wetlands. Wetland areas keep storm surge down by dissipating the force of the incoming water and the vegetation of the wetland areas slow the winds by attrition. Since Betsy, the wetlands have been all but destroyed by commerce. Since the 1930's, America's ever-increasing gluttony in matters of petroleum has caused widespread utilization of wetland areas by the petroleum industry. Canals have been cut. The consequent intrusion of salt water has killed vegetation. Without vegetation to hold the land together, it has melted into the Gulf. Are these companies the villains? No. They were simply doing what the nation demanded— produce oil.

The failure was one of vision. The true failure was an inability to grasp the fundamental inter-connectedness of all life. We are part of nature and responsible to nature. We have known that for thousands of years. (I exclude from this all those who deny that an environmental crisis even exists, for there is absolutely no way to breach defenses that are impenetrable by the weight of evidence.) Today we have begun to face the fact that we have squandered our environment, not simply in America, but in the world. Aside from a certain amount of hand-wringing and pious pontificating, no significant action had been taken. There were plans. There was talk. There was no significant action. From this realization, it is but a short step to understanding the role played by all these natural features in making possible life as we have come to live it, both in these United States, and around the globe. This short-sightedness led to the disaster that we lump under the umbrella called Katrina. Things were going to have to change. We were going to have to reverse this. Someone was going to have to step up.

Former President Bill Clinton in his book, *Giving: How Each of us Can Change the World*, cites several examples of people who intentionally set about to create a change in their lives as well as in the lives of others. He cites examples such as the establishment of the Gates Foundation by Bill and Melinda Gates, a foundation that addresses education in the United States and the availability of health care in third world countries. President Clinton tells the story of a man who started his own bank to help impoverished Bangladeshi workers create their own companies. Giving need not be the province of the wealthy, nor need it consist of dramatic actions. Giving can be something as simple as the 6 year old girl who organized beach clean-ups on the California coast.

In his book, President Clinton suggests that we all have the capacity to give of ourselves. We may give of our money, our time, our expertise, or our experience. It is in the process of giving that we discover that we not only give to others, but to ourselves. It has taken a long time and a gigantic disaster to my home state for me to fully understand this simple lesson: What I give to another, I give to myself, and, secondly, that it is only through giving that I truly know what I have. Perhaps I was the one who was going to have to step up.

I have always thought of myself as someone who was a giver, especially in my role as a teacher. I saw myself as a person who gave understanding to difficult subject matter and showed patience to my students as they struggled in their learning processes. And, though I have received praise and thanks from countless students and learners in my many years of education and training, it was not until my experiences with this project, Riding the Rim that I truly understood what is meant by the act of giving to others. When that awareness came to me, when my eyes were opened, my hand and heart opened as well. By taking action, by giving of my time and effort, I offered a gift to my fellows and because of what I gave; I was able to receive the gifts that others had for me.

I was struck by the message in Steven Covey's *The 8th Habit: From Effectiveness to Greatness* in which he urges all of us to find our voice and to help others to find theirs. That "voice of greatness" provides significance for us, and that significance helps us lead a life centered on passion. However, as Covey points out it is important that we help others to find their voice, so that we, as a collective consciousness can effect change.

This, then, is the story of a trip I made around the perimeter of the United States, speaking about the wetlands, asking that all of us take individual responsibility for the environment, being an exemplar of what one person was willing to do. This book also reflects my growing awareness, and then my deep appreciation, of what I discovered about the act of giving. It reflects my appreciation, in turn, for the wonderful gifts I received from those whose lives I touched on my motorcycle trip around the perimeter of the United States. Although I did not know it at the time, this trip became one of the most significant moments in my life.

The Wind from Katrina

Most people don't understand the way events unfold. We see the devastating power of a storm, but we don't know that it began as little more than an eddy in the dry Saharan lands of North Africa that spun over the Atlantic. Then, sucking up water vapor, its rotation tightened until it built, then grew, and then became a killer storm. In the same way, if a few clods of dirt are swallowed by the Gulf because of a boat passing their banks, it hardly matters, but when those clods become football-field sized and the coast shrinks and barrier islands disappear and the Gulf approaches your doorstep, it matters. Katrina's winds were churning the Gulf and they would soon directly impact me and those I love. I didn't know any of that just then. I was enjoying myself at a motorcycle rally many hundreds of miles away from home, from the wetlands, and from Katrina.

The Worst of Times

Friday, August 26th: It was one of those days that remind me why I am a motorcyclist. As a breed we may differ. Certainly, I hope the public perception of us has changed from the terrorizing gang of Marlon Brando's "The Wild Ones." For those who are not bikers the attraction of motorcycling may be hard to grasp. There are several attractions for me. There is power in the engine of a motorcycle. There is a kinetic thrill in riding down the road with the wind pummeling your body. But there is also the connection with the natural world that has deprived those who experience the land from inside the metallic bubble of an automobile. I think it was that connection to the world around me that I prized the most.

If someone wanted to connect with nature while riding, I was in a great place to do it. I was attending a national motorcycle rally in Chattanooga, Tennessee and had spent a full day riding through those beautiful Tennessee hills on my 2005 Harley Davidson Road Glide which I affectingly called the "Glide". The green of the vegetation, the faint blue haze where the earth met the sky was magic. The connection I felt to the swooping landscape of the hills propelling me up and down in an earthbound glide had been invigorating. After a full day of riding, I returned to the hotel and turned on The Weather Channel. The weather reporters were talking with increasing alarm about what was supposed to have been a mild tropical system, but had now become a growing cyclonic system that was threatening to turn into a full force hurricane. I watched for the next several hours with increasing concern as Katrina became a tropical storm that was making headway into the central gulf. I debated whether I should go home early or wait to see where the storm would go. That night I had a somewhat distracted dinner with some friends. The storm was on my mind and I decided to leave early Saturday morning to make the run back to Louisiana.

The trip back was uneventful, but I kept the radio on the local weather channels trying to catch an update on the storm's progress. At the Mississippi – Louisiana border I was almost turned back by State Troopers who had started to implement the system that we all dread in my part of the world. It is called contra-flow, a system that turns all lanes of the interstate into a one-way route away from the storm's path. It is well-named. When a major storm hits, the flow of your life is turned counter to what you had expected. My fellow citizens were fleeing the projected course of the storm, but the path of the storm was the exact place I was going.

At my last stop for gas before reaching my home in Mandeville, Louisiana, I noticed that the Coast Guard was transporting several small rescue boats to the north— away from the impending bad weather. It is never a good sign when the military starts to leave, but, having been through many storm "scares," I was not overly concerned. I continued on my way back to Louisiana. When I arrived in Mandeville, I was greeted by a scene of panic. The roads were jammed. Stores were packed with frantic shoppers seeking to provision themselves for the storm. The air was heavy with ever-growing humidity and an equally heavy burden of fear that was almost palpable.

Several friends were making plans to evacuate. Fortunately, Linda, my wife, was out of town. Her job as a traveling Speech Pathologist often requires her to be in residence at a health care facility far away for extended periods of time. It wasn't always a happy time when she was away, but today, I was glad she was well out of harm's way. Only my college-age son Adam and I were at home. We kept ourselves busy with the usual storm preparations: getting gas in our vehicles, buying water, laying in a supply of non-perishable food, boarding up windows, and securing items around the house that could otherwise become potential projectiles during the storm. Then we were done. The streets grew quiet. The wind grew louder. We waited. It wasn't looking good.

Sunday, August 28th: After spending a sleepless night at home, glued to the television, Adam and I made the decision to evacuate to the northern part of Louisiana where Adam was enrolled in college. A normal four hour trip became an eight hour ordeal as we, and what seemed like the entire population of New Orleans, battled it out on the interstate. Even with the contra-flow plan in effect, traffic was slow. Tempers were short. The faces of the families in neighboring cars were distraught. There was nothing to be done. We were doing all we could. We were running.

No one is ever prepared for the kind of evacuation that was underway. States like Florida and Louisiana that are subject to hurricanes have tried to plan ahead, but few government entities have any useful experience of moving people in that kind of mass. Supplies of food and water had been stripped from store shelves. That was not too bad. We could go hungry. The vehicles that were our means of escape could not. Gas was already getting scarce. As I looked at the inching line of cars ahead and behind me, I started to realize that this was the real deal.

Monday, August 29th Katrina made landfall. For a short while, everyone breathed a sigh of relief. The damage seemed marginal. We had dodged another bullet. Mississippi, poor Mississippi, had again taken the brunt of the blow. We waited for the media to provide the damage report. It did not take long. You expect wind damage. You expect minor flooding. What you do not expect, would never expect, and was now being reported. The reports of broken levees around the City of New Orleans, major breaks that were sending walls of water into one of the world's great cities, began to reach our astonished ears. We stared at the television, watching as homes, then neighborhoods, and then the entire city started to flood. That doesn't happen. That happens in disaster movies. We watched. The movie unspooled before our eyes.

Aftermath

Like everyone in the area who had television, and a lot of people around the world, I was glued to the TV over the next few days. I know you've seen the images on TV and so you think you know what it was like in New Orleans. You don't know. You can't know.

Television is a wonderful tool. It informs us. It entertains us. But it deadens us, too. And that is the horror and the pity of it. When we first saw images of war from Vietnam, a country turned against it. Even Walter Cronkite turned against it. Since then, unfortunately, hungry Vietnamese babies look much like hungry Bosnian babies or hungry Somali babies. Then the news moves on. It sounds harsh, I know, but it's true. I know, because I saw the Katrina images that you saw, but, in this case, those were our hungry babies.

So Canal Street is flooded. Canal Street? The Canal Street that Rex rolled down during Mardi Gras surrounded by thousands, tens of thousands, hundreds of thousands of happy, laughing celebrating people? Yeah, that Canal Street! People are dying in the Superdome. The Superdome? Where the Saints play? Where McCartney and Jagger rocked the rafters and we were all young again for a few hours? That immense roof covering those acres of entertainment is ripped apart by wind, pouring water down onto cowering, hungry thirsty people. The Superdome? Yeah, that Superdome! Dead bodies covered by newspapers are lying in front of the Convention Center that housed the 1984 World's Fair. The World's Fair? Where food of every kind and oceans of drinks could be had while you strolled under bright lights taking in the best the world has to offer? There are crying babies and dehydrating old women and mothers holding out their children pleading for water, for food, for shelter, for somebody to help, somebody to give a damn. The Convention Center? Yeah, that Convention Center!

Don't get me wrong. New Orleans wasn't destroyed. The French Quarter and the Garden District weren't touched. The working class neighborhoods in between were habitable because the early settlers had built along the river at a time when the Gulf was held at bay by marsh and barrier islands and the landscape hadn't yet been raped by human beings. What was destroyed was my complacency and the complacency of other people. The cameras moved on (except for Anderson Cooper and Brian Williams who, bless them, wouldn't let the story die). There was some new crisis, something the people hadn't yet heard about, the new flavor of the month that could be hawked on the TV like deodorant or a new breakfast cereal and Katrina faded for everyone but those who had lived it and those who understood. I was, I still am, living with those images. They haven't left me. I pray they never will.

Those of us, who returned, had to deal with the aftermath. There were two problems— to rebuild one of the great cities of the world, a city that was instrumental, through its port and its culture for making America what she is. Imagine our society without the music of Bing Crosby and Frank Sinatra and George Gershwin and Ellington and Basie and Miles and, Elvis and the Beatles; the other was to determine why it had happened and to keep it from ever happening again. I didn't want an America without New Orleans. I didn't know what I could do to keep it from happening again, but I was going to find out and, when I found out, I was going to take action. I didn't know what that action would be, but I was determined to respond to the call.

Thursday, Sept 1st, Adam and I decided to head back home, not really sure what we would find in Mandeville. Initial reports varied from no damage to complete destruction. Pulling a rented trailer loaded with generators, large quantities of water, nonperishable food, and every gas can that we could lay our hands on, we made our way home. As we approached our small town, the destruction became more and more evident. Everywhere there were trees felled. Downed telephone and electrical lines crisscrossed the road. Our town had become a jungle of bent and toppled trees, looking like toothpicks snapped in half by a giant hand. It was very quiet as we drove through the streets in a zigzag pattern around the debris and destruction. We were more than a little nervous as we neared our neighborhood. Then we breathed a rather guilty sigh of relief. Our home was spared major damage. We were able to pick up our lives, though, like the rest of the area, we relied on generators for many days until utility services were gradually restored.

Over the next several weeks, life revolved around recovering from the storm. The City of New Orleans was in total chaos, though the flood waters had started to recede. During this time, as radio, telephone, and TV services were restored, we watched with shock the destruction created first by Katrina, and then with Rita. The unimaginable became the norm. Daily, the routine in New Orleans and, indeed, in all of Southeast Louisiana, became established as we started the long process of rebuilding. The physical damage was easy to see and easy to deal with, the psychological damage was not. What had just happened? Why had it happened? Could it happen again? What kind of world was it when such a thing can happen? There were more questions than debris, and there was a lot of debris.

My Response

Sometime in October of 2005, when life in Mandeville began to resume some semblance of normality, (though normal was still a foreign concept in

New Orleans and much of the Gulf Coast) my wife Linda and I started to realize how blind we had been to the gradual and insidious assault on our coastal wetlands. Like so many others, we had no idea of the crucial role the wetlands played in protecting our area from tidal surge. In the ensuing months, we would become all too aware that wetland and coastal erosion had played a major part in contributing to the destruction brought on by Katrina. We decided during this time that we would step up and become part of the solution in the long task of restoring the wetlands of Louisiana.

At first we absorbed as much information as we could lay our hands on regarding wetlands and coastal erosion. It was during this period that we learned about the role of oil and gas exploration in exposing fresh water wetlands to salt water intrusion. There had long been talk of this, but now in the wake of Katrina what had been discussion, sometimes heated, turned to outrage, and citizens started to point the jagged finger of blame at the federal and state governments, the oil companies and the Army Corp of Engineers. While both Linda and I could sympathize, and, maybe even share that feeling, we decided it was the time to lay such an easy response as blame aside. We started looking for an avenue of action, some means by which we could make a difference in rebuilding our area.

One night in late October 2005, during a discussion of our futures, both immediate and long range, and where that future would land us, Linda brought up my often-voiced plans to take a leave of absence from work. We had discussed this many times in the past. Even before Katrina, I had already made the decision that I needed a break from medicine, teaching, and the business world in general. Linda (a most understanding and long-suffering wife where my motorcycle mania was concerned); knowing that my plans inevitably included some sort of an extended motorcycle tour around the country during my leave, came up with what I seized on as a novel, even brilliant, idea. Why couldn't I combine our new-found passion for restoring the wetlands with my experience as a professional speaker? I would go on a motorcycle tour to raise awareness about wetland destruction. As she put it, "If you can run that motorcycle half as much as you run your mouth it will be a breeze" I think she was joking. I hope she was joking. Well, joking or not, the observation had more than a kernel of truth in it.

My excitement grew as I began to seriously think about it. I knew exactly how to map out the trip. The route would be one that my friend and fellow rider Dennis and I had dreamed about, a ride around the perimeter of the United States. My route would follow the oceans and borders of the lower 48 states from the tip of Maine to San Diego, from the northwest corner of Washington State to Key West, Florida. Of course, the project needed a name and Linda and I went through several possibilities over the next few weeks. Then while riding one day, which is always a good way for me to process ideas, it came to me. I was going to ride the perimeter of the country so why not call this adventure Riding The Rim. I liked the "rim" concept, probably after hearing it so often associated with economics. The Far East is often referred to as the Pacific Rim. The name fit perfectly, at least I thought so. Linda was in agreement, so Riding The Rim (RTR) it became.

Though Riding The Rim was in direct response to Katrina, the more we looked at it, the more we came to view it as a way to help avoid another disaster from the next major storm that would someday hit our coastline. It seemed to be a great idea to us, but I knew that not everyone would share the enthusiasm Linda and I shared. The idea was still new and I had not fully worked everything out, so we shared our plans with only a few close friends. It was too early for me to fend off the critics and doubters who greet any new idea with skepticism

Those we did share our plans with were mostly receptive, and several indicated they were eager to help. My riding buddies, of course, were a little envious about my coming adventure, but I began to realize that even some of them did not understand that this was more than just another ride. It was bigger than a vacation from the daily routine. Although I was never directly confronted with it, some of my friends probably thought I was being selfish by taking a hiatus from work and leaving Linda alone for such a long period of time. It was a point, but I was not really overly concerned with these attitudes. Linda and I were frequently parted by our work. She is no shrinking violet. Being the independent soul that she is, she was fine with the plan; after all, it was our plan. We had laid it out together.

Though I did not ignore the discouraging words of others, I decided not to let the voices of those who doubted the project obscure our vision. Linda and I continued to plan and dream. Eventually we expanded the circle of friends we shared the project with, knowing that the more people who became aware of RTR the better our networking opportunities would become. The issue of credibility was important to us.

Forming the Team

During the months following Katrina, the Greater New Orleans area and the Mississippi Gulf Coast took on the air of a Wild West town. As relief workers started to stream into the area along with Federal troops, we became accustomed to seeing tent cities pop up overnight. Hand-made signs advertising recovery services adorned the local highways and streets. Makeshift showers, kitchens, and basic conveniences were available, at a price, to those who ventured back to their shattered homes in an attempt to reclaim some part of their past lives. Joining the paid and professional relief workers were church groups and social organizations that brought with them essential living and building materials to help in the rebuilding effort. Unfortunately, communications were limited and quite unreliable, as were the regulatory processes of local governments. Scam artists and con men started to infiltrate the area under the guise of "relief workers" or "fund raisers" for the relief effort. It was reminiscent of the "carpet baggers" who came south after the Civil War. It was in this environment that we started to put the pieces of the plan together.

My point in all of this is that we did not want to become just another fly-by-night charity asking for contributions for the wetlands. During the fall of 2005, I started to research wetland organizations in Louisiana and across the country with an eye toward their becoming potential partners. Linda and I felt that the raising and collection of funds should be channeled through a non-profit organization that had a local, regional, and national reputation. This proved to be the first of many hurdles I would experience in getting RTR off the ground. I was sure there had to be some sort of national organization dedicated to wetland and coastal restoration. While I found several governmental agencies that were active in wetland projects and education, I could not find a national group to approach as a partner for the project. Our lack of experience was starting to show.

With my limited experience in marketing, publicity, and organizing media events, I knew a partnership with one of these organizations was essential to making the project successful. Neither Linda nor I had ever taken on a fund raising project, let alone a national media event. Our lack of experience clearly showed itself once again, especially in the early planning phase. We did what we could. I had a little marketing experience from previous business ventures, and I knew that a web site would be the quickest and most effective method to let others know about our project. I put together a rudimentary web site, made a logo, and started to spread the word. By early December of 2005 I was still seeking an alliance and, perhaps naively felt that something, or someone, would step up and guide me in the right direction.

Meanwhile I had another issue to deal with. Economic winds were blowing too. The ride would require me to resign my current position, or to take an unpaid leave of absence for approximately four months. Linda, bless her, left the decision up to me. I decided, wondering how I had gotten so lucky in a spouse, to bite the economic bullet. I was determined to make this a focal point of my life and if that meant leaving my current employer, or, at the very least, going without an income for several months, so be it.

Finding employment and making the proverbial "almighty buck" had never been a problem for me in the past and, over the last several years, my perspective on having a life while making a living had undergone a radical change. After reading several books on the subjects ranging from "creative visualization" to the power of affirmation, I started to realize that we create many of the events in our lives. Putting energy into what you believe, in fact, leads to its creation. The key is accepting how an event becomes manifest in your life and to not become tied to a particular outcome. I once heard that keeping your expectations low and your acceptance high opens the doorway to inner growth.

When I was a young boy, I decided that my gift of gab, as my mother put it, was my ticket to finding employment. As it turned out I became a college professor, medical product trainer and professional speaker, all of which were based on this gift of gab. I had no idea where I would end up using this talent, but fully believed that it would play an important role in my life. It was the same with this project. When my youngest son Adam entered college, I started to visualize (and so, create) a time, someday near the end of his education, when I would take a break and leave my current employment to explore other interests. It wasn't that I no longer wanted to be involved in medicine and training, but I knew that I needed some distance from this part of my life.

Initially, it was simply telling me that I deserved, and needed, the time away. This was followed by some freethinking exercises centered around a "what if" scenario. Never quite knowing what that future had in store for me, I stayed open to whatever was coming my way. I should add also that, during this time, I became interested in downsizing and simplifying my lifestyle. A few of my family members were less enthusiastic about this than I, because they viewed downsizing as living in depravation, while I saw a simplified life style as one of needing less and having more. Thus, the employment issue, while important was not a major concern at this time.

As I put more energy into planning RTR the reality of taking a "leave" from my current routine became more and more feasible. I started to practice what I had preached to so many audiences— it is far more important to have a life than to make a living. I could now see that it was time to make a conscious decision about redesigning my life. From the many books that

I read on how to make a second career in your life, I gained confidence in my ability to start over again, either by necessity or by design. Helping me through this process was the fact that I had a job that, for the most part, I enjoyed and, above all, having a loving wife who believed in me. By the end of December, 2005 I knew it was time to take the next step in making Riding The Rim a reality. But before I went "public" with my plans I had an important issue to resolve.

It was January 2006 and I was ready to approach my employer and tell him about the project. While I had no idea how he would respond to my request to take four months off from my current position, I was completely prepared to resign if it came to that. I was working with a great group of people and felt a strong tug of loyalty toward them. In my role as a consultant, educator, and trainer, several people depended on my services to help them be successful in their position. I did not want to jeopardize their income if it could be avoided. Fortunately the president of the company shared my passion for restoring the wetlands and was very supportive of my plan. It was decided that I could take up to six months of unpaid leave beginning in the Spring of 2007. This would give me time to iron out the details of my absence and come up with a transition strategy. (I should also mention that the president of the company became one of the larger contributors to the project and was instrumental in getting other sponsors aboard.)

All of this went much more smoothly than I could have ever imagined, and I believe it was primarily due to the creative forces I had been putting into place over the last several years. Of course, it is also possible that it was an idea whose time had come. Then again, maybe I just got lucky.

With the employment issue resolved, I turned my full attention to developing a partnership with a wetlands organization. I was a lone reed in the wind. If I could find someone recognized in the field to partner with, RTR would gain credibility and I would feel a little less like a lone wolf. Finding such an organization, and turning the trip into a reality was a frustrating time for me. In sharing my frustrations, I intend, neither to disparage any group nor to weary you with the story of the struggle, and certainly not to glorify myself. It is just that, in order to appreciate the dawn, it is necessary to know how dark the night has been. I didn't say that, Sophocles did.

I began close to home. Through my research, I found some local groups who had an established track record in wetland issues and, while they were not connected on a national level, at least they were organized. One group in particular, Lake Pontchartrain Basin Foundation (also known as Save Our Lake) seemed like a good fit. I was aware of their many activities in our area and, after researching them on the internet, I made an appointment to visit with one of their staffers. While I was warmly greeted, the farther I got into the description of the project, the more I could start to see the doubt in the staffer's eyes.

I tried to make it clear that I was not seeking money or financial support, but just an organization to partner with. I explained that I needed media and public relations support. I was looking for an organization that had a tax-exempt status along with a positive track record in wetland restoration. I don't think I impressed her with the worth of my project. I didn't really hold it against her. Here I sat at her desk, a guy riding a motorcycle, who wanted to ride the countryside speaking about the wetlands! It was easy to visualize her reaction. "You want to ride a motorcycle and talk about the environment?" "Who will you talk to and do you think they will listen to you?" In any case, we didn't close the deal. I don't really know why. In my heart, I wanted to believe that this organization, as was the case with many of the others that I talked to, was so overwhelmed with requests for assistance, and so short of staff, that they needed to be somewhat suspicious when it came to taking on a new project.

Nevertheless, I was determined to continue on with the project even if it meant being my own charity, which was an attitude that my accountant strongly discouraged. We persevered. Neither Linda nor I wanted to become involved in the collection of donations. I needed an organization that came equipped with public relations, event planning, and media outreach experience. After approaching several more groups, I was still coming up empty-handed in finding a group that shared my vision. Katrina's winds were still blowing hard and I was being buffeted by their force.

Fortunately, help was on the way in the form of an organization called America's WETLAND Foundation (AWF). Though I didn't know it just then, in a matter of weeks I would be in contact with them. There's a great deal that I need to say about them and what they contributed to RTR, but that will be saved for a later time. For now, I just need to say that, with their organizational support and expertise, I would soon be riding out of New Orleans and around the perimeter of the United States— just as I had dreamed.

Part II:
On the Road

The Southwest Rim

Rim Day 1: Elapsed mileage 0

Setting Out

It was April 21ˢᵗ 2007 and I was being escorted out of town by a covey of motorcycles from the New Orleans Police Department, but it wasn't as bad as it sounds. A lot of dreaming and a lot of work by a lot of people had made RTR a reality and I was setting out to ride the rim of the United States from coast to coast and from the Gulf of Mexico to Canada. There was a long haul ahead, but there had been an even longer haul just to get to that point. If you think a trip to the beach takes planning, try this one on for size.

Linda was working out of town at this point on another assignment, so I had to deal with the logistics of having someone look after the house, collect my mail, and generally take care of any emergencies while I was away. My friend Roy volunteered to "watch the ranch" while I was away and handle any homeowner situations that came up. My plans were to use on-line banking to pay the utility bills and my other expenses, and to handle the expenses of a small company that I was a partner in. On the advice of my attorney, who is also my daughter, I had revised my living will, medical directive, and power of attorney, and made notarized copies to carry with me. Additionally, I made an Emergency Information card that listed contact information for Linda and several friends. I copied my health insurance information and put this along with the other information in a secure place on the Glide.

I had read that carrying electronic equipment across the border into Canada could create problems with U.S. Customs. They could demand proof of purchase showing that the equipment was purchased in the U.S. and was not purchased in Canada in order to circumvent paying U.S. taxes. I could either carry receipts with me for the gear, or go to the Customs Office in New Orleans to get a document showing proof of ownership. I opted for the latter to avoid carrying, and most likely losing, the proof of purchase receipts. I also needed to obtain copies of the Glide's title and a Canadian Insurance card from my insurance carrier. I decided to bring my laptop computer with me to handle internet access and also to update the RTR website. Its carrying case served as my mobile office and filing cabinet. It seemed, at times, that my "to do" list would never end, but, eventually, I swam through the sea of endless paperwork, and reached the shore of "everything put together."

As the departure date got closer, I was ready to hit the road and get past this planning phase. At one juncture, when I was dealing with some troubles coordinating the kick off event, I considered chucking the whole thing and slipping out of town a day early. Once again, Linda's voice of reason outweighed my frustrations, and the day of the kickoff event finally arrived.

The planners at America's WETLAND Foundation and the Coast Guardians (more about both of them later) wanted to have a sendoff event. I thought this was a good idea because it would attract media attention, and was a great way to involve motorcyclists from the area. We planned to stage the event at Audubon Park in New Orleans and invite local politicians, motorcyclists, the press, and whoever else wanted to participate. Starting in mid-February, I contacted the local chapters of Yamaha Star, BMW, and several other independent motorcycle groups. Flyers were posted in all the motorcycle shops, and I tried to spread the word at every opportunity that I could. The Northshore H.O.G. (Harley Owners Group) chapter was one my greatest supporters and several members volunteered to ride over to the park with me. This group had already made a sizable donation to AWF on behalf of RTR, and their continued support meant a great deal to me. Additionally, several of the chapter's members made donation to AWF on their own, without any solicitation from me.

The last couple of days before the kickoff event were filled with buttoning up the house and making some final arrangements for the event. I went over my to-do list several times, carefully checking and rechecking each item. I had already packed the Glide with tools and extra equipment, and now it was time to pack my personal gear. My carefully planned-out clothing and other riding gear were laid out on the floor of my home office. Additionally, I assembled all of my electronic items making sure that I had the proper chargers and cables. In a waterproof pouch, I packed important documents, contact lists, and insurance papers. Now, on the evening before the kick off event, I found myself going over everything for one last final check. Mid-day on Friday, I got a call from one of the event organizers informing me that a local TV station wanted to interview me in the morning. Unfortunately, they wanted me at their studio at the same time that I was scheduled to ride over with my H.O.G. chapter to the kickoff event. I suggested that perhaps they could do a live spot at the kickoff event. I explained to her that I could not make both events and that riding with my H.O.G. Chapter was more of a priority than the TV interview. I could hear the disbelief in her voice. I explained that my friends had been so supportive with their time and money and had given up their Saturday to ride with me, and felt that it would not be right not show up even with the excuse of doing a TV interview. My boss and friend Duke Johns, who was also a member of the Coast Guardians, came to the rescue and agreed to fill in for me at the TV station. I had another reason to thank him. Agreeing to my leave got things started, putting me in touch with the Coast Guardians got things moving, and, here, at the kickoff, thanks to him, everything eventually got worked out.

Sleep did not come easily that evening, and by 0500 I was wide wake and ready to go. After a final packing of the Glide and locking down of the house, I was off. David, one of my friends from Northshore H.O.G., showed up to ride over to the dealership and my friend Roy was there in his Miata taking pictures as we made the short trip to our rendezvous with the other riders. Flipping on the XM radio as I rode to the dealership, an old Beatles song starting playing— "I get by with a little help from my friends ..." As I sang along, I wondered if this would become the anthem for the trip.

The plan was to ride into New Orleans and then stage the group close to the kickoff event area at the Riverview near Audubon Zoo at the rear of Audubon Park. There was a good turnout from the H.O.G. chapter, and our ride to Audubon Park was organized and uneventful as we passed through the light Saturday morning traffic. The turnout at the park, although small, was enthusiastic. Riders from the local BMW and Gold Wing clubs were there, as were several riders who showed up on their own. I was grateful for my friends and co-workers who took time out from their day off and showed up to cheer me on. The plan for the event was to have a couple of presentations on the wetlands, and then I would address the crowd. Following my presentation, we would depart as a group with a police motorcycle escort. With the ceremonies and speeches over, we were set to depart with our escort. At the last minute, though, AWF wanted several photos taken, and, also, to do a taped interview for a local TV channel before we left. The police escort was anxious to get the show on the road, and they were in no mood to wait while I was being interviewed. I, too, was not keen on the photo shoot, and hurried the process along as much as possible.

Once underway, my police escort was truly exciting. I was riding with sirens and flashing lights and accompanied by the roar of 50 plus motorcycles. Regrouping on U.S. 90 on the West Bank of the Mississippi River, several of the District K Gold Wing Road Riders Association (GWRRA) and H.O.G. members joined me for the ride to Morgan City. After a lunch at a local restaurant, we parted ways and I bid everyone a final goodbye. It felt good to be solo as I headed towards Abbeville, Louisiana on LA 14. It was mid-afternoon, but it sure felt like the dawn after a dark night to me.

The long hours of planning, endless email and phone conversations, and tilting at the windmills of what seemed liked insurmountable roadblocks to the project, now became secondary to the activities that would come to dominate my days over the next months— finding my next fuel stop and lodging for the evening. It would take several more days before my routine fell in line with the rules of the road and riding became a part of my life. Even then, and much later in the trip, I would sometimes have a "pinch me, is this really happening" conversation with myself. But it was.

Leaving the group and heading towards my first night's destination, the sudden realization that I was leaving my home, family, and friends for over three months set in. I had a job I liked, a home I had settled into, friends whose company I enjoyed, and a wife I loved dearly. I had put all those behind me. It was hard to realize all that had transpired. I had not done it. "We" had done it. And now there was no longer a "we." There was only "me" and the road. It was what I had wanted. It was what I had dreamed. Now it was here. I faced it with both eagerness and regret. I shook it off, all that was in the past. The road was my new reality. I had miles to travel and an environmental message to get out to the world. I hoped I was ready for both.

The first leg of my travels over the next several days took me through familiar territory. I had often ridden into southwest Louisiana where the moss-draped trees and languid bayous of my adopted state were always a source of delight. I had gotten to know my adopted state and to love her lush landscapes. Louisiana is an undemanding lady; she spreads herself open before you. There is such a proliferation of plants and wildlife. There are so many sensory triggers for the eye, the ear and the nose. Her flowers are rich and full, heavily perfumed. Her trees wrap you in an embrace that is almost suffocating. I wish I were artist enough to explain it. One of the great experiences in life is to travel Interstate 10 West across the Henderson

Swamp near the Atchafalaya Basin at sunset. Punctuated by cypress trunks large and small, the placid waters of the swamp are painted shades of red and gold and orange by the setting sun, creating a scene that is worthy of the paintbrush of any painter who ever lived, if he was blessed with abundant talent. Nature is a pretty good painter herself.

In Cajun Country

In Southwest Louisiana, I had my first night on the road. I stopped in Jennings, Louisiana. I had planned to find a motel in Lake Arthur, but discovered from two riders I met while fueling up in Gueydan that there was nothing in the way of lodging there. These were the first new friends I made on the road. There were to be others. In the early days of my trip, there was something comforting in the brotherhood of bikers. I never felt alone. Throughout the trip they would pop up, bringing comfort, joy, and information. As I was pulling into the gas station, these two burly riders came out of the convenience store and strolled over to where I had parked. At first, they just checked me out, but when one of them (who I later learned was named Big Daddy) saw the "Save the Wetlands" decal on the Glide, they quickly warmed up and asked me about the trip. Big Daddy had a Honda and his friend Bud rode a Yamaha Star. As I told them about the trip, I could see the envy in their faces when I talked about the places I would be visiting. They wanted to know where I was heading, and, when I told them about Lake Arthur, they laughed and wanted to know why I would want to go there. Evidently, Hurricane Rita had pretty much wiped out any businesses in Lake Arthur, including places to stay. This had become a common occurrence along the coast. Communities that had existed for years were no more. If they did still exist, they were often shells of themselves. The storms had not wiped out places, they had wiped out history. These were the ancestors of the people who were exiled here from Canada. They had found a bountiful place of fish and fowl and game. They had wrested farms from the fertile, marshy soil. Theirs had been an existence built on and enabled by the wetland area they lived on. It provided them sustenance, clothing, and shelter. Then the land they loved was eroded by the engine of commerce. They couldn't resist, for they came to rely on the industry that destroyed the land for jobs. It was a vicious cycle that contained the seeds of the latest disaster in the first rig towed through their marsh.

I didn't say all that to Big Daddy and Bud. I probably didn't need to.

Everyone in Southwest Louisiana knows the truth of this in their bones, even if they can't articulate it. Anyway, we met as fellow citizens of the state. We met as fellow road warriors. We chatted for a little while longer and they suggested I try Jennings for a place to stay for the evening. After a big hug from each of them, I was on my way.

My first night on the road was unremarkable. After the events of the day and of the last several weeks, I was ready to lay my head down for a good nights sleep. I can't say whether or not my sleep was dreamless, because I recall nothing until the next morning. My eyes opened on my first real day away from home. It gave me a sense of purpose and urgency. Meeting Big Daddy and Bud had reminded me why I was on the road; I had places to see and a message to spread. A quick breakfast and I was off. After finding LA 82, I pointed the Glide in a southwesterly direction into Cameron Parish where I witnessed first hand the devastation that Hurricane Rita had created.

The land is low, without any significant flood or surge protection, and as I rode through the small towns of Pecan Island and Cameron the countryside was completely devoid of anything other than open marsh. I tried to visualize the land in its natural state. There should have been grass and reeds, cypress and cat-tails, muskrat and nutria, and little camps where trappers and fishers stayed while pursuing the abundant game of Louisiana. There was nothing here, just nothing! With little or no traffic to break the silence, I stood with the wind in my face, looking out onto the Gulf of Mexico. At one time, I would not have been able to see the Gulf. It would have lain beyond a horizon of vegetation stretching for miles. Now it was right there. Louisiana has lost more land to coastal erosion than make up some of our smaller states. Football field-sized parcels of land, vanished, as if they had never been. That thought was even more depressing than the barren landscape. Taking a few pictures of what was left of the wetlands, I tried to imagine what this area must have looked like before Rita. Louisiana's motto is "The Sportsmen's Paradise" and I knew enough of the state before the summer of 2005 to imagine what had been. Even in the wreckage of what had been, I knew that this was once a lovely spot. I was sorry that I had never come this way before.

Waltzing Across Texas

Soon, I left Louisiana behind me and entered a new state. It was Texas, but it was more than that. It was a step over a threshold of the life I had been living and into the reality of the new life I had chosen. I was to experience this rite of passage many times on my trip, but this was the first.

It being Sunday, the traffic was light and the ride into Texas was uneventful. Texas Hwy 182 cuts through a thin strip of land dividing Galveston Bay from the Gulf of Mexico. The strip was sparsely populated with a few stores and gas stations, and there was a noticeable wind blowing from the east. At least, I thought at the time that the wind was noticeable. Compared to what I was going to experience later on the trip, this was a gentle breeze. In fact, the wind was to become my greatest nemesis, but that was later. Near Port Bolivar, I waited in line to take the Bolivar Free Ferry over to Galveston where my first media event was scheduled at Moody Gardens.

The whole issue of media attention had consumed me during the planning stages. In February of 2007, I received a call from a local wetlands advocacy group, the Coast Guardians, who are a group of New Orleans business men who banded together to promote the economic, as well environmental, importance of the wetlands. They had learned about my project from Duke Johns, the president of Medical Specialties, my employer. He was as passionate about the wetlands as I was and had wholeheartedly supported my plans for an extended leave of absence from the company. It appeared that he had done more than that. He had put out the word where it would do some good. I cannot say enough about how his intervention helped the project in the long run. The Coast Guardians prime objective was business to business education on the wetlands, which fit in nicely with my plans to hold educational events along my route. Additionally, their organization was under the America's WETLAND Foundation umbrella. AWF had been my first sponsor of note (and you're going to hear a lot more about AWF as we go along). It was a natural fit to have the Coast Guardians affiliated with RTR through America's WETLAND Foundation. It was getting a little brighter out.

Gradually details for some of the media events started to get firmed up. I was contacted by organizations in California, Oregon, Washington, Ohio, Connecticut, and Florida who expressed an interest in hosting an event. I was relieved. In the short period of two months, I had gone from despair about ever getting anyone to pay attention to RTR, to now having a partnership with a nationally recognized organization, sponsorship that would cover a large portion of my expenses, and the promise of upcoming media coverage for the project.

As media attention started to grow, I set up a television interview with a local access channel and had several commitments from local newspapers and magazines to run the story. My health club, which puts out a monthly newsletter, agreed to include a short piece on the ride with a health/fitness slant to it. My reasons for mentioning the above is to let others know that you should not leave any stone unturned in searching for media attention. Persistence and patience are two highly desirable attributes for promoting an event.

Now as I was pulling into Moody Gardens I faced for the first time what would become a frequent dilemma, where to safely park the Glide. It is a biker's common concern; was someone going to mess with the bike while I was in the Gardens? It makes sense. She is, after all, my boon companion, especially on this trip. I scouted out a parking spot. Finding a spot close to the entrance and open enough so that the Glide was easily seen, I stripped off my touring pants and stored them along with my riding jacket in my top rack luggage bag. (My concerns about the Gide were unfounded. Not once on the trip did I experience any problems with someone messing with her)

Moody Gardens is actually a complex of buildings including a rain forest, an amusement area, and several walking paths. My event was part of an Earth Day festival that included local environmental groups and agencies. I checked into the Earth Day festival registration table and met my contact there. She was a bubbly young lady who immediately apologized for the small turnout. It was safe to assume that Earth Day celebrations are not a big attraction in Galveston and, even with some local advertising the organizers had a hard time drawing a crowd. I assured her that, whether the crowd was one or a hundred, I would be delighted to make my presentation and that I appreciated the opportunity to make an appearance. I had a little time before my presentation and decided to check out the rest of the Gardens. Walking through the huge enclosed rain forest, I was surrounded by brightly colored parrots a mere five feet from where I stood. Lush vegetation intersected by the walking paths led me to several fish ponds that were stocked with a variety of species. The place was alive with visitors and the mood was quite festive.

Then, a small but enthusiastic audience, consisting mostly of other Earth Day exhibitors, assembled for my talk. This was my first formal presentation on RTR, and although they had provided a projector for the PowerPoint presentation I had prepared, I decided to just tell my story and engage the audience while I spoke. That turned out to be a good choice and I never again considered using a computer for my presentations.

I knew all the facts about the reasons for the disappearance of the coast and the economic impact on the country if New Orleans was not rebuilt. I certainly had passion for my subject. Still, there was a sense of feeling my way through this first presentation. I felt a sense of urgency. The message, at least my mind, was critical and I needed to give my very best. I wasn't overly concerned. I had made my living as a speaker for a long time. Probably, it was just as well that my first presentation was to a small group, and one already pre-disposed to my message. I thought it went well, but I knew there would be opportunities to fine-tune my talk further down the road. If I had not converted many newcomers to the cause of the environment, I had gotten my feet wet. I was doing what I set out to do. I was riding the rim and spreading the word about the dangers to our environment. I roared into town on my Harley, found the local environmentalists, and made my pitch to a public who were strangers to me. Well, maybe it wasn't as dramatic as that, but RTR was launched.

With several hours of daylight left, I followed the thin ribbon of highway down Galveston Island and turned north onto the mainland at Surfside Beach. My destination for the evening was Clute, Texas where I found lodging and had a great meal at a mom and pop Chinese restaurant. (Yes, there is a mom and pop Chinese restaurant in Clute, Texas. Say hello for me if you ever stop there.) Journaling that evening I congratulated myself on my first media event. I felt good about connecting with the audience. It felt good to get this first presentation under my belt. It felt good to begin making my dream a reality. I felt good, but it dawned on me that, though I had given many presentations in my life, this had been far from a usual presentation. I was on a mission, and I knew that I needed to put all my soul-energy into making a favorable and lasting impression. Hopefully my assessment of the day's talk was being echoed by the audience. I didn't know. The results weren't up to me. I was here to plant the seed. Feeling a little like Johnny Appleseed, I went to bed.

It would be nice to say I slept the sleep of the just. I had intended to. "The best laid plans" and all of that; "whatever can go wrong, most certainly will;" or, to just be factual, I woke up with a scratchy throat and a headache in the middle of the night. My first thought was "this is not the way to begin a trip." Naturally, with all the many supplies I had so carefully planned and with all the gear that I had packed, Tylenol had somehow slipped my mind. I groaned a little, but there was no one around to blame but me, so I decided to deal with the problem in the morning and drifted back to sleep.

In the morning, after a light breakfast, I packed up and discovered the second setback of the trip. I had lost one of the cables used to secure my gear.

I pondered the loss as my head throbbed and my cactus throat called for attention. My decision was to deal with the security cable later, and care for my sore throat first. I headed out to find some Tylenol. Merrily medicated, I set out. Jumping onto TX 36 then to TX 55, I headed south to Corpus Christi. The wind was bellowing from the southeast, and the air hung heavy with moisture, as I rode towards Brownsville, Texas.

I stopped in Comfort Point to decide if I would continue all the way to Corpus Christi on the Gulf, or cut inland. Unbidden, two guides showed up. These two guys worked at a local plant and were winding down from the night shift. The area has many businesses associated with the petrochemical industry, and these two worked at a local refinery. Once they learned I was from New Orleans, they just couldn't stop talking about their plans for one day visiting the city. Both seemed bored with their jobs and with life. My first thought was "There, but for the grace of God, go I". I encouraged them to make their dreams come true and shared my story with them about how RTR grew from an idea into a reality. I don't know if I convinced them, but, then again, I was only planting seeds.

I kept to my original plans and followed TX 35 to its end just north of Corpus. Christi. The wind had really picked up, and I had to slow down to 55 mph with the cruise control on to keep the Glide on my side of the highway. Between the gusts of wind and the air stream from the passing trucks, it was hard work. At least, I thought at the time that it was hard work. The winds off the Pacific Ocean and the blasts roaring across the Canadian tundra into the northern plains were still ahead of me.

I stopped to gas up and met another friend of the road, a rider named Keller who was on his way back home to Marfa, Texas after visiting New Orleans. While we chatted, I asked him about Big Bend National Park and the surrounding area. He assured me that there would be adequate lodging and that the park was a must-see place. I told him I had already decided to stop in Marathon and spend an entire day in the park and he strongly urged me to spend as much time there as I could. Traveling alone on the road, not really knowing the layout of the landscape can be a bit intimidating at times. I looked at it as an adventure and, with my natural tendency to talk; my chats with the people I met helped in getting advice. I learned from past rides to trust my gut when I met someone and to take their advice if my gut told me to. Keller was one of these people and, though he, at first, eyed me with some suspicion, we eventually hit it off.

He was on a nicely-equipped BMW and was wearing an Aerostich riding suit. I could tell by the way his bike was set up that he was not just a casual, weekend rider. Through our conversation, I learned that his bike was his major source of transportation. A retired attorney, he still had a handful of clients, but mostly kicked back in Marfa and rode his motorcycle. What a life! We waved each other on our way out, thinking we would never see each other again. I should have remembered that the road has its own logic. I left in a glow of good feeling. Or it may have been windburn.

I eventually arrived in the Brownsville area and made the first of many pin stops at the local HD dealership. No, not a "pit" stop, a "pin" stop. Each dealership sells a commemorative pin and, over the years, I had made it a practice to purchase one at every shop that I visited. This was also to be the first test of the Zumo, my GPS unit (you will hear more about Zumo and its navigation voice "Jill" later). I used it to find the dealership and, as luck would have it, the dealership had recently moved to a new location that had not been updated on the Zumo's POI (point of interest) list. Garbage in, garbage out. Night was coming on, so it was time to close my third day. After finding a nearby hotel, I had dinner at Chili's and headed off to bed with a full stomach and a strong dose of Tylenol.

My route over the next several days took me on a more westerly direction, which meant that the troublesome winds would now be at my back. The lower Rio Grande is picturesque in its own way with arid stretches of land interspersed with farms. My first stop was in Zapata County, Texas to a get an ABC point. (OK, I may need to explain this one.) Harley Owners Group offers an ABC contest every year. The idea is to get a picture of your bike in front of an official sign for each town, county, and state, covering every letter in the alphabet. I needed the sign for Zapata County to get a point for the letter "Z." I completely missed the county sign, but found the county courthouse in the town of Zapata. I was delighted. With only two or three counties in the entire U.S. that begin with the letter "Z," I wanted to make sure I got a qualifying picture. After positioning the Glide in several different locations around the county court house, I took what I thought would be an acceptable picture.

The terrain was starting to take on much more of a rugged look with scrubby brush and fewer trees. It was bare and it was hot, even for a Louisiana resident. In Laredo, I stopped at a HD shop for a pin, and inquired about crossing the border into Mexico for an ABC picture. One of the salesmen, who was Hispanic, warned me about going into Mexico and said that, even though he was Mexican, he rarely crossed the border. As I was checking my gear a couple, George and Robin, from Alberta, Canada pulled into the shop. After talking to them for a bit, my reservations about riding in

Mexico were confirmed. They had been on the road since January and were now just coming back from Monterey, Mexico. Their plan was to be back in Canada by the end of May. While they had a wonderful time in Monterey, they told me that the larger border towns were not really safe for travelers. They suggested that, if I really wanted to go into Mexico, (and I'm not sure they really grasped the ABC point thing) I should select a small town at which to cross over.

I was amazed at how little baggage they packed on their Ultra Classic, and wondered if perhaps they had shipped some of their things back home. They confirmed my thoughts and told me they also shipped ahead to places on their route. This seemed to be a very good idea and I eventually did the same thing. The climates that I travel through changed, and my gear had to change with them. I was comfortable with the luggage and gear that I had at the moment, but knew that the weather at this time of year can change at a moment's notice.

Traveling towards Eagle Pass, I passed through areas of blooming cactus and swarms of small yellow butterflies. At one point, I pulled over and let them fly around me like flowers on the wind. This was so beautiful that I didn't care about the mess they made on my windshield. I found a really good motel in Eagle Pass and, after unpacking my gear, I walked over to a small restaurant that served up a great plate of spaghetti with a tangy meat sauce. The sky in the western horizon was washed with hues of red, orange, and purple as the sun sank slowly out of sight. It was a serenely beautiful sight.

Back in my room, as I checked the weather forecast for the next day, a tornado warning popped up on the screen. I went outside and the beautiful sky that I had just been admiring had turned into angry-looking thunderclouds that were racing across the sky. All of a sudden, the tornado sirens filled the air with their loud, piercing alarm and the wind started to pick up. I wanted to get the Glide under some cover, and asked the motel manager if I could park her under the covered driveway by the office. I just managed to get the cover on the Glide before a strong, but fortunately brief, hail shower struck. Along with a couple of other guests, I watched the storm from the motel's office.

The rain and hail was actually blowing sideways, and I was thankful that the Glide's cover held fast. Although I did not see any funnel clouds, I learned from the news the next day that six people had lost their lives in the tornadoes. Once the storm passed, the sky turned into a melancholy pink hue, with a bright rainbow, as if the events of the last hour had never occurred. I marveled again at the changeability of the weather and, for that matter, of life. I had gone from serenity and beauty to violence and concern in a matter of minutes, then just as suddenly, to this melancholy mood. There's a lesson there. I'm not sure what it is. After all, I'm only a motorcycling environmentalist.

Expecting a clear morning following the severe weather of the past night, I was surprised to find myself riding in a dense fog outside Del Rio. Finally, the fog burned off, and I was riding under a brilliant blue sky as I made my way on U.S Hwy 90. (Check last night's entry about the changeability of things.) U.S. Hwy 90 was the same road that I had taken following the kick off event just four days before. Here, the road was wide open with a posted speed of 75 MPH. After crossing a large reservoir at the Amistad National Recreational Area, I stopped at a scenic overlook by the Pecos River where I read about the "Silver Spike." This was the commemorative spike placed to tie together two sections of the Pacific Railroad. As I studied the sign, I realized that I was reading about how my country had grown from sea to sea. Americans have always had this urge to see what was on the other side of that mountain, or river. By doing that, we had claimed a continent and built a country. All because of people who wanted to travel from one place to another. I felt good. We travelers have a place in the larger scheme of things.

As I was reading the plaque, a car from California pulled up. The driver and I started talking (You knew that was going to happen, didn't you?) and I learned his name was Raphael. He was coming back from Mexico and returning to his home in Los Angeles. As we talked, I learned that every year he returns to Mexico to visit his family and to see his somewhat frail mother. He had emigrated to the U.S. several years ago and eventually settled in California with his wife and children. He proudly told me of becoming a U.S. citizen in 1997 and that, even though his family lived in Mexico, he considered the United States to be his home now. This made me realize what so many of us take for granted. Our citizenship in this wonderful country is a given to us. It is ours by birth. Raphael had chosen our country over his native land and over every other country in the world. Who's the better citizen here?

My destination was Marathon, Texas, one of the entry points into Big Bend National Park. I located the Marathon Motel RV Park that had been suggested to me by Keller, my rider friend from Marfa, a couple of days ago. The motel was a collection of individual cottages and one four-plex unit where I was assigned a room. Although it was only mid- afternoon I was weary, and decided to close my eyes for just a couple of minutes before going out to clean the Glide. Two hours later I woke up to the sound of several motorcycles pulling up in front of the building. Three riders from Illinois had just arrived and were in the process of unpacking their gear and lugging it upstairs to the room above mine. One guy named Ed was with his girl friend Gail and with them was Buddy, a friend of Ed's from work. They had been on the road for a couple of weeks and had ridden here to see Big Bend National Park. Buddy gave me a happy face pin which, Ed explained, is Buddy's way of saying hello. It seems he had become fascinated with the "Happy Face" thing when it first became popular, and now had a stash of these buttons that he gives out. I handed out RTR pins to the three of them and they tromped upstairs to unpack and unwind from the road.

Keller told me not to worry about room reservations in Marfa, but I knew tomorrow would be a long day in the saddle and, suspecting there were limited options in Marfa, I definitely wanted to have a place to crash. I strolled over to the motel office to get advice on lodging in Marfa and restaurant suggestions for dinner that evening. The clerk suggested Riata Inn and called to make a reservation for me. She then gave me directions to the local cantina, the Oasis, that had, in her opinion, the best Tex-Mex around. After a quick clean-up for the Glide and myself, I headed back into town and located the Oasis.

Marathon is a typical western town, with a highway lined with local businesses running down the middle of town, so finding the Oasis was not difficult. Inside was a group of riders just finishing up and, once they cleared out, I grabbed the only available table. While not a huge fan of Mexican food, I thought the meal was superb, and nothing like the stuff we get back home. Of course, it's possible that I was just ravenous after a day on the road. If you ever eat there, let me know what you think about the food at the Oasis.

After eating, I wanted to stretch my legs, and also to see the town. I walked the four blocks that made up the downtown of Marathon. For a small town, Marathon has several interesting businesses, including several art galleries, a classy hotel, and a museum. Just as I was saddling up to ride back to the motel, a group of riders from Texas and Florida pulled in next to me. They asked about the food inside and, after giving the Oasis a rave review, I found out their group gets together once a year for a week-long ride, alternating between the Florida and Texas areas. As we were talking, one of the guys from Florida recognized the RTR logo on the Glide and told how his buddy at work had showed him a story on RTR with my picture.

We couldn't believe our paths had crossed in Marathon, Texas. Given the circumstances, I gave the quick, drive-thru RTR pitch and handed out ride pins to everyone.

I have mentioned RTR ride pins several times and should explain about them. The RTR ride pins had been my idea. Originally, we were going to use them as a "thank you" for anyone who made a contribution to the project. Once on the road, the idea of asking people for money did not appeal to me. I decided to use the RTR pins as a goodwill gesture and as something to leave behind, so those I met would remember the project. Perhaps the pin will bring to mind the plight of Louisiana and the need for coastal restoration. In that case, they would have more than served their purpose. At the very least, they may remind people of the crazed stranger who carried on about the wetlands. It was a win-win either way.

Later that evening, under a sky filled with stars, several of the guests met at the open pit fireplace, which crackled with mesquite wood, for some quiet conversation and contemplation. I found out that one of the riders from Texas works for Harley Davidson as a regional manager. He was hesitant, at first, to talk about his job with the Motor Company and explained that he was on vacation and didn't want to talk shop. I totally understood his point and could only imagine how he could get swamped with questions and complaints from disgruntled Harley riders. A couple of folks had brought their jugs with them which were passed around for those who wanted a nightcap. I politely declined and, with night getting along, I headed back to bunk down for a long, restful sleep. I wanted to get an early start, because I was more than ready to explore Big Bend National Park in the morning. As I drifted off, I said a prayer of thanks for such a wonderful day. Life can be good on the road and I was filled with satisfaction as I fell asleep.

First light comes late in Marathon I discovered as I rolled out of bed at 0630. The sky was dark and full of stars. The crew from Illinois was up and stirring around as I heard them packing up overhead. We had breakfast together and got the bikes ready to roll. They were also going into the park and invited me to join them. I was still in the solo mode and declined, saying I'd meet up with them later although I did get a great photo of Gail wearing a cap made of a wolf's skin complete with its head. As I left the motel, Zumo was reading 46 degrees. I got a couple of guys on BMW's to take an ABC picture of me at the entrance to the park. I could tell by the expression on their faces that they were either amused by my request or puzzled by the Glide with all its wetlands signage.

Big Bend National Park is a fascinating place with winding roads that go from a base elevation of 3000 ft to 5500 ft. Many of the roads have hairpin turns with steep grades. Deer and rabbits roam freely, as do snakes and lizards. At the park's visitor center I met Kevin, a rider from San Diego, who was just returning from a trip through Central America on his Kawasaki 650 motorcycle. He shared a few of his adventures and then was off to hike the numerous trails which crisscross the park. I met another couple who were backpacking in the wild for three days. I learned from them that the length of time that they could spend camping was based on the amount of water that they could carry with them. There is very little water in the park, other than that supplied at rest stations, and in this arid climate, hydration is always a concern.

I wanted to visit the Santa Elena Canyon which is touted as one of the most majestic sights in the park. Although it is only 30 miles from the visitor center, it took me almost an hour to arrive at the trailhead. The roads are in very good shape and, even with the rising temperatures, the ride there was enjoyable. At the trailhead I shed my riding pants and joined up with a group of high school students from Laredo, Texas who were on an end of school year trip. We first crossed Terlingua Creek, which is only a couple of feet deep at this time of the year. I struck up a conversation with one of the teachers chaperoning the group and he filled me in on the history of the area. The canyon was formed by the slow-moving Rio Grande River which, at times, actually flows underground, and then through the steep canyon walls. He pointed out that the Rio Grande was high just then, due to the fact that we were in the rainy season, but that, during the summer months, it dwindles down to a mere trickle in some places.

The climb was steep. We followed the river bed and then took a heavily wooded trail. The scenery was beautiful and the kids in front of us were having a great time exploring the area. It was about 1330, and I foolishly had not brought drinking water with me, so I was getting hot and a bit dehydrated. I bid my companions goodbye and headed back to the Glide and a very welcome slug of water.

Heading out of the park, I passed numerous cacti in bloom and could not resist taking more pictures. I had never seen a desert in bloom and it captured my imagination. I hadn't made a formal RTR presentation for several days, but I didn't feel guilty about it. I was seeing an unfamiliar, but beautiful, part of the country and getting clued in to the realities of living in that countryside. That was good. Though my primary interest was in wetland restoration, it would be foolish of me to ignore the bigger picture. I now had an insight into what it was like to live in an arid environment totally different from hot and humid Louisiana. If I wasn't teaching at this point, certainly I was learning. In my experience, the two go together.

My exit from the park was through Study Butte, and then on to the much-anticipated highway, TX 170. Since the early planning days of RTR, this road had been on my definite must-do list and I was not disappointed. The road follows the Rio Grande with steep ascents and with just as steep declines. At one point, I saw a sign warning of a 10 percent grade, which is quite significant, and I believe my average speed was no more than 35 MPH as I made my way to the small town of Presidio, Texas. Even after a whole day of riding in the park, I could have spent another two days there, along with a revisit to Hwy 170.

The road started to straighten out as I headed towards Marfa which was 60 miles away. It was almost 1630 as I passed through Presidio and, between the hours in the saddle and the hike, I could feel my energy starting to fade. Once in the Riata Motel in Marfa, I got directions to another cantina and, again, the food was great. This made two nights in a row that I dined on Mexican cuisine, but, here in Marfa, as in Marathon, I found the local food very different, and much more exotic than the typical Mexican fare that we have in Louisiana. Back at the Riata, I met a couple of guys who were stationed at a military base nearby. They were not wearing any uniforms and both carried side arms with them. They warned me about keeping an eye on the Glide. I thanked them for the information, and made sure that I set the alarm on the Glide before going in for the night. I didn't see the famous Marfa lights, but then again I was too tired from the day's ride to see anything but the underside of my eyelids. Nobody beamed me up, so maybe the UFOs were taking the night off. I certainly was.

El Paso would be my first two day break from the road. Past experience had taught me the wisdom of building those breaks into my route. The ride there from Marfa was a short one. I was on U.S. 90 with almost no traffic, and my thoughts were looking ahead to my next long ride. In the early planning stages of another trip, I had considered taking U.S 90 from beginning to end, starting in Florida and ending up, well, wherever it ended. Something about following a road from its starting point to its final termination touched the adventurer in me. I imagined all the small towns that I would pass through and the people that I would meet along my way. It hadn't happened, but it was nice to dream about as I tooled down the road. Snapping me back to reality was the impossible-to-ignore signal that it was time for a biologic stop. The Glide, also, was demanding some premium grade ethyl.

After filling up at a local station, I met a lady who was also traveling to El Paso. In the course of our conversation, she told me about her many attempts at kicking the nicotine habit and how she wished for the determination that I was showing in this ride. I gave her some tips on how to successfully quit cigarettes and qualified my statements by telling her that I was once a two pack per day smoker. No doubt she had heard my suggestions before, but it never hurts to hear them again. We parted ways, she with her promise to give it another try, and me thanking her for the opportunity to help her. I hope she made it this time and kicked the habit. If nothing else, it validated my own long-ago decision to quit. Whatever I had done for her, she had given something to me. It all goes back to my fundamental belief that everyone we meet has a gift for us.

Relaxing In El Paso

For a big town, El Paso has got a small town feel to it and with Jill's help (the voice on my GPS unit) I found a nice Holiday Inn to stay in. I was not far from the famed Barnett Harley Davidson dealership (famed, at least, among bikers) and I stopped in for a look-see. It was a huge place with many bikes, and a lot of older models, for sale. Some of these could, or soon may, qualify for museum status, and it was fun checking out the bikes in person. I saw one of the famous (again, among bikers anyway) "Black Cow" Softail Heritage, so named after its cowhide upholstered seat. There were several Evo models, and even a couple of Shovel Heads in the mix. Well, it meant something to me.

I really enjoyed my stop at Barnett's, but it was time to get a move on. Now it was back to the hotel to get some rest and start on the laundry. My plans were to relax, catch up on correspondence, and, perhaps, take in a movie over the next two days. I couldn't believe it had been almost a week since I left New Orleans. It wouldn't be long before I reached the spot where I would be meeting up with my good friend Rob. He was joining me out of friendship, a keen interest in the environment, and, mostly, because we had always wanted to ride California's Highway 1 together.

The way things were going, I would be there soon. I was far ahead of schedule. Journaling that evening, I congratulated myself that, other than losing a couple of things, I had not encountered any major problems.

Having overcome high winds, tornadoes, and some very twisty roads, I was now starting to feel "at one with the highway". I hoped the highway was at one with me. I still had a long way to go.

In a return visit to Barnett's HD, I stumbled in on their weekend picnic which included burgers, dogs, and good conversation. A couple of locals gave me some good advice on getting over to New Mexico Hwy 9 and, as we talked, several more riders joined us. This was an eclectic group of riders; a mix of whites and Hispanics, some obvious weekend-only bikers, and a few older guys who had many miles under their belts. Everyone was extremely nice and interested about the trip. I passed out ride pins to all, and met the father of one of the riders. He was a seasoned rider, and I could see the pride in his eyes and hear it in his voice, too, as he talked about riding with his son. There is something about that kind of generational bond that is somehow rare, and very special. I think he knew it, too. He was a lucky guy to have an avocation that he loved, and a son to share it with.

I needed to purchase a replacement part for my gas cap cover, but Barnett didn't have it in stock. The salesman in the parts department offered to order one for me and he assured me he could get it in about a week. I politely declined his offer. I didn't tell him that in a week I would be somewhere on the California coast. I went out to rig something up as a temporary fix, and found out it was just a loose nut that only required a little elbow grease to make it new. I made a mental note about thoroughly investigating a fix-it option before rushing out to buy a new part. This is, I suppose, a sad commentary on our "throw away society" where I, like others, am far too eager to buy a replacement or a "new, improved model" when the old one will work just fine with a little ingenuity and effort.

Just behind the hotel was a movie theater and I took in the new Nicholas Cage flick. His character can see 10 seconds into the future. Good show, but definitely not for everyone. Following the movie, it was dinner at Logan's Steakhouse where I met another local guy, an ex-Marine just back from Iraq. Interesting people just keep turning up in my life since I started this trip. Or have they always been there and I never took the time to notice them before? The ex-marine was now a bartender, but wanted to move to New Orleans to check out construction opportunities. El Paso was his home, but he yearned to experience living somewhere else. I encouraged him to follow his dreams and to take a chance on adventure. I was.

New Mexico Desert

After my two days of rest, I was ready to hit the road. The morning brought windy and chilly weather, with a threat of rain. Following a light breakfast, I packed up the Glide and put on some warm riding gear, (I still had not broken out the heated gear) then headed towards New Mexico and Hwy 9. The sky was grey with a chilly, but inviting, bite to the air. Luckily, the threat of rain never materialized. My first stop was Columbus, New Mexico, which is a small town close to the border. The Glide needed some petrol, but the only gas station in town was closed, it being Sunday morning. I spied an open café and went in for Java and conversation. The locals said the station would open soon, so I settled in to get some local gossip. The coffee was weak, but the conversation was great. The town folks were very friendly and eager to tell me the history of their town. I found it interesting. As we don't know enough about our environment, we often know too little about our history. Ignorance in one area can be as harmful as ignorance in the other.

It seems that, in 1916, General Ramon Banda Quesada led more than five hundred men in an attack against the town, apparently on the orders of revolutionary leader Francisco "Pancho" Villa. Stationed in Columbus was the U.S. 13th Cavalry Regiment who fought bravely against the invading Mexican forces. The raiders seized 100 horses and mules, burned the town, killed 14 soldiers and 10 residents, and took much ammunition and weaponry before retreating back into Mexico. The United States Government responded by sending a massive force into Mexico to pursue Villa. This was known as the Punitive Mexican Expedition. After a long period marked with several missed opportunities to catch Villa, the expedition was eventually called off.

As I was listening to this narrative from a local guy named Barney, a lady in an RV pulled up, and we talked about her adventures as a "full-timer". She and her husband had been on the road for over three years, and were camping just down the road in a small park. She said the life of a full-timer was not for everyone, but, after an initial period of adjustment, they couldn't see living any other way. Like so many other road warriors, they made the rounds to friends and family throughout the U.S. and had traveled to most of the states, including Alaska, but, unfortunately, and maybe, obviously, not to Hawaii. Somehow the cost of shipping their RV across the Pacific was not practical. I could see her point.

As she was finishing her story, a guy came into the café and told me that the gas station was now open. Somehow the word had spread through the local grapevine that a motorcyclist was in town and in need of gas. They called the owner of the station, and he came in early to open for me. You got to love small town hospitality. As fond as I am of New Orleans, and as friendly as its people are, there is no way that I could see that happening there.

Border Issues

With the Glide filled up to the over-fill mark, I was on my way to Douglas, Arizona, about 150 miles away which was the next town with fuel. I was a little concerned about the distance, but made it with fuel to spare. On the way to Douglas, I did find one open station, but it only had diesel and 87 octane, neither of which the Glide likes. Although, later, in the wilds of Canada, I discovered that the Glide does pretty well on 87 octane and even 90/10 ethanol. Oh, and I saw my first, road runner. Now where is that coyote?

As I traveled down this lonely road, I saw several observation points manned by what must have been National Guard troops. They sat in elevated baskets high above their trucks, scanning the border. I could only imagine how boring this task must get, and was grateful that I was on the road and not involved in some mindless job. You cannot really tell where the actual border is, because everything looks the same. At one spot the road was narrowed down to a single lane with orange cones and, out of nowhere, a check point appeared. National Guards with M4's politely asked me my destination, citizenship, and home address. I just as politely answered them, remembering the advice that my friend Dave Arthur gave me; "Yes sir, no sir, and thank you." Good advice in a lot of situations.

In Douglas, I once again considered getting an ABC point in Mexico. It is just across the Rio Grande and would take all of 15 minutes. However, the words of caution from the HD salesman in Laredo kept echoing in my head, and I figured it was not worth the risk and the insurance hassle. I now headed north on U.S. 80 towards Bisbee, which is an old copper mining town. I passed a huge open pit mine, but couldn't find a good spot to pull over and take a picture, so I continued on to Tombstone.

Tombstone was larger than I imagined and I decided to stop and play tourist. Walking through the old, restored, part of town, I visited the OK Corral and took several shots of character actors reenacting the famous shootout between the Clayton brothers, Doc Holiday, Wyatt Earp, and his three brothers. What a great place to finally visit after reading about it for so many years! Fremont Street was lined with old-time shops, many of which had not changed since the 1860's. One shop had an amazing collection of guns and knives for sale, and the proprietor gave me a very informative history lesson about the firearms of that era. Since no one challenged me to a gun fight, I guess I hadn't offended anyone, so I got back on the road.

The day was warming up and, by the time I reached Tucson, Arizona, I had the leg vents open on my pants and had switched gloves. Taking the advice of a local, I found a Quality Inn for only $57.00. I could finally get cell phone service, and retrieved a message from Rob. He had run into mechanical trouble and was stuck in West Texas with a bad battery. I called him and we talked about our options, agreeing that I should continue my ride as originally planned, and meet him in Los Angeles. This meant that we could not ride Route 66 together, but circumstances always dictate our path, anyhow, and, in the end, the road always wins.

When I went out to clean the Glide, I, somehow, dislodged the wires to my fog lights. Unknowingly, I put them in backwards, which shorted out a fuse every time I switched on the ignition. It took me three blown fuses to discover my error and, after thinking about Rob's situation, I figured it was Karma. I hoped it would be as quick a fix for his bike as it had been for mine. We had talked so much, and planned so long, for this ride together, that it would be a major disappointment if it could not happen. I've come to realize that all the best things in life are shared. Well, aside from being philosophical about it, there was nothing I could do for Rob, so I went to eat.

Dinner was at a Mexican Seafood restaurant in Tucson. Now, I put it to you, and I leave it to you, is this a world-class oxymoron or what? Where'd they get the seafood? An arroyo! At least, the ambiance was nice. The live entertainment was a guy playing lounge music on an electronic keyboards accompanied by a female vocalist, both pretty good, but I understood very little of the Spanish lyrics. What a day! Taking into consideration the weather, wind, scenery, and temperature, this had been one of the better ones. But then, I've said that before. And I'll probably say that again. This adventure is turning into so much more than I had even dreamed.

I got up early, because I needed to find a HD shop to buy replacement fuses, and, also, because I wanted to get through Phoenix before the day heated up. They don't call it the Valley of the Sun for nothing. After locating a HD shop and purchasing three very expensive fuses to replace the ones from yesterday, I took scenic routes, Hwy 74 and 79, that, as it turned out, were not all that scenic, but I did get a chance to take some great pictures of cacti in bloom. It was amazing to see color and life spring out at you from a dry and arid place like the desert. Life is found everywhere, and it is often humbling to encounter it. I was, and remain still, in awe of the desert landscape that was in full bloom all around me just then. Of course, this desert ride had offered me a lesson. Again! With all of my preparations, I had not bothered to look into the seasonal changes that I would be experiencing, and I made a mental note to pay more attention to that for my next trip.

Phoenix was big and hot and I was worried that the Glide might overheat but, once again, my worries were for naught. The change in temperature was surprising in that, just two days ago, I was contemplating wearing my heated gear. I didn't dally in Phoenix, but headed out to my next stop. North of Phoenix, I-17 heads into the mountains and I pointed the Glide upwards as we ascended first to 3000 feet, and, eventually reached 4000 feet. My next destination was Sedona, and I was looking forward to seeing it after the many wonderful things I heard about it from my dear friend Sharon. I was thinking of her and wishing her well as I rode. I was filled with anticipation at seeing for myself sights I had so often heard about from her. Taking Hwy 260 off of I-17 towards Cottonwood, then 89A into Sedona, the road gets twisty with several steep grades and, then, too, the "old devil" wind was picking up, which made it a challenging ride.

Sedona, Arizona is surrounded by mountains and the famous red rocks. While the town is picture perfect, it has a very upscale, kind of touristy feel to it. I stopped and took several pictures, one of which captures a local mountain in all of its red glory. I tried to imagine what it must be like living at this elevation and having this view of the mountains to wake up to each morning. It's no wonder that it has attracted a crowd way above my economic level. I could feel the money in the air, and decided to venture off the main drag to explore some of the other neighborhoods, wondering as I did, which one Sharon lived in. She had moved here to receive some cutting-edge alternative treatment for a medical condition. Sedona is known as a spiritual healing community, and is supposedly a focal point of energy. I am not sure about all the details on the energy thing, but I could see how living here would be therapeutic. I felt the vibes that told me this was a good place to be just walking around its streets. After a stroll around town and a quick stop for a cold drink, I headed out of town towards my night's destination, Flagstaff.

The road from Sedona to Flagstaff was a pleasant surprise. It cuts through a cool valley and follows a delightful stream which sparkled in the afternoon sun. Heavy spruce and pine scented the air and there was a slight hint of rain in the sky. The wind had died down, and my head was filled with dreamy thoughts about what a nice place this would be to live. As much as I felt I couldn't ever live in the desert southwest, this valley could easily be home for me.

Although Flagstaff was only 30 miles away, it took me almost an hour to arrive, due to a road with many sharp curves and steep grades. It also didn't help that I had spent a good part of the ride gawking at the scenery. It was the type of road that a long distant rider dreams of, wonderful for the bike, stunning to the eye, and invigorating for the soul, but by the time I reached Flagstaff, I must admit, I was ready for flat lands and a straight ribbon of concrete.

Where's Rob

Rob called to say he would definitely not be meeting me in Flagstaff. He got his electrical problem fixed with the help of a local rider he found in his BMW roadside assistance book. Although it was Sunday, he found a store that had a replacement battery that would fit his bike. Although we had pretty much decided the previous night that we were not going to meet up as originally planned, I had hoped that he would still be able to make our rendezvous so we could ride Route 66 together. Well, we can still do the California coast. I hope.

I found a Barnes and Noble (B&N) in Flagstaff, and had my first good cup of Joe in several days. Going for coffee was one of my favorite past times back home. Linda and I would visit our B&N like many folks hang out in their local tavern. It felt good to be drinking coffee and catching up on my reading while I people-watched. My motel was priced very reasonably and had quickly filled up with guests by the time I got back from supper. The proprietor tried his best to get the WiFi working in my room, but was unsuccessful. I even had him walking around in the parking lot with his laptop trying to get a signal.

Several of the guests were riders and we shared experiences, admired each others bikes, and generally shot the bull while cleaning our bikes. I noted that most of the bikes were cleaner and had more sparkle then the Glide, but I had decided at the outset of the trip that I was not going to worry about getting her cleaned up each night. However, my evening routine always included a quick walk around the bike looking for any missing bolts, nuts, or any out of place things. I also checked the pressure in my rear shocks and tires on a routine basis. These things, along with regular fluid checks, provided me more comfort than a shiny piece of chrome, and I am sure the Glide felt the same way. I am equally sure that other riders were somewhat taken back at times by the appearance of the Glide, but once they learned how long I had been on the road, and discovered the miles the Glide and I had traveled, they loosened up on any hypercritical appraisal of us.

Life on the Road

Preparing for life on the road had been no easy task. It was one that I had put a great deal of time and thought into. Over a period of several months, I put together a list of items that I wanted to take with me. I categorized them into groups– clothing, electronics, tools, official documents, contact information, computer supplies, and spare parts. As most travelers find out to their dismay, what you want to bring on a trip, and what is actually needed, are often two different things. I would later find out that I had over-packed in some categories, and under- planned in others. All I can say is, thank God for UPS and FedEx. One of my sponsors, a well-known supplier of motorcycle touring clothing and accessories, became my primary source for motorcycle touring gear. Their generous support helped me stretch my already thin budget to include some special items. Also, I shopped on the internet to find bargains, combed through my own collection of gear to use what I could, and took advantage of any sale items that I could find. A few of the more interesting items purchased included a GPS/XM radio/MP3 player that, while pricey, paid for itself many times over. To keep me dry (hopefully!), I found a pair of waterproof socks that would also ward off the cold mountain air that can invade even the sturdiest of boots. I had most of the clothing that I would need but splurged on a fleece jacket to wear under my touring jacket for any cold morning starts. I purchased a new digital camera to replace an older model that was bulky and had limited memory to store pictures. The new unit had a wide angle lens which I opted for over a massive telephoto one. I wanted to capture vista and panoramic scenes rather than distant images.

We had talked about filming the trip using a handlebar mounted camcorder. The idea came from a good friend who had watched the TV series "Long Way Around," featuring Ewan McGregor on a motorcycle trip around the world. He and his friend Charlie Boorman were accompanied by a third rider who acted as a cameraman. They also had a chase vehicle that met them periodically to film the more sophisticated shots. A friend put me in contact with the film department at a local university and, while they offered several good suggestions about how I should film the trip, it seemed they were more interested in getting a contract to edit the film once I returned than in helping me to film the project. While having a mounted camcorder seemed like a good idea, the logistics, cost, and space needed to carry the extra gear outweighed the benefits of filming the trip. There were times on the road when I wished I had a camera rolling. This was especially true on the northern portion of the Pacific Coast Highway (PCH), in the Cascade Mountains, and in the Canadian Maritimes. Ah, well.

By early March, 2007, I had purchased the majority of my equipment, and had the Glide fully serviced, including new front and rear tires and brakes. My expenses were well over $4000 dollars by this time and I hadn't even left my driveway. I was still waiting for final approval from the Coast Guardians on my budget and their sponsorship. Linda and I talked about our options should the funding not come through, and we decided the trip would go on as planned. We would handle the financial issues as they materialized. This took a lot of stress out of things and eased a burden off our shoulders. Fortunately, the funding from the Coast Guardians came through, and we were very grateful for their generous support.

The Nostalgia Express – Route 66

The motel did not provide a continental breakfast, so I got an early start without my usual coffee and cereal. The sky was clear and cold as I packed up the Glide, and then headed on to I-40 towards the Seligman exit where I would get on Route 66. Not far down the interstate, there was an exit sign for "gas, food, and Grand Canyon Harley Davidson." Needing to fuel both the Glide and myself, I pulled off, only to find the gas station/restaurant under repair and not open. Pulling up to the HD shop, I noticed two riders who were trying to shake off the cold morning air. They were from West Virginia and on their way back from the Grand Canyon, which was not far away. They both had dreamed about seeing the Canyon and had thoroughly enjoyed the experience. They were going to have to hit the road hard on the way back to make it home in the next few days. I once again said a silent thank you for not having to worry about sticking to a tight schedule at this point in the trip. Even though a cup of Joe would have tasted great, I decided to roll on.

Pushing on to William to get fuel, and then breakfast, at a Mickey D's

(McDonalds), I met another RV couple. The owner, John, told me about being a full-timer and how much he and his wife Ruth enjoyed living on the road. He was in awe of my trip and wanted to hear all about Katrina and how Louisiana was recovering. I did another 50 cent version of my RTR presentation, and we exchanged email addresses with a promise to write. It occurred to me as I left that these mini-lectures may do as much to spread wetland awareness as my more formal presentations. It's all about changing minds. If I'm only changing one mind at a time, I'm still changing minds.

The exit to Seligman was not far down the road, and I was quickly on Route 66. This was one of the many anticipated parts of the ride, and I was thrilled to be finally riding a road that I had read and heard so much about. Hwy 66 parallels I-40 and is mostly flat and straight. I thought again of my buddy Rob, eating dirt behind me as he tried to catch up. It would have been great to have him with me as I jumped on the storied route.

Entering Seligman was like taking a step back in time to an Eisenhower era tourist trap. Everything about the town was 1950ish, from the store fronts, to souvenir shops and gas stations. As I was parking, a bus was unloading a group of French tourists. They were getting ready to visit one of the shops, so I decided to play tourist with them and blend into their group. Don't ask why I was thinking about blending in with this group. They were dressed like tourists, and I was in my riding gear. They were looking like jaunty vacationers, and I was looking like a road weary biker. Angel, the owner of the shop, greeted every one with a smile as we entered his store. It was filled with Route 66 memorabilia and I got some good pictures of an old barber's chair and, of course, of Angel.

When I was getting back on the Glide, one of the French tourists came over and, in broken English, started asking me about the bike and where I was going. I used the RTR flag to show him my route, and tried to explain the wetlands angle. My broken French was far worse than his broken English, but I think we connected, albeit brokenly. I didn't think about it at the time, but I was having my first international wetlands dialogue. Eventually, we both just smiled and nodded our heads. It could have been my imagination, but as I was firing up the Glide, I thought I noticed a gleam of envy in his eye as his wife was pulling him back on the bus.

Continuing down Rte. 66, I passed through Peach Springs, which was in the middle of an Indian reservation. The town had a worn look to it, and shared none of the touristy atmosphere that I had found in Seligman. Looking for a place to stop and stretch my legs, I found a trading post which sold local vegetables, groceries, Native American souvenirs, and I am sure

I could have found a water pump for a 1960 Chevy if I needed one. The cashier was very friendly and noted that I was the fourth biker that day that had stopped. After a cold bottle of water and a quick walk down the main street, it was off to Truxton. Somewhere on the east side of Truxton I noticed a motel/café that reeked of Hwy 66 nostalgia. Outside were three riders just getting off their bikes, so I turned the Glide in for a pit stop and some conversation.

One of the guys was named Sonny and he was enrolled in truck driving school. With him were Roy, his instructor, and Sonny's girl friend Pam. They invited me to join them and, after placing our orders, the talk turned to trucking. Then, the discussion turned to my trip and they were interested in my experiences both with Katrina and also with the ride. We discussed wetlands, global warming, and a host of other things. To an outside observer, eavesdropping on our conversation, this may have not sounded like typical "biker/trucker talk," but from my perspective it was a great chat. Johnny Appleseed, that's me.

Our waiter was a huge guy with crossed eyes, maybe a bit slow, but real nice. After asking permission to take a few pictures, I set up my camera to get some shots of the inside of the cafe. One of the patrons got upset when I started to take pictures. In fact, he got a bit testy with me. Perhaps he was on the run from the law or an angry wife; maybe he just wanted to keep a low profile; or maybe he was having a bad hair day. When I assured him I would delete the pictures of him, he calmed down. I didn't want to ruffle the feathers of a local. I had a long road in front of me and nobody to cover my back. Awww, Roob, Maaan! Where are you?

Pushing on, I stopped for gas just outside of Kingman. There I met four riders on Victory (Polaris) motorcycles. They were not all that friendly as I walked over to check out their bikes, but, gradually, they opened up and I got their story out of them. It was a great story as far as I was concerned. They were employees of Polaris and were road testing the yet to be released 2008 models. Their explanation of how they, and another team, rode eight hour shifts to put the bikes through their paces, made me instantly envious. Now I understood why they were a little bit reserved, and I jokingly asked if I could take their pictures! They, rather elaborately, and with deadpan faces Buster Keaton would have envied, made an elaborate attempt to cover the bikes with their bodies so I couldn't get them on film. We all had a good laugh.

Then, it was onward to Kingman where I located the local HD shop which also sold Victory, Honda, and Yamaha bikes. After picking up a pin, (of course) I headed towards Parker, Arizona my evening's destination.

I was not initially impressed with Kingman, which was touted to be one of the better stops on Rte. 66. However, once I got into town, my opinion changed. It was truly like stepping back in time, and it looked just like all the books I ever read had depicted it. Motels, diners, and gas stations were everywhere, all claiming to be the "official" Route 66 location. The wind was picking up, so I didn't stop to take any pictures, but headed west towards the mountains.

Just south of Kingman, I again made the unhappy acquaintance of an unwanted riding partner, the wind. I started to get blown all over the highway. Something inside of me said, "turn around and get a room for the night and relax." It was only 1400, and I was in no particular hurry, and was actually a day ahead of schedule, so I listened to that voice. Back I went towards Kingman, and found a ground level room with WiFi. There was a great restaurant across the street where I chatted with the waitress and learned that, though she had recently moved to Kingman, she couldn't wait to leave.

I was glad that I had trusted my gut about getting off the road, because the wind continued to pick up. I have a tendency to be overly cautious when it comes to the wind, but I was glad that I listened to the voice of reason and caution. My new friend, the waitress, informed me that, each day, about that time, the wind picked up, but, by the morning, it would be calm. I think she might have been hitting on me (unlikely) or perhaps looking for a way out of town (more possible) or it could be that I was just looking for attention because I was missing my lovely bride (Oh, true, how true!). In any event, life was sweet!!

She turned out to be right about the wind. Leaving Kingman in the morning, the temperature was in the high 50s, with a clear sky, and no wind to speak of. I quickly shed my fleece jacket as I made my way towards Needles, California. Gas there was $4.19 per gallon for premium grade which turned out to be the most I paid for a gallon of gas in the U.S. The attendant, trying to be conciliatory, told me that I could wait until the next station, which was a mere 89 miles down the road, but that the prices might be even higher there. That wasn't the case, as it turned out. Nevertheless, not wanting to risk it, I shelled out the cash. Then I took a picture of the station's sign for my friend Dennis who works for Shell Oil. I certainly hope he appreciated my contribution to his retirement fund. This was also my first experience with the awkward gas pumps they use in California. They have a special nozzle adapter that requires you to press down on it as you fill up. It was very cumbersome for a motorcycle gas tank, but, after several attempts, some of which ended up with me spilling gas all over my tank, I got the hang of it.

You might wonder why I choose the route that I was on considering the conditions that I faced so far on the trip. Well, for one thing, it is part of long distance riding. Not everything is a walk in the park. Also, my route had to take in a number of considerations. By early January of 2007, I started to plan the particulars of the trip in earnest. While I had a definite direction and route outlined, I needed to start planning daily mileage based on media and speaking events. Though these were still few in number, I had shored up several meetings with H.O.G. chapters and a couple of wetland organizations. We were still waiting to hear from the Harley Davidson Corporation on their level of involvement, but I was sure that they would want to be part of the project. Additionally, the Coast Guardians were going to reach out to their business contacts around the country to schedule meetings with business groups and organizations. Scheduling, at times, proved to be much more of a chore than I ever envisioned. My motorcycle contacts, while enthusiastic about meeting up with me, were often limited to weekend dates or, at the very best, an evening dinner ride. Business groups had designated dates for their meetings which often conflicted with my schedule. One group on the East Coast was very interested in having me speak at their monthly business meeting, but, unfortunately, my route had me in northern Minnesota at that time.

In my innocence (read "ignorance") I had no way of anticipating these stumbling blocks, but, after a few such incidents, I developed a bit of savvy in my scheduling. By early February, I had a definite route which targeted overnight stops. By design, I would rarely travel more than 300 - 400 miles per day and planned a two night stop every five to seven days. I had learned from previous rides that it was best to set an easy pace up front, and to "get into the groove" of the road before attempting longer mileage days. Additionally, I learned several years back that, if I got off the bike for a fuel and biological break every 100 miles or so, my energy levels sustained themselves and I had a more enjoyable ride. These frequent stops would also provide opportunities to meet people and talk about the wetlands. Also, the RTR, AWF, and CG logos on the Glide were real attention getters and became the catalyst for many impromptu presentations during my frequent stops.

From Needles, it was on to Ludlow, California on I-40 and that is when the wind started to pick up big time. I met another rider in Ludlow who said it was gusting 40-45 mph and I believed him. That set the tone for the rest of the day's riding. The landscape in the Mojave Preserve is brown and sandy and very little else. In its own peculiar way, it has a certain type of beauty to it, even for someone like me who identifies so strongly with trees and forests. However, I was not into any "beauty" of the desert as I hung on tightly to the Glide as the crosswinds blew us over the highway's center line. Finally, I reached Barstow and turned onto I-15. Thinking that the winds would now be on my back, I was ready for a reprieve from two hours of doing battle with the tempest. Unfortunately, this was not the case because the side gusts swept me back and forth across several lanes on I-15. I had the cruise set to 65 mph, but needed to throttle up to 70-75 mph to keep in my lane. The far right lane was reserved for trucks and slow moving traffic, and I tried to keep the Glide in line as the road twisted and turned its way south.

It took me a while to learn how to gauge when the next gust would come, and then to accelerate to counterbalance the wind. Once, I didn't respond quickly enough, and I went into the far left lane. Luckily, there was not another vehicle there. "Are we having fun yet" was the only thing I could think of as I tried to relax my death grip on the Glide's handlebars. If that wasn't enough, Jill kept on telling me to take I-215, but the road signs kept saying I-15 to Los Angeles and San Diego. After five miles on I-15, I decided to pull over for gas and directions. I found a very nice UPS driver (Go Big Brown!) who assured me that I-15 was the way to go and not I-215. It was the first, though not the last time, that Jill proved to be a sometimes flighty lady.

Finally, as I turned Southeast from my Southwest route, the winds switched to my back and the Glide and I sailed down the road for the next 110 miles and I arrived at my friend's house around 1445, right on schedule. With a sense of relief I parked the Glide in the driveway and unwound from the day's ride. This, by far, had been the most challenging day, in terms of the weather, and riding, that I had encountered. The day was a real test for me. From putting aside my fears about the wind, doubting that I could make it around the Los Angeles area, and finally finding my friend's house, it had been one tough day, but I made it!! I was proud of the skill I had shown in handling the conditions. I was happy I had weathered the adversity that faced me. Above all, I was grateful I had come out safely on the other side. I knew too much to believe it had all been about me, and I took the time to give thanks for my success before I joined my friends for some camaraderie.

The Rims End: San Diego

San Diego is one of my favorite places to visit. It has the great weather of southern California, but is more laid back than Los Angeles and some of the cities farther north. My friends Glenn and Margee were wonderful hosts, and we caught up on each other's lives. They moved there from New Orleans several years ago, raised two fine sons, and now were fully assimilated into the California scene. Glenn managed to get some time away from his business, so we walked the rugged beach areas around San Diego, visited a rather large and smelly sea lion colony, and got some great pictures of wetland areas in and around the San Diego area.

I don't know how many people think of wetlands when they think of California, but there are places where it is an issue, too. For that matter, failing levees are not the sole province of New Orleans. The California state capitol, Sacramento has its own reasons to be concerned about levee failures. If experience teaches us anything, it teaches us that a lot of people don't learn from experience until it is too late. I had driven half-way across the continent doing my part to help change that. Maybe what I was doing was only a drop in the big ocean I gazed at, but I didn't believe that. I, rather, chose to believe that, in time, all the seeds we sow will blossom.

The Glide got a much needed cleaning and maintenance check. After 13 days on the road and almost 3,000 miles, it was necessary to check and tighten critical bolts and fasteners. True to the spirit of American engineering, the Glide was none the worse for wear and neither was I. I had my first home-cooked meal in almost a month, and thoroughly enjoyed being a couch potato while Glenn and Margee handled the cooking duties. It was nice just to absorb their domesticity, but it made me more than a little lonely for my own domestic hearth. Though she was with me in all the ways that count, Linda was a continent away, and I felt her absence.

That evening, while reflecting on the last 12 days, I realized how much I had accomplished. I successfully made it around the Southwest Rim, avoided several close calls on the road, dodged a killer tornado, and kept the Glide and me rubber side down in a windstorm. More importantly, my life had taken on several small, but important changes. I felt a sense of oneness with the road, and with those I met along the way. Some of my long-standing suspicions and prejudices had been dispelled, and I was starting to shed some of the control factors that for so long had dominated my life. I was able to appreciate the trip and to see it as a wonderful gift that had been laid in my lap.

A feeling of humility came over me as I realized that there was still some 13,000 plus miles left in my journey. While that distance seemed daunting, I was not overwhelmed. That evening, as I wrote those thoughts, I had a feeling of cautious optimism that, no matter what or who would cross the center line of the road, I could handle it. In all of literature, the open road has been a symbol of freedom, most especially, freedom from the bondage of self. I was beginning to experience that freedom and was hungry for more. I was ready to begin the next phase of the trip.

Santa Elena Canyon in Big Bend National Park.

Continental Divide in New Mexico.

Texas Badlands near the Pecos River.

Old time barbershop in Seligman, AZ on Route 66.
To view additional pictures of the Southwest Rim go to www.ridingtherim.com

The Pacific Rim

Rim Day 13 Elapsed mileage 2,965

HOW IT HAPPENED

It was great to stay with my friends in San Diego, but I was raring to go as the Glide and I pulled out of their driveway. Ahead of me stretched one of the world's most beautiful roads, Hwy 1 up the California coast. I thought of Rob who had ridden a couple of thousand miles to ride it with me. We were now supposed to meet in Los Angeles. I hoped his mechanical woes were behind him.

I hopped on the I-5 towards Huntington Beach to meet up with Lisa Noble my America's WETLAND Foundation (AWF) project manager. It occurs to me that I haven't said enough about the efforts of AWF, Val Marmillion, and his entire staff. A lot of people put me where I was, and I needed to acknowledge a debt of thanks to the people who had made RTR possible.

One day in late January, 2006, as I was researching wetland groups on the internet, I came across a group called America's WETLAND Foundation. Their name intrigued me because it indicated a national wetland organization. (Later on I discovered that America's WETLAND refers to the Mississippi River basin wetlands which are primarily in Louisiana.) Using the AWF web site to learn about the organization, I was surprised to see that they were a Louisiana-based group established by Mike Foster during his last term as the Governor of Louisiana. The more I read, the more AWF seemed like a fit. They had extensive public relations and media resources and a strong reputation as a leader in wetland and coastal restoration. I had a lot of hope that this might be the group that could help me make RTR a reality. At first, it seemed as if I would be disappointed again. I sent off an introductory letter to their office in Baton Rouge, Louisiana and patiently waited for them to respond. The silence was deafening. For some reason (inspiration, perhaps?), I didn't want to give up on this possibility. After two weeks, and hearing nothing back, I decided it was time to change my approach. This grew out of my business experience. Although I am employed by a sales organization, my job did not entail selling a product. I "sold" ideas and concepts, and let the real professionals sell the product. Even in this limited sales role, I had learned the benefits of an ear-to-ear initial conversation that leads to setting up the first face-to-face appointment. I decided to put it all on the line and call the AWF office. I felt strongly that AWF, in my case, could become a key element to the success of my project.

Initially, through nobody's fault, the results were unpromising. At first, I got transferred to the automated message center where I left my contact information. Over the next several days, I continued to call until I was connected to a live voice and got an introductory meeting set up. (I need to clarify that the AWF office was not dodging my calls. They had a limited staff at this location, and those few were out in the field on most days overseeing a large number of projects.) The first meeting with the AWF staffer, Michael, proved to be very beneficial. He was young, enthusiastic, and his father was a motorcycle rider. My kind of guy!

After listening patiently to my plan, Michael fired back with several organizational questions for which I had very few specific answers. At the end of this brief meeting, he promised to take my concept to his boss, and said that they would get back to me. I waited and waited, and then waited some more. That was a very long month and half for me and I became increasingly frustrated with the pace of the planning and my difficulty in getting AWF involvement. I tried to remember that the bright dawn comes after the dark night. It took until April of 2006 before we could arrange a conference call with Val Marmillion, the president and owner of the public relations company that manages AWF. The phone conference went well and I came out of it with a plan for several action steps to be initiated in the near future.

It was during this initial call that we decided to use Earth Day Weekend, April 21st, as the departure date. This decision was based in part by discussions with other riders who had ridden through west Texas during the summer months, for I had decided to make my initial approach to the rim going west which would take me into Texas. The other riders had strongly suggested that I tackle that portion of the trip in the spring to take advantage of the milder weather. Having had the experience of hot weather riding, it seemed sensible. I also wanted to experience a southwest spring in order to see the desert in bloom. Earth Day also seemed liked a logical choice for a day to kick off an event that was tied so closely to the environment. America's WETLAND Foundation was in agreement with both my choice of time and with the direction of the route.

Following this meeting I was primed, pumped, and ready to go. With a start date selected, my excitement, if possible, grew ever more intense. I felt that the project was finally starting to take shape. There was still a lot to be done, and not a great deal of time in which to do it. My first task was to put together a budget for the trip and send it to AWF. As the weeks passed, I eagerly waited further contact from Michael or Val. One month, then another, passed without any word from AWF. I grew frustrated, always a fault of mine. I was incredibly eager to get some sort of official recognition on the AWF web site which would be of enormous help when I approached potential sponsors and media organizations. (Dark night comes before bright dawn. Say it again.)

To say that I waited patiently for these events to unfold would be both an understatement and less than factual. A gnawing voice in my head kept urging me to do something while I waited for AWF to take the next steps in developing our partnership. I started contacting anyone who was writing about wetland and coastal issues in the local and national press to pitch my RTR project. When I came across an article on the wetlands or related topics, I would clip it for future reference, and then send off a quick letter to the author. I also called on any media contacts that I had and tried to get myself invited on local radio or TV shows. This was all occurring in the spring of 2006, a full year before the planned departure date of April 21, 2007. By mid September of 2006 I was no further along than I had been in April.

I would later learn that media interest is measured in days if not hours, and that while my project might have been novel, it was way too early for any real interest from them. For those who may be contemplating their own campaign or quest, I want to let you know that my experience has taught me to stay focused, not become discouraged, and trust in the process. I urge you to learn from my experiences, whatever your cause may be.

On September 11, 2006, I decided to contact Val Marmillion directly. I wanted to know if the relationship between RTR and AWF was going to proceed, and at what pace. I was completely ready to go it alone if necessary, but I would rather have AWF as a partner. A response came quickly from

Val. He explained that their plate was very full, but they were still committed to partnering with me. Shortly after this RTR got a new logo, a place on the AWF web site, and things started to happen. Marketing materials were jointly developed between RTR and AWF, and I finally felt that we were gaining some traction in making the project a reality.

Frustration, I later learned, is a common theme in the planning of any project. For example, I got my first bite for media attention after contacting a friend who was a reporter with a local newspaper. He was excited about the project. We met in mid-October for an interview and photo shoot. I was told that the article would come out in late October or, perhaps, early November. By mid-November the article still had not been published. I started to get concerned, even more so, when my newspaper contact stopped returning my emails and telephone calls. It was not until January of 2007 that I found out that the article would not be published because my reporter friend had taken an early retirement due to health problems. It seemed like I was taking one step forward and two backwards. I gave myself a pep talk. At least I was on the radar screen with AWF and had their promise that RTR would soon have a place on their web site. When that occurred, there would be a mechanism for sponsorship and media recognition.

During the summer and fall of 2006, I could have easily become discouraged with the whole fund raising and media awareness aspect of the project. At times, I was ready to chuck both concepts and just take off on the Glide and ride into the sunset. Thankfully, Linda kept me on track. Also, something in the back of my mind kept telling me to be patient and allow things to unfold on their own. I continued what I had been doing through the early spring of 2006— seeking media contacts, shoring up the relationship with AWF, and planning the trip. I was still uncertain about many aspects of the trip, but knew that having AWF in my corner was a crucial component to the success of RTR.

With the appointment of Lisa Noble as my project manager things started to move forward at a rapid pace. Lisa became one of many RTR champions. With her help, RTR grew from a vision into to a reality. Though she had no experience as a motorcycle rider, her expertise in dealing with the media, organizing events, and coordinating all the details of the project proved invaluable. She quickly became my advocate and advisor. Much of what RTR had accomplished so far, and what I still hoped to accomplish, was a direct result of her efforts. To be accurate, I must add she was not alone. Since I've acknowledged her efforts, it would be less than fair if I didn't say the same about the efforts of the entire Marmillion staff. A lot of people put me where I was, and I owed a debt of thanks to a great many people. Lisa and all the folks from AWF were riding with me as I headed towards Highway 1.

Meeting the Pacific

Huntington Beach was near Lisa's home, and she treated me to a great lunch, followed by a stroll on the beach, including (of course) a picture taking session. It was a windy day with an overcast sky, but I was actually standing on a California beach, decked out in my biker gear, in a photo shoot. The blue Pacific unscrolled itself at my feet, and, although the ever-blue California sky was hidden overhead, Balboa and I had both made it to the Pacific. (I know it was Hernan Cortes, but, in his poem, Keats says it was Balboa, and who am I to argue with John Keats?) Of course, I wasn't thinking that at the time because I was being pummeled by winds that started as gentle breezes in Japan, and grew as they sailed across the vast expanse of the Pacific. It was still a great moment, though no one was ever going to write a sonnet about it.

I was concerned about getting around Los Angeles, but, with Lisa as my guide, I was able to negotiate the maze of off ramps and freeway entrances without incident. The "freeways" as my California friends call them are five to six lanes wide, and traffic moves at 55 – 60 MPH. Concentrating on following Lisa, I barely noticed the downtown skyline of Los Angeles. I was too busy sweating, gritting my teeth, and hoping no one on the freeway on that day had a beef with bikers. I planned, one day, to come back to see the city in a more relaxed manner. Maybe in an Abrams tank!

Hooking up with I-10 was like greeting an old friend. This stretch of tarmac started in Jacksonville Florida, was a major artery through the heart of New Orleans and shot across the desert to the Pacific. It's a great road. It's a shame that, for many Americans, it came to symbolize the site where stranded victims waited above the flooded streets of New Orleans. Entire families, babies and grandparents, baked in near 100 degree heat for days, with no shelter and no water, waiting to be rescued. It was searing images like that, and worse, that I never wanted to see again and not let the rest of the country forget. Those images were part of the reason I had traveled across the country to meet that blameless interstate and now I followed it up to Santa Monica.

Santa Monica would be the place where I started my journey up the fabled Hwy 1, also known as the Pacific Coast Highway (PCH). All was well until Oxnard, where my old friend and nemesis, the wind, once again joined me. It was not a menace that day because the road followed the beach and the scenery was outstanding. The carving done by wind and water on the rocky shore outdid anything in a museum, and it was hard to pay attention to the road. The crosswinds, however, were a great help in keeping me focused. I rode in those crosswinds all the way to Ventura, which would be my stop for the evening.

Entering Ventura, I thought about all the Beach Boys and Jan & Dean songs I grew up listening to. Here I was, riding along the same highways, and seeing the places that they sang about. It was an enormous rush. (And I swear I saw a '57 Woody with a surfboard sticking out its rear door. If I didn't, I should have.) The plan was to meet my long-lost friend Rob (remember Rob?) in the morning, when we would (finally) join up to travel north for the next several days. First, though, it was time to get back to the business end of the trip, promoting awareness about the state of the environment. I had an event stop coming up. After settling into my room, I prepared for the presentation to be given that evening at a Ducks Unlimited banquet.

Ducks Unlimited is a national organization dedicated to preserving the natural habitat of several bird species, including ducks. While the general public is aware that they are closely associated with the sport of duck hunting, few people outside the organization realize their support and dedication to wildlife conservationism. DU was one of the first organizations to respond to my inquiries for a media event. If not for that first flicker of support, I would have had a much harder time staying in the battle, and I owe them a lot of thanks. I was looking forward to meeting with the Santa Barbara chapter.

The ride up to Santa Barbara was a pleasant one. The evening sun was setting, its orange- red disk, swollen by atmospheric refraction into a giant, golden globe that slowly sank into the gleaming waters of the Pacific Ocean. Its dying rays were like an arrow, marking a glowing road to the west across the darkening water. It was tempting to follow the path it laid out for me, but Harley doesn't make submersibles. Arriving in Santa Barbara at around 1800 hours, I was somewhat dismayed to learn I would not speak until 1930. I was a little concerned about driving back to Ventura at night, but I decided to enjoy the fine food and conversation at the banquet and not to worry about the ride back to the hotel.

It was their annual banquet, and they had a large turnout of members. There was a silent auction that included wildlife paintings, guns, knives, and an assortment of outdoor equipment. I would have liked to bid on a couple of items, but, of course, I did not have the space on the Glide to carry any extra gear with me. As I waited for the dinner to begin, I struck up a conversation with a couple of guys who were also riders. They gave me some advice on riding the PCH, (Pacific Coast Highway) and were envious they could not accompany me. I had been asked to present the keynote speech for the evening, and, after my host introduced me, I gave a short, but, I hope, spirited talk on the wetlands, Hurricane Katrina, and what I was attempting to accomplish with RTR.

The audience was aware of some of the points I raised, but I don't think anyone can really comprehend the hundreds of thousands of acres of marshland lost by the state of Louisiana over the past fifty years. It must be hard for any state with a rocky shoreline like California to grasp the insidious disappearance of so large a part of it. I was lucky. This audience was both interested and committed. There were several questions from the audience and, as they ate, I put aside a very tasty meal as I tried to answer all of them. (Don't worry. I finished my meal before I left. Motorcycle riders rarely go hungry.)

They had a business meeting scheduled after dinner, and I excused myself because I really did have to hit the road back to Ventura. The ride back, while windy, was very scenic, with the moonlight shinning on the ocean, and the waves breaking on the beach below the highway. It seemed proper. I entered Santa Barbara in the fiery orange light of sunset, and I was tooling back to Ventura in the silvery light of the moon. If there's not a song about that, there should be.

Heeere's Robby!!

The next morning I got a call from Rob (Rob. Rob? Who? Oh, Rob!), for directions to the hotel. We had a great reunion once he arrived. I felt a little guilty that he had been battling mechanical woes while I was having so many great experiences. But he was here, and I was glad to see him. I've never been able to decide if Rob looked like a kindly old grandfather who would hand out lollipops to children, or a steely-eyed politician who would steal them out of their mouths. He has this shock of white hair and these very blue eyes. Maybe Hollywood could cast him as both. Certainly, he didn't look like a biker, but we had been on many a ride together, and I really looked forward to making this one with him. It sure was nice to have him with me at last.

I packed my gear as he filled me in on the details of his own trek across the Southwest. It was a nice, comforting sensation to be sharing again the kind of conversation we had so often had. He had been on the road for several days, and then stopped in Los Angeles to visit with an old friend. Now he was here. It felt like old times with him. After riding so many solitary miles, I believe we were both ready for some companionship as we headed out, taking Hwy 101 to the north. Our destination for the night was San Luis Obispo, which was inland off the coast.

California Dreaming

Green foliage covered the hills and wild flowers were everywhere. With the crashing waves of the deep blue Pacific on our left, and the craggy cliffs on our right, it was hard to concentrate on the road and keep the bikes in line but we had to, especially with the wind blowing as it was. Hwy 101 was everything that I imagined it would be, but, even with the beautiful scenery, the wind was taking a toll on us.

By mid afternoon, with 50 miles still left to go, we were both ready to settle in for the evening but we pushed on. Arriving in San Luis Obispo, we discovered there were two motorcycle rallies going on in the area, and hotel rooms were scarce. After getting turned down at a couple of motels, our luck changed, and we landed a room at Motel 6. We took it gladly, although it was a smoker. My allergies would just have to cope for the evening. Bikes of all makes and models lined the motel's parking lot and there was a lot of eye candy for us to enjoy. Some guys read Playboy. I read biker magazines. After supper at a local diner, it was off to bed. The weather forecast for the next day was for lower winds, and we both agreed it would make for a much nicer ride. We hoped the weather man would be right this time.

There was a definite chill in the air the next morning as we chatted with several other riders at the motel and traded stories with them. Most of the bikes were sport touring models, and the Glide seemed out of place in this pack of German and Japanese machinery. We learned one of the rallies had begun in San Francisco and was an annual event open to all makes of bikes. The rally planners laid out a course over two days that went from the interior of the state out to the PCH. (Pacific Coast . . ., oh, you remember.) Everyone was in high spirits as they packed up their bikes, and Rob and I bid them safe riding as we went our own way.

Hurrah! Hurrah! No wind as we pulled out on Hwy 1 towards Salinas.

We could enjoy the ride without being blown off the road and becoming part of the scenery. Both of us needed fuel, so we stopped at a gas station in Salinas where we met a group of Hispanic riders called the Salinas Valley Road Saints. Initially, we eyed them, and they eyed us, warily. Then, I decided to walk over to introduce myself. I was on their turf, after all, and it was my place to make the first move. (Anyway, any group calling themselves "Saints" has instant appeal to a New Orleans boy.) After a few awkward moments, everyone relaxed, and I found out about their group. The newly-formed "Saints" had, as their mission, helping needy children and families, while letting others know that bikers are concerned about social issues, just like anyone else. Boy, were they singing my song!

They were meeting to go on a club ride up the coast, and I was amazed that some of the guys were only wearing thin tee shirts or vests without anything on underneath. (One macho point to California riders) As we got ready to go our separate ways, they insisted on having our picture taken with them. During the picture-taking, they kept on saying "queso." I probably looked either foolish or concerned, because I did not know what "queso" meant. They got a big kick out of telling me it was Spanish for "cheese!" In one shot, they insisted I hold up a vest with their colors on the back, quite an honor for an outsider. I told them I would include a picture of them on my website. As we parted, they gave us some really useful directions on how to get over to the coast by taking a local highway. We parted, all friends, combining our passion for biking with a desire to improve the world, even though we met as wary strangers. There's another lesson from the road for me.

We traveled Hwy 68, which cut through the low mountains, and took us over to the Monterey Peninsula. Rob and I both commented on how great the scenery was. Lush trees and foliage lined the road, blue California sky overhead, a perfect day. Then, suddenly, we were in Monterey and looking for the Hog's Breath Saloon. Jill did a great job guiding us there by routing us towards Carmel-By-the-Sea. The Hog's Breath was smaller than I imagined, but nice. We met a couple from Oregon who gave us some suggestions for riding and dining in their home state. They made it a point to tell me about a local cheese factory, and how I must stop to take a tour of the facility. I promised to consider it.

After hanging around, hoping to run into Carmel-By-the-Sea's most famous resident, Clint Eastwood, (whom we did not see) we decided to get back on the PCH and travel north towards the evening's destination. As we left Carmel, I marveled at the upscale shops, expensive automobiles, and the feel of wealth that was everywhere.

Back on the 101, the scenery just kept getting better by the mile. I pulled off by Davenport, and we both took pictures of the sea and the cliffs, with the waves crashing below our feet. The air was filled with the aroma of sea pine, and rosemary. I kept looking at the sandy beaches, framed by towering cliffs and craggy rock formations, all of which were pounded by the endless surf. Despite the seeming permanence of that place, I knew it was just as susceptible as my part of the world to natural disaster. We had hurricanes. They had wildfires and earthquakes. I knew Californians had rallied to New Orleans after Katrina, just as New Orleanians had hustled up to New York after September 11. We are a caring people and it was that spirit of altruism I wanted to tap into. Earthquakes and hurricanes may be unavoidable, but preparations for them and the proper use of natural resources were not. A heavy thought for a beautiful scene, but it was really what the trip was about.

Hwy 1 is not only beautiful, it is also well-traveled. The road was busy with traffic. There were lots of motorcycles that were mostly sport bikes and crotch rockets. We ended up in the midst of another rally. We soon found out that its headquarters, once again, were in our night's destination—Half Moon Bay, California, a fact that did not bode well for our prospects for an evening's lodging. I'm a biker. I like bikers, but this was becoming inconvenient.

After finding a nice room at the Holiday Inn, we unwound from the road and talked about the great day of riding we just had. Rob misplaced his wallet in the hotel room, or, at least, he thought he did, but we found it under the bed where it must have fallen when he was unpacking his gear. Rob got frustrated with himself. It had been a rocky trip for him, what with his mechanical delays, but I tried to let him know everything was all right. When it's just you and your bike on the road, keeping track of important papers, having an adequate cash flow, and making sure you don't leave things behind becomes an important part of each day. I understood. I tried to plan it so that wouldn't happen to me. I'm sure Rob did, too. It happened; Another life lesson from the trip.

A stroll through town took us to a bistro for dinner. We thought the place would be filled with bikers from the rally, but, instead, it was mostly an upscale crowd. They gave us a wary look as we strolled in wearing our riding gear, and looking exactly like two guys who had been on the road for a couple of weeks. (I looked fine, of course. Probably it was Rob who scared them.) The meal was just okay, and we had enough of the "beautiful people" crap, so we headed out, tough bikers that we were, to find ice cream for a nightcap.

San Francisco is a mere 17 miles north of Half Moon Bay. That stretch of Hwy 1 was spectacular and very twisty. It was the road I remembered from when Linda and I drove the PCH several years ago. For a moment, I pictured Linda, missing her, feeling the distance between us keenly, then I turned back to the scenery. I decided, if she couldn't enjoy it with me, I'd get a good mental picture of it and tell her about it when we were together again. The steep cliffs dropping off to the ocean, countered by the high cliff on our right, required our full concentration as we rode into the fabled City by the Bay. (Otherwise know as San Francisco to us southern boys.)

Getting through San Francisco was a breeze with Jill guiding us through the light traffic. We made our way to the Golden Gate Bridge and then to Sausalito. It was only 1030 as we checked into our hotel, which made it my earliest day off the road since leaving Louisiana. After unpacking the bikes, we were both ready to do some exploring. We headed out to Muir Woods, which required driving a twisty road that was a delight to navigate. John Muir was instrumental in creating the Sierra Club, and also played an important role in developing our National Park system. This small remnant of the once vast Northwest redwood forest was, fittingly enough, named for him.

Muir Woods remains the magical place I remembered it to be, with its towering redwoods, heavily shaded walks, and numerous plant species growing everywhere. As close as you are to San Francisco, it's like being in another world; walking among trees so tall it would break your back if you leaned back to see the tops. Deep in the trees and foliage, even on the trails, you are cocooned in silence. It was possible, closing your eyes, to imagine the United States when a squirrel could travel coast to coast by jumping from tree to tree. OK, maybe that was never possible, but it is sad to realize how much we destroyed in the process of building our country. This stand of redwoods was unique in its close proximity to a large metropolitan area and was almost lost to residential development. That would have been a tragedy.

I think Rob felt some of the enhancement of Muir Woods, too. We spent well over two hours walking the area. During souvenir shopping at the gift shop, my first on the trip, I got my first National Parks Passport stamp and then headed back to the hotel. There was a great restaurant, bordered by a small stream, and, fortuitously, some wetlands, within walking distance of the hotel. Gazing on the wetland area as we ate, I wondered how many Californians realized their wetlands were in the same danger as Louisiana's, though not to the same extent. I was glad they were there. They kept me focused. Enjoying Rob's company, the ride, the beautiful sky and landscape, still lost in the spell cast by Muir Woods, I could not escape a conclusion so obvious that it seems silly to state it. I will, though. What a great day!

That evening, I decided to lighten my load and get rid of the tour-pack trunk. I had planned on using the trunk to temporarily store my riding gear and helmet while on the road. I thought it would offer a safer alternative than just leaving my gear on the bike when I stopped for a media event, to get a bite to eat, or explore an area. Now, after several weeks, I found I was not using it as originally planned, and, at times, it made the Glide a bit top-heavy, especially in high winds. I sorted through my gear and divided it into what definitely could go back, those items I could possibly live without, and those I absolutely needed. After moving items back and forth between the piles, and with some input from Rob, who was lounging comfortably on his bed watching me work, I was able to set aside a considerable amount of items to load into the tour pack trunk and ship back. That would be the first of several times I would ship back to Louisiana unneeded gear, gifts, and other items to lighten my load.

The next morning, we were both excited about exploring San Francisco, but, first, I needed to find a FedEx or UPS store to ship back my unneeded gear. The hotel called a cab for us, and the driver knew of a shipping place. Fortunately, it was close to the terminal that we would use to catch a ferry to cross the bay. The shipping clerk was very helpful, and suggested I simply use the tour pack as a shipping container rather than a box, which would save me some money. He even used plastic ties to secure the zipper pouches so prying hands couldn't raid the pack. The cost was minimal, even at a weight of 15 lbs, and, in no time at all, we were heading down to the Larkspur Ferry for the ride over to San Francisco.

The ferry ride over was crowded with many locals, including business men wearing suits and riding bicycles. (Yes, Toto, we are in San Francisco.) The combination was incongruous to my eyes. Rob, who traveled extensively around the world, including a stint in Singapore, was unfazed by the sight. The bay was windy and cold, but, just the same, the boat ride was great. Rob had planned our day in San Francisco because he had been here several times before.

We walked up to Union Square, took a cable car ride up Knob Hill, and past the shortest, narrowest, testiest street in the world, Lombard Street. Even for San Francisco, it was a sight to see. We commented on the steep streets and speculated on the difficulty that would be faced by a novice motorcycle rider attempting to maneuver the streets and park a bike on the steep inclines. On our walk to the wharf, we were both grateful it was a downhill, versus an uphill, climb. Along both sides of the street were brightly painted Victorian homes the area is so well known for. I wondered how much one of those beauties would sell for. (The answer was— a great deal more than I would ever be able to afford.)

Finally, arriving at the wharf, we played tourist, taking in all the shops lining Pier 47 and Rob purchased a fleece jacket to ward off the cold Pacific air. Lunch was at a 50's style diner and the burgers were great. After several more hours of sightseeing, we made our way back to the ferry terminal. There are two ferry boats that cross the bay, and we decided to take a different one back to Sausalito.

While waiting for the ferry, I heard violin music, and discovered a fellow named Mike playing in a small room next to the ferry landing. Mike worked at the ferry terminal and had picked up the violin at a yard sale. He taught himself how to play about three years before. While I was not a music critic, he sounded good to me for only having three years experience playing what seemed to me to be a difficult instrument. I asked him to play some Beethoven, which he did while he told me his story. He has been working for the ferry service for 20 years and, also, as a part-time school teacher. His music was a way for him to give something back to the people waiting for the ferry, and for him to experience a different part of himself. (Very Zen-like was this fellow Mike. Of course, we were in California.)

On the ferry ride back, I managed to bend a few ears with my AWF pitch, and most people listened politely. Once again, I had to ask the rhetorical question of myself, am I making a difference? Then I thought of Mike and his violin, and suddenly knew, just as he did, the important thing was my intention, not the response to it. (Keep that in mind, Johnny Appleseed.) Thanks Mike. Once again, the Universe connected me to someone who gave me exactly what I needed at exactly the right moment.

After several days of riding, with only minimal cardiovascular exercise, both Rob and I were exhausted from our day of touring the fine city of San Francisco. After a dinner spent planning tomorrow's route through the wine country, it was off to an early night's sleep. As I dozed off, I wondered if I was beginning to experience sensory overload. I had seen so much and met so many people. There had been so many gifts along the way. I didn't want the inevitable passage of time, to say nothing of the daily routine of work, when I went back to it, to steal any of it from me. Well, I had the pictures, and my journal. That would have to do, I supposed. Then, just before I drifted off, I recalled a lesson I had learned long before— intense experiences stay with a man, because they change a man. I knew I was changing and that was a great comfort to me. I'm pretty sure I had a smile on my face as sleep took me.

We left Sausalito around 0800 with a mild layer of fog hovering over our heads, and headed north on the 101. The plan was to take the 101 to Santa Rosa, and then cut over to the Hwy 1 at some point. As we traveled further north, the weather held, and the fog layer, while thick, did not hug the road, so visibility was not a big problem. Past the town of Petaluma, Hwy 116 came up on the Zumo's screen. The highway took a westerly direction towards Sebastopol, and, since that was where we wanted to go, we took it. I'm going to save you a description. You can figure it out. It was California. The road was great.

In Sebastopol, we located a Starbucks for a quick cup of Joe, and used the rest stop to get some local advice on the roads. The folks were nice and woodsy, almost a throwback to the 70's (sans the leisure suits.) We continued west on CA 12/116 to Bodega Bay, enjoying the tight sweeps and turns through hills dotted with modest homes. At Bodega Bay, a turn north put us on the Hwy 1, and I quickly noticed how different this part of the PCH was from the southern route we had previously been on. On the east side of the road, the highway was lined with trees. They had the most wonderful fragrance. The west side of the road dropped off to rocky crags, with the dull waters of the Pacific lashing small beaches and rock formations. The turns were tight, and, with the wonderful scenery, it was hard to keep our attention on the driving. After fueling up in Bodega Bay, we headed towards Fort Bragg, approximately 100 miles away. It was already 1100 hours and we had only gone 72 miles in three hours. Sightseers!

The further north we traveled, the better the scenery on either side of the road became. It was a challenge to look at it, because the road was pretty testy. We would come up on a tight turn, a steep incline, or a fast down grade that often required we slow down to 10 MPH. It was hard to keep my eyes on the road and not be distracted by the lush vegetation that lined the highway. The scent of fir trees filled the hollows, and bright purple plants sprung out at us when we crested an incline. This was sensory overload in the highest degree! I glanced over to Rob and we laughed. We both felt like kings; tooling down a great road, taking in fantastic sights, with no one to answer to but ourselves. It's good to be the king! There was no urgency to our travel and we relished taking as much time as needed on this portion of our trip.

Around noon we arrived at Moss Point and stopped at a deli/gas station/ grocery/hardware store. It was a delightful place with a deep, heavily forested ravine in the back that also served as the outdoors bathroom facility. While it may seem contrary to the message of my trip, I had little choice. The store did not have any public restrooms. I felt bad about peeing in such a beautiful place, but figured I was only adding fertilizer for future hardwood growth. The deli was great and served us a heavily-stacked sandwich of turkey, bean sprouts, and cheese.

As we ate we were joined by a rider named Scott who was traveling from Los Angeles to somewhere in Oregon. Scott told us he bought and sold furniture from the 1940-50-60's periods, hot items in California. He was on a heavily loaded Honda CB 750, and told us he had two other bikes in Oregon. We invited him to join us for the ride north, cautioning him we probably would be taking a much slower pace than what he was used to driving. He happily followed us, and stopped with us when we took a photo opportunity at a pull-off. Here we met a couple on their honeymoon, and together we all marveled at the beauty of this unusual place. We set out again, putting miles behind us, but savoring the scenery as well. After a while, I think our pace got to Scott and, a little bit below Mendocino, we parted ways. (The honeymooners left much earlier. I think they had pressing business that didn't require our presence.)

Rob and I headed towards Fort Bragg, now going 50 MPH which was our fastest speed of the day. Gas at Fort Bragg was only $3.59 a gallon, the lowest I had seen in several days. We located a Holiday Inn, and they directed us to a nearby laundromat which had a pizza joint close by. While our duds were spinning, we dined on an excellent pizza and talked about the day's events. It had been a fantastic ride and we hoped it would continue. The remaining miles of the PCH did not disappoint us.

Land of the Giants

Both Rob and I felt a noticeable change in the energy as we traveled north up Hwy 1. In Sebastopol the crowd at Starbucks was less "Yup" and more "Hip." Moss Point had more of a frontier feeling and, now, in Fort Bragg, it seemed every spent flower child of the 60's and 70's and their spiritual descendants were there. In Stewards Point, we saw an American flag with the peace symbol that proudly flew over a government building. You won't see that often in Louisiana. I had to marvel at the energy there. What a wonderful part of the country this is. Pinch me, is all this real!

Leggett, California is famous for a giant redwood tree that you can actually drive through. We went to investigate, but the road down to the tree was gravel and very steep. With our heavily loaded bikes, it did not seem like such a good idea to push our luck by navigating it. Stopping for a break at the Leggett convenience store, we met Windy, a rider from Los Angeles, who was coming back from an advanced rider's course in Oregon. She was a freelance writer for one of the sport touring magazines and was riding a Honda ST1300. After chatting with her, there was little doubt she was a very accomplished rider and it seemed safe to guess it was also true of her as a writer. After some good-natured ribbing about riding a Harley and not trying the road down to the famous redwood, we got pictures of each other, and went our separate ways.

At Leggett, we bid our fond farewell to that glorious stretch of road. It had taken us almost 725 miles from Los Angeles. We hopped on Hwy 101, which went inland away from the coast, however the scenery was just as beautiful. Our destination was a place called "The Avenue of the Giants". After pulling off for a picture and a biological break, two German dudes rolled up in a rental RV. They were on a cross-country trip and had the entire summer to make it to the East coast. They asked about our trip in flawless English, and were rewarded with my 15 minute RTR presentation. I didn't realize it at the time, but it was my second international RTR pitch. Of course, it may not have been as good a preparation for my eventual foray into the Maritime Provinces as the French tourist in Seligman, Arizona, because I didn't think that I was going to find that many people who spoke German in Quebec.

Five miles down the road, we entered the Avenue of Giants, which is CA 254. The road is canopied by huge redwood trees for almost 32 miles, all preserved in their natural state in a protected environment. Several small towns dot the road and, again, we picked up energy from a time gone by. A stop at a visitor's center close to the town of Mudflats treated us to exhibits on the history of the area. While we were there, I met a very politically active lady from Eureka, our next stop. I took a final look at the redwoods as we left. Once again, I was overwhelmed at the majesty of the redwoods and could not understand why anyone would want to destroy these graceful giants.

Our destination that evening was Eureka where I encountered my first lodging problem of the trip. There was a large festival being held that weekend, in addition to graduation at a local college. We could only find lodging for one night, though my plans called for us to be there for two nights. Eureka has a long history of wetland preservation and the city was surrounded by several reclaimed wetland area. I wanted to touch base with one or more of the wetland groups in the area. I was also scheduled to meet up with a group from the Eureka H.O.G. chapter who had been enthusiastically corresponding with me over the past few months. We were going to join them on a ride up to Steelhead Lodge, an annual event their chapter sponsors. Unfortunately, after calling my contact, I learned their plans had changed. I explained about the room shortage. After much debate I expressed my thanks to them and explained we were riding north in the morning to find a room for the next evening.

This would be the first of several H.O.G. events that did not work out as planned. Initially, I felt a sense of failure, but I soon realized I was trying too hard to make things work out. Yes, I should have made a room reservation in Eureka, knowing it was an important stop, but it was too late to do anything about it, other than to make sure that this would be a mistake I would not repeat again. I also regretted I would not be able to hook up with a couple of local wetland groups. I was still feeling a bit down at bed time, but sleep came easily enough, for there was always the promise of a grand adventure waiting for us tomorrow.

Before leaving Eureka the next morning, we visited the local Harley dealership where we met two guys from Hamilton, Ontario, Canada— Big Bob, and Everett the Wanderer. They were on a three week trip that would end with them crossing the Golden Gate Bridge. So far, they had traveled 5600 km, about 3500 miles. I was impressed they were riding that far just to cross the Golden Gate Bridge. How does that old saying go, something about the journey being more important then the destination? I guess that was true in their case. I asked them about traveling in Ontario, and also got some good tips about where to go in Nova Scotia and Prince Edward Island. We parted ways. Rob and I did manage to visit some of the wetland areas on the outskirts of the city before heading out to Crescent City, California.

The road up to Crescent City was more of the same, meaning some of the best riding I had ever experienced. We stopped at the Redwood National and State Park, which are one of the few national and state parks sharing the same boundaries. A walk on the beach at the visitor's center gave Rob and I the opportunity to ham it up for some pictures. The road through the park was shrouded in fog and we saw herds of elk grazing in pastures of fir trees that filled the air with a very strong, and pleasant, aroma.

At the "Big Tree" we stopped for pictures, and to gaze at this mighty giant which had almost been cut down to be used as flooring for a dance hall. There was a young couple with their children hiking the path with us. They were out exploring the area, and letting their kids experience the wonders of this enchanting place. "Good for them." If you plant the seed of ecology in children early in life, there is a better chance it will sprout in them as adults. We all agreed this was a magical place for kids of any age, including big kids like we adults. As we talked, the kids checked out my riding gear which seemed to fascinate them. Later, I hoisted them up on the Glide for some photos.

In Crescent City, we found lodging at the Curly Redwood Lodge, a 1960s type of motel. It was built from one redwood tree! It was well maintained, and had internet, and covered parking. It was late afternoon when I got a call from Mary Lousteau (my media manager) letting me know a TV station in Eureka wanted to do an interview. My spirits took a nose dive. I explained the lodging situation and our current location, which was almost three hours (88 miles!) away. I had already cancelled with the Eureka H.O.G. chapter and the Steelhead Lodge. I called the TV station back, but they did not want to do a phone interview. However, a Eureka newspaper did agree to one.

While the event was not a total loss, once again, I felt I could have done a better job of planning. The perfectionist in me was trying its best to rule the day. In the scope of just five minutes all the great events of the day evaporated, and all I could think of was how I let down the project because of a scheduling error on my part. With some gentle advice from Rob, I talked myself out of this morass and tried to keep the focus on the here and now, not on the "woulda" and the "shoulda." Oh brother, every day is a learning day!

Using the strong internet connection at the lodge, I tried to get some information on my brother John. I had been unsuccessful in my previous attempts to contact him to arrange a visit when I got to Washington State. We had not had much contact over the past several years, and I wasn't even sure he still lived in Washington. Even with the power of Google, I was not able to verify his location. All I had was an address which was over 10 years old. It was another disappointing turn of events. It had been a long day, filled with a wide range of emotion, but it was time to get some rest and have dinner at the diner across the street.

Once again, the morning skies were cloudy and wet. At breakfast, Rob and I met a couple from Minnesota who were traveling on a Gold Wing and pulling a trailer. I introduced myself as an associate member of the Gold Wing Road Riders Association (GWRRA,) and we traded riding stories and compared touring notes. I was sure they were a little bit confused by my membership in the GWRRA, so I explained about the trip and how the Metairie, Louisiana GWRRA Chapter had paid for my membership as the club's contribution to the project. I had been invited to speak at their chapter meeting after one of their members learned about RTR from a Coast Guardian. She was so enthusiastic about my ride that she volunteered to pay for an associate membership in their national organization for me. The Gold Wing Road Riders provide road side assistance to their members, and I would be able take advantage of this benefit if I had any mechanical problems. This, along with my membership benefits with H.O.G and the American Motorcycle Association (AMA) roadside assistance program, covered almost any type of breakdown assistance that I would need.

I asked my Gold Wing friends if they were familiar with the Aerostich factory in Duluth Minnesota, and both said they had never heard of it. I told them it was well worth a visit the next time they were in that part of the state, and that, I was planning to visit there later in the month. They looked doubtful that I would make it to Duluth in such a short time frame, but when I further explained the nature of my trip, they started to grasp the magnitude of what I was undertaking. They were interested in what I had to say and listened attentively. It was occasions like this that brought me down to reality and made me realize what a grand adventure I was on.

Solo Again

Every meeting carries with it the seeds of a subsequent parting. That was happening now. After fueling up, Rob and I said our goodbyes. He was turning back, heading to Louisiana and his most patient wife who had agreed to share him with me for some hundreds of miles. It had been great riding with him for the past week, but I sensed he was ready to see his relatives in Truckee, California and then trek back home. I would, once again, be a "lone rider". Rob turned east on Hwy 195, and I headed north on the 101. We waved to each other through the fog and drizzle. It has been said nothing is worth the wear and tear of winning, except for the friends you meet along the way. That had been true on my trip, but I had the further advantage of a good friend who chose to journey with me. Another gift.

Crossing the border into Oregon was another milestone for me, and, before I left it, I felt I should give thanks to the great state of California for the exceptional riding experiences I had on its roads over the past several days. At the Oregon State welcome center, I stopped to get a map, take some pictures of the rugged coastline, and change riding gear. The drizzle had increased to a light rain and the temperature was in the low 50's. I decided to pull on my heated gear. This was the first time on the trip that I used my heated jacket liner and gloves, and they did a great job of keeping me warm and dry.

Continuing towards Coos Bay, Oregon, I followed the rugged coastline as I drifted back in thought to the time my family and I visited the area with my brother Curt who lived in Portland. I was only 12 years old but I still remembered coming down the coast and walking along the beach. It was the first time I had seen an ocean and, like most young lads, I had scurried around collecting seashells and driftwood. The coast was similar to that of California, but more populated, with towns that popped up about every 45 miles.

At a fuel stop, I made friends with a local biker and asked him about the many small towns on Route 101. He explained they were settled in the days when travel was done on horseback. A good day's ride back then was about 40 to 50 miles. and, thus, towns sprung up at those intervals to support the overnight needs of travelers. I was not sure whether this was fact or fiction, but it was an interesting story in any event. He told me Coos Bay was not far and the road was in good shape. He cautioned me about wet surfaces and told me to keep my speed down in the small towns because many of them use speeding fines as their major source of income.

In Coos Bay, I located the HD dealership. The H.O.G. chapter was having a cookout and, after I introduced myself, they invited me to join them and tell my story. The editor of the newsletter did a short interview with promises of an article in the next edition. They, of course, were familiar with the destruction resulting from Katrina, but, like so many people, had no concept of how important the wetlands are in protecting coastal areas. After Katrina, most of the national media attention was centered on the levee system and the failed pumps. I explained how the wetlands and the barrier islands were the first line of defense when a storm comes in, and the loss of this natural barrier to storm surge was responsible for much of the destruction they had heard about.

The discussion, as it often did, finally got around to my project, and what I expected to accomplish with RTR. I told them, along with a general misunderstanding of the wetlands, most of the country did not realize the economic importance of the gulf coast and the Port of New Orleans. Almost 40% of our nation's energy comes across the gulf coast, and the vast network of pipelines, drilling platforms, and supply channels rely on a stable coastline. As the wetlands disappear, so does the coastline, and, with each tropical storm, more of the land mass is lost back into the Gulf of Mexico. Additionally, the Port of New Orleans is a major import and export center for farm and industrial products.

My informal presentation was peppered with questions from the group and, as I reeled off the statistics of land loss and economic importance, I could sense their appreciation for the project. I concluded by telling them my mission was not only to bring awareness about the environmental impact of wetland and costal destruction, but, also, to highlight both the economic importance and the security issues of preserving the gulf coast. I felt at home with these new friends and, following a hearty lunch of dogs and burgers, everyone got an RTR pin for listening to my story.

After I had finished up, I remembered an old Chinese fable that went something like this:

"A master and his students came to a swift river where they a found a young girl who wanted to cross but could not swim. This particular order of monks had sworn off all physical contact with females, but when the master learned of the girl's plight, he picked her up and carried her across the river. Once on the other side, he put her down and continued on his way. After a few miles, one of the students protested. He asked the master why he had carried the young girl across the river, thus breaking his solemn vows. The young acolyte wanted to know what the master was going to do to rectify this grievous incident. The master quietly looked at the student and said," It seems that you are the one still carrying her. I put her down several miles ago."

I felt as if I made up for the missed media opportunity in Eureka with the presentation in Coos Bay. It was time for me to stop carrying that load and get on with the rest of trip. I decided to leave regret about all that behind me.

It was only 1300, and one of the H.O.G. members suggested Florence as a good spot to spend the night. The drizzle had stopped, but I fired up my heated gear anyway. In less than two hours, I was checking in at the Chateau Motel. They advertised WiFi in every room, but, somehow, mine was not included and, no matter what the desk clerk tried, I could not get a connection. Actually, it was okay, because I knew there would be times, especially in Montana and Canada, when getting a connection would be almost impossible. I had become dependent on the internet as means to stay grounded with events back home, but I would have to stay a little less connected in those places later in my trip. Perhaps it was the universe's way of letting me practice for that.

That evening, I reflected on my time with Rob and the twinge of sadness I had felt when we parted in Crescent City. Now, after a day of riding solo, I was back in the groove and hoped Rob had made good time towards Truckee. I had been on the road for three weeks and, though comfortable with my schedule, I really missed Linda. Well, this was the path I had chosen and I still had work to do. I tucked Linda and Rob away in a pocket I could reach easily if I needed their sustenance, and got back to the business of the trip.

I do not function well without a plan, and planning ahead would keep me from looking back. I needed to get myself and my plans in shape. I made a few resolutions. I decided to cut back on the calories and try to increase writing down my thoughts and feelings. I had barely turned on my digital tape recorder, so I decided, in the future, I would try using it to interview the people I met during my travels.

I was a couple of days ahead of my schedule, and was not exactly sure which route I would take up to Seattle. The planned event with the Seattle H.O.G. groups was not coming together, so it was back to plan B once again. The next morning, before leaving the Chateau, I chatted with a young fellow named Jeff who was a pre-nursing EMT student. As we chatted, I let him know I was a Respiratory Care Practitioner and, after some hesitancy, he asked me about a tetanic contraction of the chest wall muscles that was mentioned in one of his text books.

Strangely enough, he was the first person on the trip that I spoke with about my professional life. Not making my professional life known to those I met was by design. My career as a Respiratory Care Practitioner had been fulfilling. I was proud of my profession. Prior to Katrina, though, I had decided I needed to get away from medicine, training, and the business end of the profession for a while. I had been in the medical field for over 30 years and, while it had been very good to me, enough was enough. I had planned on a six month leave of absence, during which I would do some serious motorcycling, perhaps some writing, and explore some of my other interests.

The tragedy of Katrina served to focus my energies, and I was determined to leave the field of medicine in the background for now. Yet, there I was, talking shop with a guy in Oregon, discussing a respiratory disorder, and giving him some tips on a presentation that he was preparing to give to a local group. We talked about public speaking and our mutual love of speaking to groups, and motivating others to improve their lives.

An Unexpected Encounter

Outside my room were three riders getting ready to load up and hit the road. One guy had a 1984 Roadking (the first model year) and it had a chain drive. They suggested I check out the sand dunes just outside of town. I easily found the dunes, using their directions. These dunes are part of the Oregon National Recreational Area and are protected against intrusion from commercial development. Many are quite steep and, after parking the Glide, I hiked up one and got some pictures of the surrounding area. Behind the dunes was a small area of wetlands which, I could only guess, had been formed by the Siuslaw River, which I would soon be following on my way to Eugene. The wetland areas I encountered on the trip always brought back to me the destruction of the wetlands I had seen in Cajun country. They were like a shot of adrenaline that kept me going on the road.

Traveling inland on Hwy 126, I followed the Siuslaw River east towards Eugene. With the river bubbling on the south side of road, the Glide and I purred down this delightful road taking in the gorgeous scenery. At Mapleton, I took Route 36, a suggestion from a local, and headed towards Triangle Lake. Again, the Siuslaw accompanied me, complemented by a heavy forest on my left flank. With almost no wind and the temperature in the low 50's, it was turning into a great riding day. I stopped several times to take pictures of the river and forests. Somewhere on Route 36, I passed a covered bridge that could have come out of Madison County, Iowa or some place in New England. It was traversed by a one lane road, and the bridge's sign indicated a construction date of 1928.

At a roadside park, I chatted with a family out for a Mother's Day fishing event on Triangle Lake. Unfortunately, they could not find a public area to fish. Even in the wild northwest, civilization had encroached on the public's access to nature. I felt bad for this family, whose plans had been spoiled. Seeing them bound together, first in anticipation, and then in disappointment, I felt again the joys of family. I made a mental note to call Linda and wish her a great day. I got a motel recommendation from them, and also a suggestion to view the nearby fish ladders. In an adventurous mood, I made the short hike to the fish ladders and was rewarded with several good photo opportunities. The Siuslaw was running very fast here, and the fish ladders were built to aid the fish as they swam upstream to spawn. The water was crystal clear and the brightly colored rocks sparkled under the swiftly moving river. Without the ladders, the fish would have gone extinct. It was another one of those all to rare moments where the encroachment of man on the environment was contrasted by his attempts to preserve it. Yes we are capable of striking a happy medium.

The road just kept on getting better as I headed towards Eugene and the Valley River Inn which the couple had recommended. It was a ritzy-looking place with a nearby mall and restaurant. I did not want to pass it up. Inside, the desk clerk quoted me a rate higher than I was accustomed to paying. I negotiated the price down with a promise to mention the Inn on my web site. She gave me an upgrade to a room with a view of the Willamette River, and I made it a point to find the evening manager and to tell him about the fine customer service that I had received.

After cleaning up and securing the Glide for the evening, I took a short walk through the mall and found the movie theater. The only thing playing that looked interesting was a movie called "Georgia" that was just okay. I found going to movies while on the road had a grounding effect on me. Somehow, it satisfied that part of me that wanted familiarity and routine. Linda and I both enjoyed going to the movies, especially with friends, and then getting coffee afterwards to chat. I had seen a movie. Now, where was that Starbucks, and Linda!

The next morning, I took a walk along the Willamette River, and then towards the college campus. Eugene is the quintessential college town and, while I did not have time to take in all the sights, I enjoyed the students milling about and the energy rolling out from the campus. Finally, after packing up, it was off to Portland and my next media stop with a local H.O.G. chapter. The interior roads were rather boring, compared to the coastline. I arrived in Portland after lunch and located the local HD dealership where we had an event planned. I had tentative plans for a ride with the local H.O.G. chapter, but my contact was unable to gather any interested riders because it was a weekday evening. The few riders who did show up filled me in on some good riding routes for my trip up to Washington State.

Checking into a motel, I received a call from my friend Roy and had a nice chat with him. He caught me up on the local gossip in Mandeville, and we dealt with some issues about the house. Then Roy told me that our mutual friend Hilly was also in Portland on business. Hilly and his wife Jeanne left Mandeville shortly after Katrina and moved to North Carolina. Like many Louisianans, they had enough of the aftermath of the storm and were in a good position to retire from their jobs and explore some new horizons. At dinner that evening, Hilly and I had a nice chat as we caught up on each other's lives. It had been over a year since I last saw him, but Hilly had not changed in the least. To a third party listening in, our conversation might have seemed a bit scattered. We lapsed into a familiar dialogue, ranging over topics from spirituality to the plight of the education system, depression, kids, wives and his move to North Carolina. For Hilly and me, this was life as usual, and it felt like the old days when we would have morning coffee on the shore of Lake Pontchartrain. It was just the kind of unexpected lift I needed that day.

I woke up feeling restless and wanting to get back on the road, even though there was no hurry to do so. I was ahead of schedule and Seattle was less than two days away. I still felt as if there was something I needed to take care of. I had not shaken the old "doing" thing. It was still with me. I had a phone-in radio interview at 0930 with a station in Eugene which went very well. The reporter was interested in my perspective on the attitudes of people concerning the recovery from Katrina. We talked about the apathy of some Washington politicians, and about the misinformation related to recovery issues in Louisiana. She was well-informed on the wetlands issue, and it was enlightening to talk with someone who shared my passion for change. Hopefully, we got some good air time out of the interview. Plant those seeds.

Leaving Portland, I stumbled my way through the morning traffic, and emerged on the west side of town to take Hwy 26 towards the coast. The more miles I put between me and Portland, the cooler the temperature became, as buildings gave way to lush green forests. I was once again enthralled with the country side. The road opened up to pasture lands, then to forested hills and low mountains. Checking the Zumo, I saw that the elevation was changing frequently as I passed through Saddle Mountain State Park and into the Tillamook State Forest. Near Elise, I spotted a museum that had several odd pieces of logging and lumbering equipment, but I saw the turn too late, and decided to push onwards. In no time at all, I found myself at Seaside, Oregon where Hwy 26 ends.

At Seaside, I once again picked up Hwy 101. As in northern California, there was a definite 60's feeling about the place. Several shops carried all-natural products. Co-op bakeries and grocery stories were prominent, and I passed several VW Vans adorned with flower power decals. After a brief lunch stop at the Bigfoot Bar & Grill, I pointed the Glide towards Astoria and the Washington State border. A short detour east took me to the Lewis and Clark National Park. This was the location of their winter quarters during their epic journey to map and survey the western frontier. I walked the grounds, and snapped pictures of the re-creation of their camp. I also got my National Parks Passport stamped. Then it was off to Astoria.

I was about to cross into Washington State, a fact which held several meanings for me. I would be ending my journey here, as had Lewis and Clark. Well, actually, though it was the endpoint of my Pacific leg, I was not ending anything. There would be a short break in the trip, however. I was going to fly back to Louisiana to see my son Adam graduate from college, and I would have a chance to spend time with Linda and my other son Phillip. Those twin events seemed to help power the Glide on its way into Washington.

After going just a few miles up 101, I saw in the distance a very long and high bridge. I suddenly realized that I would be crossing that monster to reach the other side of the Columbia River! There was no problem. I knew I could do it. With no other options, I took a deep breath and guided the Glide onto the access ramp, or, as I thought of it just then, the point of no return. As I rode onto the bridge, I kept saying to myself "I know I can do this," and, of course, I did. (I am proud to say I kept my eyes open all the way.) The crossing was, actually, not that bad, even with cross winds of 18 mph and gusts from passing logging trucks buffeting me and the Glide around. On the other side, I congratulated myself and took an ABC picture for Washington State.

The wind got better as I rolled inland and started to shadow Willapa Bay, eventually arriving in Aberdeen on Gray's Harbor. Aberdeen is a shipping town with a very obvious logging and industrial feel to it. I recalled this was the home of the grunge- rock group Nirvana. The town is nondescript, or at least what I saw of it was, and I could understand the somber lyrics and angst of Nirvana's songs. My lodging for that evening was the Hummingbird Motel. After unpacking the bike and getting a Diet Dr. Pepper, I noticed a lot of activity on the second floor balcony of the adjacent building. After observing this for a few minutes, it hit me that I may have stumbled on an "adult" entertainment enterprise there at the Hummingbird. Several men were hanging outside one of the rooms. Periodically, the door would open, one guy would come out, and another would enter. I tried not to be conspicuous as I took all this in, and decided to mind my own business, which, in my case was cleaning up the Glide.

The internet connection at the motel was poor, at best, so I decided to explore the area on foot. A local grocery store had a Starbucks coffee shop, so I finally got to enjoy a real cup of Joe. Nearby was a Denny's restaurant which I decided to visit for dinner. I was having difficulty deciding what to order, in that it all looked the same. After so many meals on the road, the selection was just not very inviting. The waitress patiently waited for my order, and I finally gave in and asked her what the specials were. With a bored expression, she reminded me that this was a Denny's and there were no house specials. She did suggest I try an omelet because it was a safe bet that the cook wouldn't screw it up. Taking her suggestion, I was rewarded with a tasty omelet. I ate it and counted my blessings that I had not been more adventurous in my selection.

Summing it up at Denny's

It was almost 1930, and, at this latitude, the sun had a long way to travel before it set for the evening. Sitting in the Denny's, I reflected on the past several days on the road. Crossing the bridge at Astoria was a big deal for me. Ever since my battle with the winds in the Mojave Desert, I had been overly cautious when confronted with high winds. I recalled a presentation at a H.O.G. Primary Officers Training meeting where one of the speakers told us about his fear of crossing the Mackinaw Bridge in Michigan. The bridge's decking was constructed of steel grates that tended to grab your front tire and make the bike wobble. There is actually no real threat with that, but the feeling of losing control can be very discomforting. He, as had I, used the voice of calm and reason to get him across the bridge without letting the incident get the best of him. To that extent, the bridge at Astoria had been yet another lesson. I thought, too, about my meeting with the Salinas Valley Road Saints in San Luis Obispo, California, and my initial fear of being the only non-Latino in the group. I smiled thinking of how they ribbed me when I did not know that "queso" was Spanish for cheese when we were taking photographs. Putting aside my fears and anxieties had become a theme of the trip. These were the real gifts I was finding on the trip.

Life had fallen into a routine for me. I was getting used to not having a great deal of responsibilities, other than getting on the road, maintaining the Glide, making my media stops, and taking care of expenses. Updating the web site and writing "Notes from the Rim" had become a welcome part of each day, and I hoped the readers were enjoying it also.

On the other hand, I still felt a sense of urgency about making good time on the road, and I had found myself passing up stops like the logging museum.

I needed to slow down, experience the unexpected, and live in each moment that the road offered. Also, my plans had initially included talking with people about their passions in life and then recording those conversations. I had not recorded many stories because of my self-imposed pace. Perhaps I should slow down. Perhaps there were real stories out there for me to record. I didn't know. As I continued summing up, I began to have the feeling that my trip was more about finding something inside of me rather then discovering someone else's story. The road can get lonely and I was sitting at a Denny's because the alternative was the hotel room. I was feeling the need for some much needed companionship, but the prospect of starting up a conversation with my waitress seemed more dreadful than my room back at the Hummingbird. In time, of course, that is just where I had to go.

Once back in my room, I started to make a list (I love lists.) for my upcoming trip back to Louisiana. I was really looking forward to reuniting with my family. Making the list somehow brought that a little closer to me. Besides, my other choices were the waitress and the "adult" entertainment suite. The Coast Guardians, AWF, nor Linda would understand the adult entertainment item on expense report. Since the waitress and I had already exhausted our conversational possibilities in our discussion about the menu, making the list was a good way to end the day.

The first thing to consider was the Glide. We still had a long way to go together and I had to be sure the old girl was up to it. I considered those things that needed to be addressed including: scheduled service items, suspicious engine noise, tire and rear shock pressures, and approving any items in advance that were covered by the extended warranty. There might be other things that would arise, but I was pleased that I had a grasp on what it would take "ter get Ol'Paint and me ready to ride off into them thar hills."

I also had to plan for the personal items that I would need to take with me to Louisiana. That list wasn't nearly as extensive, because, as I was writing it, my thoughts kept drifting to my family and the upcoming reunion. Besides, I needed less care and attention than the Glide. I don't have as much horsepower as she does.

The Rims End: Seattle

Finally, it was daytime and I was back on the road. After leaving Aberdeen, I decided to head towards Port Angeles and go to the northernmost point of Hwy 101. At a fuel stop in Kamliche, Washington, I received a message from my friend Shirley who lived in Seattle, and we made plans to meet on Thursday. There was also a message from Mary Lousteau informing me that a radio station in Seattle wanted to interview me on Thursday morning, which was the next day, or, at least, I thought it was. I was having a hard time keeping up with the correct date, probably because I decided not to wear a watch. However, my confusion about the date didn't seem to be enough of a reason to start wearing one. After verifying which day it was with another motorist, I quickly made a change in my route in order to go back towards Seattle by way of Olympia.

In Lacey, Washington, I stopped to purchase a pin and get an ABC picture at the Harley Davidson dealership. One of the salesmen volunteered to help me set up the picture and took one of me with the Glide. It was one of the friendlier dealerships I had encountered, and I hung out for a while, chatting with several of the customers. It was still early in the day and I wanted to confirm the location of the radio station. With directions from a rider at the dealership, I headed into downtown Seattle to scope out the station and to find a hotel nearby.

My interview was at 0800. I had the choice of staying in the suburbs and getting up very early to beat the rush hour traffic, or finding a room nearby, which I knew would be pricier. After deciding to stay in town I located a nearby Holiday Inn Express at $161 a night. That was a lot of money for a room, but the alternative of getting caught up in rush hour traffic and potentially missing my appointment, made the choice a little bit easier. As it turned out, that was my most expensive room for the entire trip, but, looking back, it was a good choice. I got the usual stares from the desk clerk as I strolled in wearing my riding gear to inquire about a room. Her attitude quickly changed once I identified myself as a Platinum Club member. My room was pleasant, and I was able to park the Glide in the parking garage which had 24 hour security. Once I settled in, I called Shirley and we made plans to meet that evening.

Seattle is an exciting city. As Shirley and I walked the downtown area to Elliot Bay, which is part of Puget Sound, I could feel its energy. The fish market was full of tourists and a vendor entertained us by tossing huge fish into various piles as he filled customer orders. After finding out it was Shirley's birthday, I insisted that we go to one of her favorite restaurants on my dime. Her selection was a small Asian restaurant, and the cuisine was superb. Making a decision on what to order was not a problem, and, after so many greasy diners, this was a real treat for me. After catching up on each other's lives over a lazy meal, we walked back towards her high rise, and parted with a promise to keep in touch. Seattle would be an interesting place to live one day, and I wondered if it would be a place that either Phil or Adam might like.

I made my way over to the radio station the next morning and had a great interview. The program's host was very friendly and showed a lot of interest in the project. We covered a lot of ground during the 20 minute taped interview, and she thought I had a good chance of getting some good air time later that day. As I later found out, they ran the interview a couple of times during the day, and also during primetime that evening. Much later, in Montana, I would hear from a long lost relative who lives in Seattle and heard the interview. The synchrony of life never ceases to amaze me. I can't remember the name of the show's host, but I am grateful for her efforts in getting the word out about the wetlands and my project. Sitting in the studio, wearing the headset, and hearing my voice from a high quality microphone, was great. It had me thinking that being on the radio would be a nice gig. I wondered what subjects I would cover, and whether or not I would run out of things to talk about. I had to laugh. Anyone who knew me would know that I would probably run out of listeners long before I ran out of topics.

After the interview, I headed towards my hotel in Tukwila which was right across the street from the HD dealership and, after unloading the Glide, I turned the bike in for service. The service writer was a nice guy and showed a lot of interest in RTR, which, of course, got him one of our limited edition ride pins. I expressed my concerns about having the bike ready when I returned, where it would be stored, and whether or not my gear would be safe. I let him know that I had an extended warranty, and that he need only to call me if they found any problems. As it turned out, they stored all the bikes in a secure area during the day and in the building at night. I left the Glide in his good hands, but with mixed emotions running through my head. While I was looking forward to flying back to Louisiana to see Adam graduate, and while the Glide did need service, I was still uneasy about not being with her. For almost a month, the Glide and I had been constant companions, and now we would be separated for several days and a few thousand miles. It was like a leaving a good friend on the side of the road— maybe worse. What a strange range of feelings, but, it is what it is!

With nothing much to do, I walked around the hotel and took several pictures of the blooming flowers. The locals did not the know of name of several of them, so I posted a question on the RTR web site asking if anyone knew what species they were. Dwight, a member of my H.O.G. chapter back in Slidell, had the correct answer (rhododendron). I awarded his efforts by making him the first Honorary Rim Rider.

Later, back in my room, I caught up on emails, called a couple of local TV studios to pitch the project for possible interviews on my return, and then headed back to the HD shop to browse. I also hit the local Starbucks for a cup of Joe. Dinner time arrived and there was a family diner within walking distance of the hotel. I called it an early evening after finding that the shuttle bus to the airport would leave at 0530. It was an antsy evening, and I knew exactly why. In a few short hours, I would be reunited with my family, however briefly. If you ever want to know how much something means to you, try doing without it for a while. I knew, and I was ready to reunite.

The next several days were somewhat surreal. I flew into Dallas in a cozy coach seat, and then met up with my son Phillip for the drive to Ruston, Louisiana to attend the graduation of my other son, Adam, from Louisiana Tech. In a few short hours, I had gone from being a long distance motorcyclist to being a tourist, and, now, I was a proud parent who watched his youngest son graduate from college. Linda was also able to attend the ceremonies, and after not seeing each other for several months, we had a great reunion. Here I was, with my sons, Linda and not a worry in the world, other than enjoying myself for the next couple of days. Although Linda had a horrible cold, she was a real trouper, and made it through both the three hour graduation ceremony and dinner later that night. While the rest of the crew organized a Texas hold'em game, Linda and I begged off and called it an early evening. And, to quote a line from the movie *Forrest Gump*, "That's all I'm going to say about that."

My family time in Ruston passed all too quickly. I had been surrounded in affection from my sons, and, above all, Linda. It was nice to submerge myself in family. If I could have pulled them over my head like a warm blanket on a cold night I would have. I knew that, once I got back on the road, it would begin to seem as if it had been a dream. If so, it had been a great dream. It wasn't easy to leave Linda and the boys, but I didn't see how I could give up the trip. It could be considered successful to this point, but there was still much to accomplish. After a long, uneventful flight back to Seattle, it was time to get back on the road. There was a long haul ahead of me. I was at the top of the northwest corner of the United States, and I was heading east, across the Northern Rim.

Salinas Valley Road Saints in San Luis Obispo, CA.

Mike the violin player – Ferry terminal in San Francisco, CA.

The rugged coastline of northern California.

Rob and I on the Avenue of the Giants.

The "Big Tree" north of Redwood National Forest.

To view additional pictures from the Pacific Rim go to *www.ridingtherim.com*

The Northern Rim

Rim Day 30 Elapsed mileage 4,860

Conquering the Cascades

The Glide was ready to go, but, somehow, the radio antenna had gotten misplaced, and was nowhere to be found. I rarely used the bike's radio because of the Zumo which offered its XM radio, but it still irritated me that it was missing. Chatting with several riders as I packed up the Glide, I got directions to Burlington, Washington, my stop for the evening. The ride to Burlington was pleasant, but, somehow uneventful. Maybe everything was uneventful after leaving my family. I found a motel near the HD dealership. The motel was quaint, clean, and beautifully landscaped. I was back on the road. I still had a long trip ahead of me and it was time to get to it. That evening I planned my route. I had anxiously waited for a chance to ride the fabled WA Rte 20. Now it was here.

In the early morning, I awoke with a sense of anticipation about the day's ride. I was ready to conquer the Cascade Mountains. Weather reports were favorable all the way into Kettle Falls, my destination. An early morning chill had me debating on how to dress for the ride. I elected to go with my heated gear, long johns, and wind pants under my touring pants. Dressed for the weather, I pulled out of Burlington and onto WA 20. As the day passed, I congratulated myself on this decision.

Highway 20 proved to be everything I had been told it would be. Shadowed by the Skagit River on the south, the road twisted and turned, and then swept to higher elevations with gentle curves. The Skagit was beautiful in the early morning sun, and I could hear it singing to me as I coursed over the road. After what seemed like just a few short miles, I was already at an elevation of 2000 ft and still climbing. I entered North Cascades National

Park and attempted to find the Ranger's Welcome Station to validate my National Park passport, but missed the turn-off somehow.

My first pullover was at Diablo Lake where a young man was cleaning the Port-o-Lets. He was industrious and extremely thorough in his efforts and I greatly appreciated his devotion to duty, a devotion which was, no doubt, equally appreciated by those who would follow after me. We chatted and I learned that Diablo Lake was dammed to create power for the greater Seattle area. The lake was clear and surrounded by a dense tree line. While I did not get down to the water's edge, I am sure it was just as ice cold as it was crystal clear.

Back on the Glide, I rode up into higher elevations. Nearing Washington Pass, at an elevation of 4000ft, snow started to appear along with mist coming up from the ground — very surrealistic! On the south side of the road, steep wooded hillsides were interspersed with solid rock cliffs. Small waterfalls cascaded from the rocks and splashed crystal clear water into small ponds. I looked for a spot to pull over and capture the beauty of the scene on film, but, with no pullovers and very little shoulder, it would have been foolhardy to stop and risk getting rear-ended. With some regret, I continued up the Cascades.

The snow increased, and gradually the highway became a tunnel, banked on both sides by snowdrifts, some of which were three to five feet in height. At Washington Pass, I found a pullover and took several pictures of the Glide surrounded by snow. The elevation there was 5477 ft and the scenic mountains made a perfect background for my pictures. Enjoying the scenery, I again gave a quick thanks to the universe for having worn my heated gear.

As I had suspected, the road took a dramatic turn downwards as I went over the crest of Washington Pass. The next town on my route was Winthrop, Washington, a partially-restored, partially-recreated, old frontier town. It looked like a nice place to stop and I found a great cup of strong coffee to enjoy while taking in the sights. After a quick lunch, I was again cruising on WA 20, this time going through lush green valleys filled with fertile fields and grazing cattle. The valleys give way to a semi-arid landscape around the town of Omar and I was reminded of West Texas, New Mexico and Arizona, though without the border patrols. At Winthrop, I had left the Skagit and now had the Twist and Okanogan Rivers as my companions. At Republic, another restored town, I again started to climb. This time, my route took me towards Sherman's Pass, which is at an altitude of 5575 ft.

Back in 1999, there had been a forest fire whose scars were still visible on the landscape, but Mother Nature was doing her thing, as she always does, and new tree growth was starting to show. Nature will always heal itself, if we human folk will let it. Louisiana's coastline had not suffered one devastating blow, but many. It had been used and reused and misused and never given a chance to repair itself. Now time was running out. We have to take the steps to let the healing begin. Some people talk as if the land is irreparably damaged and it would take a Herculean effort to fix it. What it will take is the desire to fix it. If we stop misusing it and let nature take its course, in the long run it will heal. Of course, this will cost some money and be a little inconvenient and that's the problem.

Well, that's what the trip was about. It didn't matter what I knew. What mattered was getting enough people to see what I did. I was convinced that, if people understood, they would demand that the correct action be taken. Perhaps I sound naïve. Well, that's a hat I will gladly wear rather than sit around and moan that there was nothing to be done. Enough of that! The trip was work and worry, but it was also a chance to see the beauty of this great nation. This had been one of the best riding days to date. (I say that a lot, don't I?) Highway 20 was excellent and the Cascade Mountains were everything I had heard about.

After a couple of wrong turns (I didn't ask Jill for help), I pulled into Kettle Falls, Washington and found a motel. It was next to a restaurant, and across from a health food store that offered free WiFi. And, as an even bigger plus, they sold Diet Dr Pepper. I have mentioned Diet Dr. Pepper before, but now I must own up to the fact that it is one of my bigger addictions. You'll be hearing more about that in the future. For now, I had an ice cold Diet Dr. Pepper in my hand. Life was very good!

I listened to the folks around me chat as I sipped my drink. I had begun to notice a subtle change in the accents around me. They sounded more "northern," with a touch of Canadian. The town, too, seemed different. While the locals were nice folks, there was less of the 70's environment than what I had experienced in northern California and Oregon. It's not a criticism of Washington, nor is it praise for Oregon and California. It is just what I noticed. A man has to be precise. A man also has to cover his butt if he plans a return trip someday. Those folks have long memories.

Later that evening I also took part in an act of near sublime physical grace, just, I must say, as some of my friends would expect of me. Finishing dinner at the Grouch Burger restaurant, I slipped on the steps outside as I was leaving, cutting the side of my face, and bending the hell out of my glasses. After cursing myself out, I stopped and said a prayer of gratitude. Here I was, in the middle of nowhere, and I had not broken anything or been knocked unconscious. After picking myself up, I hobbled over to the motel to wash my scrapes and to try to resurrect my glasses. On examination, things were not too bad, and my glasses were usable. It wouldn't have been a catastrophe in any event, because I had packed a spare pair just in case of an emergency like this. Still, I was glad that the first pair was usable.

Canadian Foray – I

Looking in the mirror the next morning, my right eye was slightly swollen and gave a strong hint that it could easily become a real shiner. I ministered again to my cuts and scrapes, and then loaded up the Glide for another day's journey. I was once again on WA 20 going east, but not for long. I turned north towards Canada and crossed into British Columbia above Metaline Falls, and headed east on Canada Hwy 3. Hwy 3 was a grand road, with broad turns that took me over Kootenay River. At its highest point, Kootenay Pass, Hwy 3 rises up to 5900 ft. Although the road was clear, snow was piled several feet high on each side of the road.

The reason for this Canadian foray was that I had decided to visit a 17,000 acre wetland area in Creston, British Columbia. It is a wildlife area and is open to the public. It boasted a wonderful visitor's center with several hiking trails and boardwalks through the preserve. Arriving at the wetland area, I met two local residents, Kasha and Farakf, who were very active in wetland and global warming activities. We talked extensively about their farm and about life in this part of Canada in general. I was surprised to learn that, as in the U.S., many Canadians do not take wetland preservation seriously and seem to pay little, if any, attention at all to urban encroachment on sensitive areas.

I didn't know if it was something about being in Canada, or if I was beginning to feel my bumps and bruises but an uneasy feeling came over me. Then it became clear. Nature was taking its course with my injuries. By the time of our conversation, my right eye had definitely taken on nice brown, orange, and blue hues, which had surely caught their attention. They were polite and did not stare, but I am sure they were wondering about my "shiner". I wondered if they thought I was some crazy biker dude invading their turf. I hope I was too well-mannered for them to think that. They both wished me well on the trip, and I continued east towards the border. Leaving Canada, I headed back to the U.S. and that night's destination, Kalispell, Montana.

Big Sky Country

The scenery on the ride was just what I had expected to see in Idaho and Montana. I kept waiting for Little Joe and Hoss to come riding out of the wilderness at any moment; Yes, I know "Bonanza" was filmed in Nevada, but this was Ponderosa Country to me. There is something about rugged places that triggers thoughts of adventure in you. That probably explains why explorers keep pushing over the next horizon. A couch potato like me is just reminded of movies and television programs he has seen.

The weather turned colder as the day wore on and on the way to Kalispell, I encountered my first significant rain storm of the trip. Arriving warm and dry, thanks to my waterproof-heated riding gear; I quickly found lodging and decided to call it a day. There was no internet connection at the motel, but a small pizza place down the road had it. Unhappily, they were ready to close. I ordered a sandwich and, of course, a Diet Dr. Pepper. (I told you it was an addiction.) Perhaps they could tell I had an educated palate, or maybe, I just looked cold and miserable. At any rate, they stayed open long enough for me to log on and check email messages.

The morning weather forecast was predicting six to eight inches of snow in the higher elevations. My original plan had been to ride through Glacier National Park on the "Going to the Sun Highway." I had been reading and hearing stories about that spectacular road for years and had made it a "must see" point on my route. Keeping my options open, I waited until morning to make my final decision. After listening to the local weather, I reluctantly decided to drive through Glacier National Park at the lower elevations, thus missing the "Going to the Sun Highway." On the other hand, I would also be outrunning the rain that was predicted for later that day. It didn't matter. I got caught in another rain storm anyway.

To those of us who are long distance riders, it is an all-too familiar scenario. Mother Nature always rules the road. Over many years, and several thousands of miles, I had learned to take the weather in stride and to be flexible in my plans. Even with rain and temperatures in the mid 30's, I could not help being struck once again by the raw beauty of this region, but it was just too cold to take pictures. I once again crossed the Continental Divide, this time at Marisa Pass, at an elevation of 5216 ft., and began my descent to the wide open plains of Montana's Big Sky Country.

It was as if I had entered a different world. Grass plains opened in front of me as far as the eye could see. Still riding at 3900 plus feet, the rain continued and my old nemesis, the wind, returned in full force. At one point, around Shelby, Montana, road construction began, and one of the most dreaded road signs that a rider can encounter appeared— "Pavement Ends in One Mile". With no other options, I gingerly picked my way over gravel and loose pavement for several miles. I am sure there were many frustrated motorists behind me, because I sometimes slowed to 10 mph. Eventually, I reached Malta, Montana, where I started looking for a place to spend the evening.

I found a delightful establishment called the Sportsman Motel with rooms that included a full kitchen, cable TV, and high speed internet. I share this information with you so you can understand, and appreciate, my decision to spend a second night there. Once in the room, I put on the Weather Channel and was dismayed to learn that the weather I had been running from was catching up to me. Friday's forecast for Malta and the surrounding 200 miles included flash flood warnings, winds up to 25 mph, and an 80% chance of rain. Old Man Nature was telling me "you can run from me but you can't hide". It was time to lie low and let the storm pass, which is exactly what I did.

Malta was a typical "whistle stop" town, with a main street that runs parallel to the railroad line. Standing on the tracks, and looking first east, and then west, it seemed as if I could see for miles. Even with the foul weather approaching, the air was clean and light and it felt good to just take it all in. That part of Montana is known for its many dinosaur fossils and Malta had one of the few mummified examples of a 74 million year old dinosaur. He bore the nickname, "Leonardo." I wanted to ask why he was so called, but I felt I should respect the privacy of anyone 74 million years old. There was a Field Station, which is a wet lab as well as a museum, and it was open to the public. There, I was able to observe one of the paleontologists actually working on a dinosaur fossil.

Surveying the town, I stopped by an auto parts store and got an antenna to replace the one that got "lost" in Seattle. There, I met the owner of the store, Dick, and we talked about over-regulation of the natural gas drilling that is a big part of the local economy. At the Radio Shack shop next door, I purchased a WiFi finder so I could scout out connections when selecting a hotel in the future. The hit and miss approach had been frustrating. The owner of the Radio Shack was a former rider, and I could hear the envy in his voice as we discussed my ride. He told me, in glowing detail, about North Dakota Rte 5 and how it was one of his favorite rides.

Montana is Big Sky and Big Beef country, so I splurged and tried each of the two steak houses in town. At the Malta Hotel Restaurant, I got a huge slab of tender prime rib with all the fixing's for $16.99— and no sales tax! Hear that, Louisiana? The restaurants there also double as card parlors and, while I was not invited to play, I am sure they would have been willing to let me sit in for a round or two, if only to fatten their wallets with my hard-earned money.

I wasn't lazing around and ignoring my responsibilities. Over the two day layover, I also stopped by the local newspaper and was interviewed for an article in the Phillips County News. Then, I dropped by a local radio station to let them know about the project. Even though it was hardly a major media market, I was on the road to spread the word. It's like a drop of water on a rock. In time, the water will wear away the stone. I was out to erode the granite of misunderstanding and apathy about the wetlands and you never know which drop is going to do the trick. At least these folks in Montana were getting the word. I felt satisfied. All in all, it had been a very exciting and adventurous two days! And I had stayed dry.

Even though I had been on the Northern Rim for several days and many miles, I felt that changing the mountains of the Northwest quadrant of the country for the plains of the Big Sky Country marked a milestone, so I logged in my stats for the ride: "Rim Day 34, elapsed mileage 5,906". Somehow, seeing it written made it more real. I had come far, but I had a long way to go.

Leaving Malta, the sky was clear. The Zumo was reading 38 degrees, and I was again happy to have my heated gear. I passed through several small towns as the Glide took me east on US Hwy 2 and then, suddenly after 30 miles, I hit a fog bank. It got real thick, wet, and cold, with visibility limited to a few hundred feet. Once again, the dreaded "Pavement Ends" sign greeted me as I came upon a section of gravel road. Although it only lasted for a couple of miles, I was happy to see the tarmac again.

Just like that, I remembered Ewan McGregor and Charley Boorman in their *Long Way Round* motorcycle trip around the world. I had read the book and seen the television series they made of their trip. In a way, it may have helped inspire RTR. I thought about Ewan and Charlie who rode hundreds of miles on nothing but dirt roads and gravel. I gained a new appreciation for what they accomplished. Imagine a motorcycle trip around the world. It was a major effort for me to get around one country. I marveled at the planning, endurance, and fortitude such a trip would demand of a rider. Recalling my own struggles to arrange this trip around the United States, my head reeled at the thought of what must have been involved in their journey.

I passed through Glasgow, then Wolf Point, where the land remained flat and wide open. As I approached the state line of North Dakota, I noticed that there was more of a roll to the hills, creating small gullies. Tidy farms dotted each side of the road and traffic was light with only the occasional trucker speeding by me, sometimes blowing me sideways as they approached from the other lane. (Thanks, Guys.) After crossing into North Dakota, I snapped an ABC picture before connecting up with Hwy 85. I then turned north towards the Canadian border on ND Rte 5. The land spread out in front of me, a panorama of cultivated fields waiting patiently for spring planting to begin, or perhaps to lie fallow for livestock grazing. It wasn't completely pastoral though; oil and gas rigs stood like exclamation points in the fields. Even after my conversation with Dick in the auto parts store in Montana, I had no idea that this part of North Dakota had so many gas and oil wells. They dotted the farm lands, co-existing with the livestock and the crops. Many had that strong fuel odor that I was familiar with from home, and one even had a flare burning off waste gas from a well. Are we in Louisiana, Toto?

If I haven't commented much about the sights, it's because there was little to see, especially compared to the recently-viewed and glorious coastline of California and the magnificent trees of the Northwest, but it wouldn't be fair not to, at least, pay tribute to the country I rode through. The plains of North America are one of the wonders of the world. To most eyes, they may not be as magnificent as, nor as colossal as, the mountains and the coast, but the very existence of my country depends, to no small extent, on what they provide us. The land I traversed was once a shallow, marshy sea that provided a habitat for dinosaurs. Today, there are rich, rolling grasslands which are farmed to feed, not only America, but much of the world. Beef, buffalo, and mutton go into our gullets. Wool and leather clothe us. Oil and natural gas power our machines. Yet, there are people who dismiss the plains as something to pass through as quickly as possible to get to something more interesting. In dismissing them that casually, they dismiss the processes of life itself. I am learning more on this trip about the fragility of all environments, and I am learning about the interdependence of all mankind. That's a lot to get from basically flat land, but, hey, they are not called Great Plains for nothing.

Canadian Foray – II

My day's destination was Fortuna, which turned out to be only a few homes, a church, and no gas stations. The port of entry into Canada was another five miles up the road, and, after answering a few questions from a Canadian Customs officer who was obviously bored; I crossed into Saskatchewan to get my ABC picture. That was really all I was there for. Those for whom an ABC picture is not important may find this strange, to which I can only answer, "But it was an ABC picture." I hope that helps explain it. The whole process took less than five minutes, and then I pointed the Glide back towards the U.S. border. I had given little thought to my excursion. It was just a short diversion to satisfy a whim. I was wrong. At the crossing, things got a bit difficult.

After running my passport, one of the U.S. officers informed me that I should tell him in advance if I had any drugs, because he would go easier on me if he found some. He also threatened to confiscate the Glide if I had any other illegal items. He repeated this warning several times. After I repeatedly denied that I had any drugs, the two officers had me completely unpack all of my gear, which they went through piece by piece— including my dirty underwear. Finding no contraband, they turned their attention towards my now, very obviously, black eye and sarcastically inquired if I was one of those "bad ass bikers" who got into barroom fights. This all began to seem very surreal and, had I not experienced it personally, it all would have sounded like a plot from a very bad movie. Finally, they told me to get on my way. That was my only bad experience with law enforcement or, in fact, with anyone else during the entire trip. It was disheartening that these were my countrymen. It contrasted unfavorably with the Canadian courtesy I had just experienced, but there it was. There was little I could do, other than to accept it, so I wrote it off. Perhaps these two guards were having a bad day. Perhaps I was just in the wrong place at the right time. It was still a bummer. But it was an experience, right? Lucky me! Well, I had to let it go, so off I went to find fuel.

The North Dakotan land was rich with wildlife, including pheasants and ducks that dotted the many ponds and lush wetlands. I even saw a small fox in the ditch by the side of the road. I had changed times zones and now was on CDT, I was getting tired, even though it was only 1500, so I put Jill to work, and found lodging in Kenmore, North Dakota, a small town with a wonderful old-time square and a museum. The motel was clean and had WiFi. Outside my room, I met a young guy from Texas who was working for a company that cleans the ballast from locomotive engines. He was homesick and missed his wife. I could relate to that. He told me that work had dried up in his home town and the offer to work for the service company was too good to pass up. I could tell he was worried about being away from his family. My heart went out to this guy, who seemed so young to be carrying such a heavy load on his shoulders.

I found a Chinese restaurant where I was the lone diner. The owner and his family seemed very happy to have a customer; the service was outstanding; and the meal, including dessert, was only 10 bucks. Needing some exercise, I strolled around the town square which was bordered by small shops, a movie theater, and the local police station. I was struck by another TV moment. This could be Mayberry. I looked for Andy and Barney sitting outsides Floyd's barbershop. They weren't there. Maybe they went fishing with Opie. There are still small towns like Kenmore all over the country. We forget that a lot of our values, and, maybe, the better ones, grew in small towns like this. I think we still long for that kind of certitude. Although it wasn't a natural wonder, it was still a gift to see it on the trip.

After a good night's sleep, I awoke to a beautiful day. My first stop was another indulgence, but one I chose to take. I had heard about the International Peace Gardens which straddle the border between North Dakota and Manitoba, Canada. While it was too early in the year to see the gardens in full bloom, I did walk the grounds and soak up the serenity of the park. The most interesting things to me were the Peace Towers. These four 120 ft tall columns symbolize the four corners of the earth. Two columns are in North Dakota, and the other two are in Manitoba. There was also a Peace Chapel where one could sit and meditate; a 911 memorial with actual girders from the World Trade Center; and a wonderful bell that chimed every 15 minutes in its tower. I loved the symbolism and promise of the place, and hoped that someday international peace gardens would cover a world that sorely needed peace. The mood was so serene that I made one more foray into Manitoba for a picture, forgetting my last border experience. This time, I had an uneventful crossing back into the U.S. Then, it was off to Minnesota.

The Great Lakes

As I rode the Minnesota highways, I noticed the neatly maintained farmlands, the well-kept fields, and the small, organized, farming communities. I thought about how hard the early settlers of these plains, probably of Scandinavian or Germanic heritage, must have struggled to cultivate this frontier land. Everywhere I had traveled so far, however easy the road is now, someone, at some time, had to carve that place out of the wilderness. We sit atop the shoulders of a lot of people and we are indebted to them. One way we can repay that debt is by taking care of the wilderness they discovered, and then settled, through their sweat and muscle. They did it for themselves, but, by doing so, they also did it for us.

I located a wonderful hotel, The American Inn: Lodge and Suites on Hwy 11 in Roseau, Minnesota. When I checked in, I was informed by the helpful desk clerk that there was a group of people having a "South Louisiana" style picnic at the hotel that very evening. I had a head-slap moment because I had forgotten it was Memorial Day! Well, ma cher, say no more to this Louisiana boy. I made my way over to their gathering to say hello. It turned out to be a very interesting meeting. These folks were part of a group from several local churches who had just come back from Louisiana where they had gone to rebuild a house in Phoenix, Louisiana (down the river from New Orleans in Plaquemines Parish). The trip was organized by the Covenant World Relief Organization. Many of the 29 volunteers were members of the Roseau Evangelical Covenant Church. Today, Londa was in charge of the seafood cooker. Londa had received Cajun cooking lessons from a local Louisianan during their stay. I guess the lessons took. She cooked up a great pot of shrimp, sausage, turkey necks, and potatoes. In addition to the seafood dish, they also had burgers, and some mouth watering brats! I love Louisiana cooking, but as a native of Wisconsin, there is a special place on my palate for bratwurst. This wonderful group of people invited me to join them in their feast and partake of some fellowship. What a lovely way to end a day!

The group planned to return to the New Orleans area in late December, 2007 and I volunteered on the spot to swing a hammer with them when they did. We talked about the ride I was making and the importance of the wetlands to New Orleans. They immediately understood why I was doing the project, having had first-hand experience with the aftermath of Katrina. As so many others have found out, it only takes one visit to feel the impact. The destruction left by Katrina gives you an appreciation for the magnitude of the rebuilding effort. I felt at home.

Canadian Foray – III

My plans for the next several days were to cross into Ontario, Canada and travel east towards Thunder Bay, Ontario. I crossed into Canada at International Falls, Minnesota. At the Canadian border, I met a very friendly Canadian Customs officer who asked a lot of questions about my trip and New Orleans. As it turned out, she was a member of Ducks Unlimited and an advocate of wetland preservation in her area. We chatted for a while since we shared common interests and learned about each other's part of the world. Fortunately, there wasn't a long line of traffic behind me as she seemed in a talkative mood. Finally, we parted with a wave. As I pulled back onto the road, she warned me about the possible scarcity of fuel on Canadian Hwy 11. The contrast between her attitude and that of the U.S. Customs Officers that I had encountered just a few days earlier was startling.

Not far down that very scenic road, I pulled over and got a picture of Lake Rainy which was, no doubt, the headwaters of the Rainy River that I had been following for most of the day. Highway 11 is a fine road, with sweeping curves and gentle, rolling hills that wound through heavily-forested land. Although beautiful and wild, the road offered little diversion as I prepared for the four-plus hour ride to Thunder Bay. Keeping the officer's warning in mind, I set the Zumo to find all the available gas stations between my current location and Thunder Bay, my evening's destination. I started to re-calculate my MPH into KPH, forgetting that the Zumo had an option that did this automatically. I did find a gas station. They only had 87 octane, but, as the old saying goes, "beggars cannot be choosers," so I coaxed the Glide into a fill up. Arriving in Thunder Bay, I settled in for the evening at a nice, but expensive, Comfort Inn. Ouch! Everything in Canada is pricey!

Journaling that evening, I realized that I was nearing the halfway point around the rim, and had traveled approximately 7000 miles. Although I was looking forward to the next two months, I missed Linda. I know I have said that a lot, but try being away from someone you love for as long as I had been away, then you can call me a wimp. Besides missing my wife, I was also, at times, growing weary of my daily routine— pack the bike, look for gas, find lodging, unpack the bike, clean up me and the Glide, journal, update the web site, and decide on where to eat. Well, given the work of all the folks who had put me 7000 miles away, and given what Linda was sacrificing for me, I decided I was being, oh, perhaps, just the least little bit ungrateful. Once again, I had to remind myself just how blessed I was to have the opportunity. Time again to quit looking at the glass as half-empty.

"Home" Again

The next morning was damp and cold as I crossed back into the U.S. at Grand Portage, Minnesota, but the rugged and raw scenery of the shores of Lake Superior more than made up for the weather. This stretch of road had made it onto my "must ride" list because it shadowed Lake Superior for 140 miles. Besides the gorgeous scenery, the road was also lined with quaint towns and resorts. I stopped at a roadside wayside, and walked the beach which was completely covered with stones and pebbles. This was the second time I had ridden a "home" road to its end, for this rocky shore marked the end point of US Hwy 61. That may mean nothing to you unless you know that US Hwy 61 actually begins at the intersection of Broad and Tulane Avenues in New Orleans. Theoretically, you could start in New Orleans and ride all the way north to Grand Portage, Minnesota, staying on U.S/MN 61 the entire time. It made me think— is there a future ride here?

The contrast in the land was striking. The distance from the marshy, endangered soil of Louisiana to the pebble-strewn beach of Lake Superior was over a thousand miles. The lakeshore I was standing beside seemed so permanent but, at one time, we believed that about the Louisiana coast. We need to be stewards of all that we are given. No matter how big and magnificent something might seem, it is inherently fragile. A few hundred miles away, the people living on the shores of Lake Erie had learned that to their cost. At one time, the lake was so filled with industrial waste that it actually caught on fire. *The lake was burning.* To their credit, they cleaned it up. It took time and it took money, but it got done. I suppose the twin lessons are that everything is at risk and, with the will (and the money), things can be restored. That's what I wanted for the Louisiana wetlands. That's why I was on the shore of Lake Superior. Standing there, I was still connected to a place that was home to me in many ways. Standing there, I was connected to Linda and my children. Standing there, I was connected to the destruction wrought by Katrina and the daily struggle to recover. We are none of us solitary. We are not "masters of our fate and captains of our soul," no matter how much vanity or ego might tell us otherwise.

Thinking of home brought family and friends to mind. Aristotle said that Man is a social animal. I'm told Aristotle was a genius. I don't know about that, but, absence from those I loved had made me feel, in a way, closer to those I loved. We can't escape our life circumstances. There is no such thing as a "geographic cure." My enjoyment of the sights I had seen, and the people I had met, had not removed me from the problems that I had left. The people in New Orleans were still struggling. They were making a magnificent effort on their own, but they needed help, and it was our, all of our, obligation to give it to them. Rte 61 connected me to all that, a reminder and a lesson. I needed to get back on the road.

Once in Duluth, I made my way over to the Aerostich factory. For those who are not familiar with Aerostich, the company is known around the world for their Roadcrafter and Darien suits. In fact, while I was there, I met two riders from Belgium who had ordered their Darien suits on-line and had come all the way to Duluth to pick them up. In addition to riding suits, Aerostich carries a large inventory of just about anything you would want for motorcycle touring. It is a true Mecca for a gearhead like me. Andy Golfine, the owner of Aerostich, had invited me to drop by to get a tour of the factory and meet his staff when I came into town. Unfortunately, he was out of the country, attending a rally in Europe, but his assistant, Lynn, graciously gave me a complete tour of the facility. I was grateful to both her and Andy for their support.

My brother lives in Superior, Wisconsin, which is just across the bay from Duluth. We had lost touch with each other over the last couple of years, and I wanted to look him up while I was there. After checking into my hotel, I tried to locate the taxi company that he worked for, but I was not sure about its name. After a couple of hours of searching, I was still coming up empty-handed. I noticed a barber shop next to the grocery store where I was shopping, and decided that my beard could use a trim. I met the owner, a very nice lady by the name of Kim. While she was cutting my beard, I mentioned that I was looking for my brother and I gave her the name of the cab company that I thought he drove for. She said it sounded familiar, but thought I hadn't got the name quite right. She called one of her frequent customers, a cop, and he gave her the correct name and the address of the cab company. What a break! With directions in hand, I gave her a big tip and headed off.

Supposedly, the cab company was only a few miles away but, even with Kim's directions and Jill's help, I could not find it. I saw a neighborhood tavern and stopped to inquire about the taxi company's location. Bars and cab companies are well known to each other, so I figured this was my best chance. The barmaid was, in fact, familiar with the taxicab company and called the number for me. I talked with the dispatcher and he got a message to my brother Bruce. In less than five minutes, Bruce pulled up and we had a reunion of sorts in the middle of the street as the sky opened with a rain shower. Later that night, we caught up on each other's lives over dinner and parted with a promise to stay in touch.

My route took me towards Madison, Wisconsin, my home before moving to New Orleans. The ride brought back fond memories of my early riding days. I passed neatly-trimmed farm lands with tall silos and red barns surrounded by rolling green pastures. In Maple, Wisconsin, I stopped to watch a wood carver create unique designs out of tree sections using a chainsaw. His dexterity was unbelievable. I especially liked his carving of Tree Beard from the *Lord of the Rings* trilogy. I couldn't help but notice the changes in the land, though. I came to the realization, though I was a native of Wisconsin, Louisiana was now my home.

Leaving Wisconsin, I took Michigan RTE 28 north into the Upper Peninsula and connected with Hwy 64, which took me into Houghton via Hwy 38. The land was not very interesting, with little to see other than tall pines and an occasional small town. I wanted to visit Copper Harbor, but was not sure how the weather would hold up, so I decided to find a room in Houghton and make plans for the next day. My motel was a small inn and I met its proprietors, Mark and Julie. They had met at the local university where Julie was majoring in Hotel and Hospitality. Mark had been a semi-pro hockey player, playing in the European league. He later taught at Houghton State University. They met, married, and were now truly living their passion. They had fulfilled their dream. They had each other. They owned their own hotel. We talked about following our dreams and I shared my story with them.

Later, a local restaurant provided a great meal of prime rib and some conversation with a local resident who was heavily into his cup by the time our food arrived. I don't know why he was in his cup. I was sorry that he was in his cup. I couldn't imagine that life looked all that good from the bottom of his bottle. I'm sure he had what he thought were good reasons for being in his cup but, having seen all that life had to offer, I pitied him his isolation. It didn't ruin my meal, but I was glad to leave. There was a lovely walking path through a heavily-forested area that led me back to my room. I was ready for a good night's sleep.

My family had camped at Copper Harbor, the very northernmost point in the Michigan Upper Peninsula, when I was a young lad and I had wanted to visit the area once again. It would be a long ride up, and then back down again on essentially the same route. I had to wonder if a little nostalgia was worth the time and effort. Finally, I decided to skip Copper Harbor because the weather forecast was for strong thunderstorms. Instead, I took U.S. 41, first going south into Wisconsin once more and then pointing the Glide east, I headed towards Green Bay. At a local roadside diner, "Butch and

Sue's," in Cedar River, I had a tasty bowl of soup and some great peach pie a la mode. At the time, it was just a good meal, but life has a way of tying people together. Several months later I received an email from the daughter of Butch and Sue. She had learned of my visit to the café from my on-line journal. She told me that her father Butch had recently passed away, but that she was pleased that I had mentioned the café on my web site. I was glad, too. Connections may be fleeting, but they send out ripples which often bounce back from a far shore. I was very touched by her message.

After leaving Cedar River, my destination for the evening was Green Bay where I would have dinner with my nephew Eric. I was glad that I was having the opportunity to connect again with family members. I had missed one brother in Seattle, but had managed to connect up with my brother Bruce in Wisconsin. It reinforced the fact that I was home again. Home offers something you get nowhere else. Just now, I was surrounded by home. The ride down MI 35 which skirted Green Bay was very nice. The rugged shoreline was dotted with a few small towns mingled with fishing camps and parks that made for a very enjoyable ride. I passed through Escanaba, Michigan where I had traveled more than 40 years before on one of my motorcycle trips to Canada. Back in those days, I was riding a 250cc HD SS Sprint and would go into Canada with just a tent, a blanket, and a canteen of water. (My tent was actually a heavy piece of plastic which I draped over a clothes line to make a lean-to. Ah, youth.) I would shop at a local store to purchase canned goods which could be heated up over a fire at night. I was young, adventurous, and I tried hard to exemplify the lone rider, the tragic wanderer and rebel. Oh the memories!!

Near Green Bay, the skies opened up with heavy rains and strong winds. I had to pull over and take refuge from the lightning at a restaurant. While I was standing under the covered driveway to wait out the storm, the owner came out and invited me to dry off and have a beer on him. I accepted his offer of shelter, but passed on the beer and opted for a diet coke (They didn't serve Diet Dr. Pepper, Cretins that they were). I was not surprised at all to be offered a beer in the middle of the day. It was Wisconsin and, in Wisconsin, it is quite normal to offer someone a beer regardless of the time or circumstances. In Wisconsin, having a beer is akin to visiting over a cup of coffee in Louisiana, Although it is my native state, I have to admit, Wisconsin makes better beer than they do coffee. How I longed for some Louisiana Joe!

When the rain let up I hit the road and, after consulting Jill located several hotels. I settled on a Motel 6. It was nothing fancy, but, it was clean and safe. Unfortunately, there was no internet. While watching the news,

I was reminded that it was the first day of hurricane season. Louisiana is a great place to live, but it does have its risks. Hurricane season ranked high on the list. It amazed me that, after Katrina, some ill-informed government officials and media types had said that people shouldn't live there because of the risk. Do they say that about the Midwest because of tornadoes? The West Coast because of earthquakes, or the Northeast because of blizzards? Since hats are no longer in style, you had to wonder what those people used their heads for, certainly not to think. Well it was the onset of hurricane season in my adopted state and I said a prayer that it would be a mild season.

While in Green Bay, it seemed only fitting that I visit Lambeau Field, home of the Green Bay Packers. Outside their newly-renovated stadium are two towering statues of Vince Lombardi and Curly Lambeau. If you don't know who those two are, you had better stay the hell out of Green Bay, Wisconsin. After a brief visit to the Pro Shop, I headed over to the Packer's Hall of Fame where I found pictures of the original 1919 team, examples of their uniforms, and several displays of Green Bay players from the past up to the present. The most interesting displays were the re-creation of Vince Lombardi's office and a display case of Super Bowl trophies. As I left the stadium, I thought about all the Packer games I had watched as a youth on TV. Even now, though I am a loyal Saints fan, I am still awed by the mystique and legacy of the Green Bay Packers. The sky continued to threaten rain and the forecast included heavy thunderstorms for southern Wisconsin. Heading out of Green Bay, I continued towards Madison on familiar roads that I traveled as a youth.

A stop in Beaver Dam at a HD shop brought back memories of my carnival days. Beaver Dam was typical of the many small towns that held summer festivals complete with a live stock show, beauty pageant and a carnival. I had started to work as a carnival "barker" at an early age and traveled with a family-based show during the summer months. I suppose that it was during this time that I honed the gift of gab my mother had recognized in me. At any rate, I think it was there that I found my "voice" both figuratively and literally. In my role as the "Guesser Man" I would "bally the tip" (entice the crowd) to try and challenge me to correctly guess their weight or age. Possibly not a great beginning to a career as a public speaker, but it was what is.

I refined my pitch over the years and learned how to engage the "mark" (customer) in a playful interchange of insults mixed with humor. More importantly though, and to my advantage in later years, I found my "voice", that is to say, I found my love for public speaking. I realized the power of my voice and how to hold the attention of my audience, blending information with entertainment in my presentations. As Stephen Covey put it; I found my significance, my purpose in life— to be a conveyor of information, to help others understand. To some this may seem a bit boastful and to others it may sound like a grand "delusion" but it was for me a very formative time in my life. These early life experiences served me well later in life. It was those experiences that were now helping me to carry the RTR message. Hopefully, my carnie-nurtured talents were also helping others to carry their message, whatever it might be.

By mid-afternoon I had pulled into the driveway of my friends, Dave and Diane. It wasn't more than 30 minutes later that the sky once again opened up with rain and high winds. Ah! Timing is everything.

I was looking forward to a few days off the bike, catching up with Dave and Diane, and, of course, seeing my old home town of Madison again. First, though, it was time to kick back, shake off the road, and enjoy sleeping in a real house. Over the next few days, due to cloudy and rainy weather, the Glide was idle, and I was quite content to let Dave drive me around as we visited some of my old haunts in the area. I had a meeting with a local Wetlands group in Madison and, later that day, had an interview with the local newspaper that wanted to run a story about a local boy (me) trying to help with the reconstruction after Katrina.

The Matter of Media

I had done this kind of interview so often on the trip that it might be worthwhile to summarize this one, because it was typical of the message I was trying to spread. There were the usual questions. How long did I ride each day, what problems did I encounter and was I enjoying myself? My response was typically; A lot, not many, and absolutely. Eventually, we would get to the real meat of the interview, that being, "why was I doing the project and was I making an impact?" (Somebody had to and I hoped I was.) That out of the way, I was usually asked the questions, "why the wetlands and what makes them so important? And, where do they tie into rebuilding of New Orleans?" That was the key point and I had a lot to say about it.

Using the analogy of parking lot speed bumps, I explained that the wetlands slow down the tidal surge created by a hurricane. I went on to explain that every two to three square miles of wetlands reduce tidal surge by one foot, and that much of the destruction from Katrina was from the tidal surge that had stressed our already inadequate levee system. Going on,

I told how the wetlands had been gradually disappearing over the years due to salt water intrusion from the Gulf of Mexico. It was a slow and insidious assault caused by both oil exploration and the building of levees on the Mississippi River to control flooding. I was quick to point out that the finger of blame lay with no one individual, organization, or corporation. It was a general misunderstanding of the natural processes creating wetlands that had contributed to their eventual destruction. I would further explain that the destruction of the wetlands had still not been halted. Every 30 minutes, nearly a football field-sized area of wetlands is destroyed.

This was always an eye opener to most people I spoke to. The reporter from the Madison newspaper asked me a question that many others had brought up. "Why save New Orleans if it was a city already destroyed? and wasn't it doomed to be flooded again by future storms?" Incredibly, she shared the same vision of many, that New Orleans was completely destroyed and there was nothing left to save. I had to remind myself that, for many people, their only reference to post-Katrina New Orleans was what was said on the evening news. In their minds were the pictures of people stranded on highway access ramps surrounded by flood waters. They had seen the corpses floating in the garbage- strewn water that filled the city after the levees broke. To many, the city was no more, merely piles of debris, rotting in the heat of the Louisiana summer.

I always did my best to explain that, while some areas of the city were still uninhabited, much of the city was up and running. I told how the French Quarter and the Garden District in Uptown New Orleans, areas so closely associated with the charm and uniqueness of the city, had escaped most of Katrina's wrath and were returning to normal. Yes, it was true that New Orleans East and the lower Ninth Ward were now, almost two years following the storm, still waiting to be revitalized. (The same is true as I write this, and it is now four years since Katrina.) The wheels of the insurance industry and the Federal government were turning at a slow pace. (They still are.)

In response to those who questioned the value of protecting New Orleans, a city destined by its location to flood on a regular basis, I reminded them that we were more than just an entrainment and convention city. I reeled off the facts and figures about New Orleans being the nation's second largest port, and its importance to the mid-west farmer who needs his corn and wheat shipped abroad, or to the industrialist who is using foreign steel to manufacture the products he sells. I reminded my audiences that 40% of the nation's energy comes to their homes and factories through New Orleans from the Gulf of Mexico. The majority of that oil flows through pipelines across the wetlands and into the petrochemical industries of the State of Louisiana to be refined for use. With all this in mind, I would turn the tables and ask my interviewer if he really wanted to see New Orleans slip into the gulf when there are alternatives, albeit costly, means to avoid its destruction? Wasn't New Orleans worth saving? What toll would our National Heritage suffer if we were to lose her? What would the homes and factories of the interviewer's area suffer by the loss of this vital port?

As the interview wound down, questions about the impact of my trip on wetland and coastal restoration came up. They always did. Many interviewers thought my goal was to raise money to be used for a specific wetland restoration project. When I explained that the price tag for restoring the wetlands was approximately 15-20 billion dollars, I could see the doubt in their eyes as to the impact of RTR. I quickly pointed out that our goal was to raise awareness about the wetlands, and not to solicit donations. My role, as I saw it, was to be a catalyst for a dialogue that would propel others to start asking the questions that needed to be addressed. When would we, as a nation, stop asking "if the wetlands could be saved?" and, rather, ask "what are the options to save them? What are other countries doing to prevent coastal destruction, and what could be learned from their experiences? What was needed to get my beloved New Orleans back on her feet to once again become the queen jewel of the south?"

Those were the questions I wanted others to ask of themselves, and I wanted them to demand answers from their local, regional, and national political leaders. The idealist in me never faltered, but I knew that most of those who listened to me did not share my vision for the wetlands. I was okay with that. Perhaps, to many who read this particular interview, I was just a "local boy" trying to make a difference for something they really didn't understand, nor care to learn more about. However, my vision was clear and my determination strong. I was making a difference, if only one mile at a time. That was the belief Linda and I had come to share in our living room in Mandeville. That was the belief that sustained me on the road. It was a belief I would not lightly surrender. I slung my pack of seeds on my shoulders and got on with the work I had chosen to do.

Pressing On

I still had family living in Janesville, Wisconsin and they had set up a small reunion at a local restaurant. While in Janesville, Dave and I stopped by the local HD shop and I found a pair of FXRG boots on sale. I had been looking to buy a pair like this for the last several years, but the retail price was a bit much for me. Besides, my current boots were more than adequate. On the other hand, FRXG gear is the best that Harley Davidson sells. The boots are waterproof and come highly-rated by many independent reviewers. After further negotiations in an effort to get the price down, I happily walked out with them and against conventional wisdom decided to wear them for the rest of the trip. Usually, it is not a good idea to break in a new pair of riding boots, or any gear on the road, but these boots were waterproof, extremely comfortable, and would serve me well in the wet Canadian weather that I knew was ahead.

The visit with my two sisters, their children, grandchildren, and great-grandchildren was wonderful. They were very interested in the ride and asked a lot of questions. Like everyone I spoke to, they wanted to know about my daily routine on the road, how I managed to ride so long and not get sore, and, also, if I thought that I was making a difference in wetland awareness. It was hard to explain to those who did not enjoy long distance riding what it is to experience the people and places that the road brings. I tried my best to impart my joy of riding and the sense of humility that I felt in being able to be part of a project like Riding the Rim. I wasn't sure if they got it, but I knew deep in my soul that I was making a difference, if only to myself. I knew in my gut that we could all become agents of change, if we chose to make the effort.

By the third day off the road, I could feel my restlessness returning, so I started to plan the next leg of the trip. The weather forecasts for the Michigan UP continued to look bad, with high winds and rain. I decided to bypass this part of my original route and instead, head over to Milwaukee and take a ferry to Michigan's Lower Peninsula. I was disappointed that I would again be veering off my course. I had wanted to ride up the UP and across the Mackinaw Bridge, but, as in the case of the Highway to the Sun in Glacier National Park, at the end of the day, it is old man weather that has the last say.

As I was packing for my departure, Mary Lousteau called with news about a media event at the Mud Hens baseball game in Toledo, Ohio. It seemed that I would be throwing out the first pitch and that the mayor would be making an official proclamation in support of the wetlands. What an arena to proclaim the message! I was really looking forward to it. Mary was really doing a great job.

After saying my farewells to Diane and Dave, I headed out towards Milwaukee and the Capitol Drive Harley Davidson Plant. Several years ago, I had toured the plant, so today's stop was to get an ABC picture. (Yes, another.) Before the trip began, we had hoped that Harley Davidson would be receptive to hosting a media event during my time in Milwaukee. Although we had reached out to them very early in the planning of RTR, and several times afterwards, we never received any communications back from them. I had made it very clear that we were not looking for a donation or sponsorship. We only wanted to stage an event to promote the wetlands and, along the way, motorcycle riding. Since I was riding a Harley Davidson motorcycle, it seemed to us like a win-win for both RTR and the Motor Company. Here I was, just a short distance from the historic Harley Davidson headquarters on Juneau Avenue and it was clear to me, anyway, what a great public relations opportunity it would be for them to show that motorcycling and environmental concerns can go hand in hand. The event never did materialize and I often wondered why they chose not to respond to our inquiries.

An Unexpected Reunion

When my plans to enter Michigan through the UP changed, I decided to take a high speed ferry from Milwaukee to Muskegon, Michigan. After finding the ferry terminal, I purchased a first class ticket. With lots of time to spare, I struck up a conversation with two ladies on bicycles who were going to ride around the lower end of the Great Lakes with several of their friends. I suggested that, on their next trip, they follow the Mississippi River to New Orleans. That was a trip that I planned to take someday, but in reverse; starting at the end point of the Mississippi in Louisiana and ending at its headwaters in Minnesota. We chatted and shared stories. They were as fascinated about the nature and route of my ride as I was with their trip. It always made me feel good to share with people I met. It was proof, if I needed it, that I was carrying a message and in turn was receiving one. Finally, the call came to get in line, and the bicycle group and I were directed to the front of the line. (It is customary on most ferry boats to allow two-wheel vehicles to board first.)

As I pulled into line a rider from Billings, Montana, who was also named Terry, (I later nicknamed him "Montana.") joined us. He was riding a recently-purchased Sportster, and was going to see his daughter in Lansing Michigan. "Montana" told me he had been battling the winds for the last several days as he headed east. I suggested that his very next purchase be a windshield, which would help protect him, and also reduce his ride fatigue. Although he agreed with me, he felt that a windscreen would detract from the looks of the bike. That was a common response from some bikers, especially Harley riders, who often chose style over comfort. At one time, in my earlier riding days, I would have felt as he did, but, nowadays, appearance takes a back seat to functionality. Not long after we got in line, I saw still another rider. This one was pulling up on a BMW. Something about him looked familiar as I eyed him in my rear view mirror. Then I recognized him.

It was Keller, the same guy I had met in Texas back in April on Rim Day 3. I remembered that he lived in Marfa (of the famous lights which I never got to see). He was going to visit his lady friend who lived in Grand Rapids, Michigan. Neither of us could believe the coincidence of meeting up like this. (Of course, there are no coincidences in life, just opportunities to experience new realities.) After boarding, we managed to get the bikes secured, once we figured out how they wanted us to do that. Their tie-down system was a bit difficult, but we all helped each other and soon the bikes were safely secured. Keller had purchased a coach seat, and I decided to join him, even though I had paid for first class passage. Going into the coach area, the attendant noted my first class ticket. I explained about our reunion and that we wanted to sit with each other. She was very nice and offered to bring us the complimentary beverage that came with my first class passage. We both felt like kings. We talked, enjoying our beverages. The other passengers looked rather puzzled at the VIP treatment that these two saddle tramps, Keller and I, were getting.

The ferry ride was great and after a while we went out on the observation deck to take in the wind, water, and birds that followed in our wake. Lake Michigan is one of the larger Great Lakes and, although we were moving at a good clip of 34 knots (40 mph), it took almost two hours for the trip. At times, the ride was rough and both Keller and I were glad we took the extra time to securely tie down the bikes.

Back inside, we passed the time chatting about his retirement and how he met Mary Ann, his friend from Grand Rapids. He rode this way each summer to meet up with her. They usually planned a long road trip while he stayed with her, and then, in late summer, he headed back to Marfa. Not a bad lifestyle, if you ask me. Towards the end of the ferry ride Keller invited me to ride with him and meet Mary Ann when we arrived in Muskegon. I decided I really wanted to meet the lady who Keller thought was worth this migratory romance, so I agreed.

Once on the Michigan side, I followed Keller into Grand Rapids and met Mary Ann, who just happened to be an independent media and PR consultant.(Remember, there are no coincidences) She was promoting a film festival that was in town and immediately volunteered to call her TV, radio, and newspaper contacts to promote my event. That was very nice of her and again demonstrated the goodwill that I had received so many times on the road. She invited me for dinner that night but, three's a crowd, and it was obvious that they wanted some private time together. (It had been almost six months since they had last seen each other). I knew the feeling.

Media Woes, Michigan Miles

I left them with a promise to come over for brunch in the morning and found a local motel. The winds were really picking up, almost to 40 mph, and the same weather was predicted for the next several days. I was thankful to be off the road, and decided to sit tight for an extra day to see if I got any media bites. My next scheduled stop was several days away, and I had plenty of time to make it to Detroit where I was going to visit some friends before going on to Toledo.

The weatherman's predictions turned out to be accurate. The next day started off with more high wind warnings. Hoping to get a hit from Mary Ann's media contacts, I spent a leisurely morning with coffee and the newspaper before riding over to have a pleasant brunch with she and Keller. Later, back at the hotel, I met a guy from Sandusky, Ohio named Marty. He was a Kirby vacuum sales trainer who was training a group of door-to-door salespeople for the area, and he was also a biker. I got an interesting education on vacuum cleaner selling as he told me all about the Kirby product line. After I learned more than I ever needed to know about vacuum cleaner sales, he started talking about a big bike rally in Sandusky, Ohio later that week. Sandusky was close to my route, so I decided to make it a stop.

I was still waiting to hear from the local press when Mary Ann called to fill me in on the media situation. It seemed I was playing second fiddle to Rudy Giuliani who was in town drumming up support for his presidential campaign. If that wasn't enough distraction for the media, I also got upstaged by "wheel chair boy," a young man in a wheel chair who got caught in the grill of a semi truck and was pushed down the road for about two miles before the driver realized that something was wrong. Fortunately, the young man was not hurt. My event now seemed trivial compared to the potential harm that the boy could have experienced. Obviously, the local media felt the same way. It seemed as if I was just small potatoes in the grocery store of life. Since I wasn't running for president, and had absolutely no desire to be hit by a semi under any circumstances, it was time to get back on the road.

Leaving Grand Rapids the next morning under cloudy, but dry skies, I once again had my old friend the wind kicking me around at 20-25 mph. (That guy sure gets around.) I decided to take a series of winding back roads, first M37 to Hastings, then M79 to Charlotte, and finally M50 down to Jackson, Michigan. All this time the wind was at my side and I had to be careful about crosswinds blowing me around. I finally took a more easterly course at Jackson and had the wind at my back. Even with the wind, the ride was pleasurably scenic as I rolled through several small communities. Finally, I was on I-94 East. Two storm warnings came up on the Zumo as I approached Ann Arbor. My destination was American Harley Davidson where I was greeted warmly by the store manager. After learning about my trip, he offered me a free tee shirt. I asked if I could exchange the shirt for a pin, due to my limited luggage capacity. He completely understood and so I garnered another pin for my collection. What I did not tell him was that I already had several Harley tee shirts that I had never worn and would probably never have the time to wear.

I talked with Rick, one of the sales guys, about the Sandusky event and he said not to miss it. He also suggested a Holiday Inn near a shopping center just up the road in Ann Arbor. With the wind continuing to pick up, a short day on the road sounded like a great idea. I was thinking that I might get lucky and find a nearby movie theater, which would be a definite plus. My luck held out, and that evening I enjoyed a great action movie. Going to see a show always brought a degree of normality to my schedule and broke the monotony of staying in my room. Piping hot popcorn drenched in butter added to the total experience and made for a completely satisfying evening.

Morning brought a clear sky and the ride to Sandusky was easy. With no wind and sunny skies, the road felt great. I had tried to book a room in Sandusky, but, due to the rally, I had to settle for a hotel in nearby Clyde. The folks at the Red Roof Inn were very nice and, even though it was only 1100, they let me check in and gave me directions to Sandusky, a mere 20 miles away. I passed several groups of bikers as I traveled to Sandusky and later found out that there was also a motorcycle race going on nearby.

Roeders HD in Sandusky was ground zero for the rally and it was full of riders. I couldn't help but notice the number of women riding solo on Road Kings and Softail Heritages. (You don't see a lot of that in the south.) The rally was typical of the many that I have attended over the years. There were the usual food vendors, along with merchants who were selling an assortment of riding gear, clothes, and general motorcycling merchandise. There was also entertainment. The rally organizers brought in a group of stunt riders who were billed as the "Wall of Death". They performed in a circular ring surrounded by high walls. Using light-weight bikes, they propelled themselves around the rink at high speeds and then, using centripetal force, they gradually rode higher up the walls until they were parallel with the floor of the rink. It was an impressive spectacle, even though I had seen it several times in the past. After walking around for a couple of hours, I was ready to call it a day.

Play Ball!!

In Toledo, my hotel, the Park Inn, was downtown and I found it without a problem. I was immediately impressed as I rode up to the entrance. It was a pretty swanky place compared to what I was used to staying in. My host had made the reservation for me and I was pleasantly surprised when I saw my room. It had an excellent view of the ball park, Fifth Third Field, home to the Toledo Mud Hens.

The Hens were made a household name by native son Jamie Farr whose character, the cross-dressing wannabe 4F Max Klinger, on the TV series "M.A.S.H", often wore a Mud Hens jersey on the show. The day was still young and I explored the downtown area on foot, including the area around the stadium. Across the street from the ball park was the famous Tony Packo's restaurant that Max Klinger often described as home to the best "dog" in town. After sampling the fare there, I completely agreed with him. Then it was off to the baseball game, one of my fondest memories of the entire trip.

The event at Fifth Third Field (named for the bank that sponsored the field) went very well. I was one of eight honored guests who threw out the "first pitch" and I actually made it across home plate, albeit with a little arc on the ball. They put me last in the lineup so that a local councilman could come onto the field and read a proclamation from the mayor proclaiming the day as "Wetlands Day" in Toledo. Next, there was an interview in the press box with the local radio announcer who was calling the game. I stayed

there after the interview so I had an excellent view of the game from the top of the stadium in the press box.

My local contact was Jennifer Ziolkowski who worked at Buckeye Cable along with Dan Penny (the brother-in-law of a friend back in Louisiana). Dan was a producer for the station and had pitched the event to the Hens and the mayor's office. Jennifer introduced me to Neal, the assistant general manager of the stadium who gave me the VIP tour of the ball park, including some areas usually off limits to the general public. We went into the tunnel the players used to access the home plate area, and there I met the team's mascot. He or she (I couldn't tell through the costume.) gave me some good-natured ribbing about my pitch across home plate. I took it in stride, knowing that my sons would be doing the same thing over the phone later that night. After that, it was up to the Buckeye Cable suite to visit with Dan and the crew from Buckeye as we watched the Hens win the game in the bottom of the ninth inning. The whole Toledo experience was one of the best organized events of the trip and I will always be grateful to Dan and his crew for making it such a success. After the game, it was time for me to head back to the hotel. From my 15th story room, I watched the post-game fireworks. What a day!!

The Rim Ends: Vermont

My route over the next several days took me through Pennsylvania, and then into New York. Day 47 was a particularly long day in the saddle, even though my travel time was only seven hours. I had made an error by not having a clear travel route planned for entering Pennsylvania and New York, especially considering the toll roads that were now starting to pop up. They made me nervous because I was unfamiliar with the process for paying tolls, having the exact change, etc. Instead, I took U.S. 20 (my old friend) but ran into many, many stoplights as I passed through one small town after another. At one point, I tried to jump over to NY 5, but, after 10 miles, there was a bridge that was under construction, and I had to backtrack to U.S. 20. Realizing I would not make my goal of reaching the north side of Buffalo by day's end, I started to look for a room and found a nice place in Irving, New York which had a diner close by. The daily special was liver and onions, one of my favorites.

I planned the next day's route with more care and decided to either go south of Buffalo and cut north or go up through the city close to the

border near Niagara. (I had no plans to stop at the Falls; been there, done that, and bought the tee shirt.) Having corrected the planning mistakes of the previous day, I had a better idea of my route through Buffalo. (RT 5 to I-190 then to NY18 and on to N104 to pick up I-81. Well, it was clear to me.). Leaving around 0730, I encountered very little traffic and easily negotiated my way through Buffalo. There was a rather high bridge that crossed the Niagara River that gave me a panoramic view of the city, but alas not the falls. I was being careful to follow the signs that would lead me to NY Rte. 18 but, at times, it was confusing as to how NOT to cross over to the Canadian side. I did not want to go through the customs routine again if it could be avoided.

NY 18 turned out to be a great road and I followed it for some time, passing through small, quaint towns, bordered by neatly-kept farmlands and forested areas. That winding road was one of the better ones that I had been on over the past two weeks, and that was saying a lot! Lined with cherry and apple orchards, well kept farmlands, and perfumed with the rich smell of conifers and birch, the road was a "must-ride" for anyone who came that way. I stopped to take pictures in a town with a small harbor on Lake Erie and then dropped down to NY 104 which took me through Rochester. I had the option of taking Route 3, which closely followed the shoreline of Lake Ontario or of remaining on 104 and hooking up with I-81. I eventually decided on Hwy 104 and made it over to Adams Corner, New York where I visited the HD dealership.

I had originally planned to have my 50k/mile service performed here, but could never get them to a commit to a service date over the phone. It had been frustrating, but I decided I didn't want to mention this while I was visiting the store. I purchased a pin and was rewarded with some good advice from the salesman He suggested Route 3, which goes through Lake Placid, where I could catch a ferry that crossed Lake Champaign to Burlington, Vermont. After looking at the map, this seemed like a good idea and I silently congratulated myself on not getting pissy with the dealership about the service appointment.

Finding a room in Watertown that evening proved to be somewhat difficult. There was a military base close by and a large contingent of troops had just arrived from Iraq. All the motels were filled with family members anxious to see their sons and daughters who had been away for a long time. Fortunately, at one motel that had already filled up, the owner made some calls and a found a room for me at the Davidson Motel, only 10 miles away. It was a mom and pop establishment, and I met the owners and their three

children as I was checking in. They all came out to check out the Glide and, I also suspect, to make sure I was not one of those "bad ass bikers". They had an inviting pool on the premises and I enjoyed a quick dip before dinner. The kids were great and we all clowned around in the pool. The entire family apparently pitched in to run the motel, and everyone seemed to take the work in stride. They asked a lot of questions about my trip and New Orleans. Later, after scouting out the area for a place to eat, I discovered that there were no open diners close by. The motel owner suggested a place that delivered and I had a feast of tasty Italian cuisine in my room. That was truly room service— RTR style.

It often pays to take advice from the locals, and my route the next day was no exception. I started on Rte 3 into the Adirondacks region and passed through several charming and quaint towns. At Natural Bridge, New York, I found a café that was open and stopped for a mid-morning cup of Joe. Behind the counter was a delightful lady by the name of Marie who had lived in the area on and off for most of her life. I inquired about the town's name, and she told me about a series of caves below the town that formed a "natural bridge". It was too early to see them that day she told me, but said that if I waited for another hour, they would be open. Enjoying my coffee, we continued to chat and I took her picture standing next to a well-worn countertop and cash register. At one time the café had been a hardware store and she remembered coming in with her father to buy supplies. She let me in on some of the local gossip, who was doing what to whom while I had my second cup of coffee. As we said our good-byes she loaded me up with cookies for the road.

Continuing on Rte 3, I passed through heavily-forested mountains, with frequent streams and rivers that flowed under the smooth ribbon of highway I was traveling on. Unfortunately, there were not many turnoffs and those that were available for picture-taking were not very scenic. I did stop in one town and take a picture of a very calm lake dotted with fishing boats. The scene could have come straight out of a promotional tour magazine for upstate New York. Rte 3 eventually landed me in Lake Placid, which has on two occasions been home to the Winter Olympics. No one of my age will ever forget the hockey game there several years ago when Team USA defeated the highly-favored Russian squad. ("Do you believe in Miracles?" Believe in them! I was living one.)

I was somewhat disappointed by the "touristy" nature of the place, so I continued on, turning onto Rte 87 towards my next stop. Driving north, I cleared the eastern edge of the Adirondacks and approached Port Kent

where the ferry to Vermont departs. It was still early and I decided to try to make the 1225 crossing rather than my planned time of 1445. At the ferry landing, I met three riders from Quebec who were on their way to the annual bike event in Laconia, New York. We had fun joking around with each other as the ferry pulled out and I am sure that the other passengers were thoroughly entertained by the ribbing we gave each other. They proved to be a wealth of information for my ride to Quebec the following week. Parting, we exchanged email addresses, and I handed out RTR ride pins to the three of them.

Arriving in Burlington, Vermont, I settled in for the night. Preparing for my long excursion into Canada, I decided to get Canadian cell phone coverage. Then I spent some time repacking the Glide, making sure to put my rain gear close at hand. After a quick check of my border documents and a great dinner at a nearby restaurant, my thoughts turned to my son Phillip who was celebrating his birthday that day. I always tried to keep in touch with all of my kids while on the road, and to call as often as possible. Usually, it is a late night call, letting them know where I am, and filling them in on the day's events. I reached Phil and we chatted about his birthday plans. He wasn't going to celebrate that night because the following day was a work day, but I was sure he would make up for it on the weekend.

The next morning, the Glide got its 50k service at Green Mountain HD in Essex, Vermont, a suburb of Burlington. The wrench who did the work was an old seasoned rider, and we shared road stories as he did the job. The total charge, including parts and labor, was a whopping $460. What a deal! They even had a bike wash, and the Glide looked pretty spiffy as we rolled out of the shop. I got on the road and pointed the Glide's nose north. We were leaving the United States and heading into our neighbor to the north. Whether they were ready or not, our Canadian neighbors were going to get a healthy dose of RTR.

In the snow at Washington Pass - Cascade Mountains, WA.

The final resting place of Leonardo - Malta, MT.

The second time crossing the Continental Divide – Marias Pass, MT.

Peace Towers at the International Peace Garden.

Wetlands proclamation at the Mudhen's game in Toledo, OH.

To view additional pictures from the Northern Rim go to www.ridingtherim.com

Into The Maritimes

Rim Day 49 Elapsed miles 9521

Lost in Two Languages

Then, like an explorer sighting land after a long voyage, I sailed into the Maritime Provinces. Okay, actually it was a ferry into Vermont, but I wanted it to be impressive. The truth is that I rode into Canada on the Glide. Even though I wasn't really sailing and I wasn't actually an explorer, I faced the next few days with the same kind of excitement. Although it was close to 1500 when I pulled out of the dealership in Burlington, I decided to head straight for my night's destination, Saint-Hyacinthe, Quebec. My Maritime adventure was beginning.

Soon, I was riding under a very blue sky through picturesque farmlands. The strong, pungent odor of manure was heavy in the air as I let Jill guide me through one small community after another. At my first stop, I encountered a language problem for the first time. It wasn't an especially opportune moment, because, when it happened, I was asking if I could use the "men's room." It happened to be an urgent need just then. My request was met with a quizzical look from the attendant, until I mentioned "toilet," which she quickly repeated in French as "toilette," and then pointed to the back of the store. Quebec is bi-lingual and French is the predominant language. It is spoken everywhere, though not by me. After I was there a while, I thought it would have been a really good idea to have taken a course with the Berlitz language school or to work with the Rosetta Stone computer program before heading into a country that took great pride in their language. The Québécoise are seldom willing to take the first step across the language barrier. For anyone from my adopted state who is considering a trip there, I offer a hint— a few days in Southwest Louisiana will be of some help.

On the other hand, if you are a Louisiana Cajun, you would probably fare pretty well there.

In Saint–Hyacinthe, I found lodging at a simple, but clean, motel run by a nice Asian couple from Toronto. (An Asian couple from Toronto? The world is becoming increasingly multi-cultural wherever I go.) At a local diner, I met up with a group of riders who gave me suggestions about making my way over to Quebec City. I was already impressed with Quebec and I was really looking forward to several days of bi-lingual adventure there.

Maintenant! (That's French.) Off to Quebec City! After a few wrong turns, I got on Rte 132 and followed what I believed was the St Lawrence River heading northeast. The Glide and I were once again greeted with lush farmlands. The ever-present smell of manure mingling with the sweet moist smell of the morning dew wasn't all that offensive. "The year was at the spring, the day was at the morn, and everything was well with the world just then." (I read that once.)

On the spur of the moment, I decided to cross the river at Cop-de-la Madeleine and take a different route into the city. I had a vague idea as to where I was going, but relied on Jill to get me through the tangle of country roads as I continued east. I noticed a tourist information sign and pulled in for directions. After dealing, once again, with the slight language problem that never really left during my stay in Quebec, I got maps and directions to Rte 138, which turned out to be a delightful road. As it turned out, I was not the only rider to discover this road, and I waved to several other bikers who passed me, though few returned my wave. I figured it must not be a Canadian thing. On the other hand, perhaps I wasn't waving in French. Maybe I was waving with a bad American accent. Nearing Quebec City, I stopped for lunch at a Mickey D's (I wondered if they called McDonald's that in Quebec. What else would it be "fils de Donald?) about 20 miles outside the city.

I had been somewhat successful at avoiding fast food on the trip because, over the last several years, I had learned that my stomach, inside and out, could not handle high-fat, calorie-rich foods. I decided to try some chicken tenders, which turned out to be none that tender, but they did fill me up. While eating I met a delightful retired guy who gave me some suggestions on what to do and see in Quebec City. He lived there during the summer, and then went to Miami for the winters. I congratulated him on a successful retirement and what seemed to be a very contented life.

So many people, especially men, find retirement less fulfilling than they had imagined it would be. I suppose you can only play so much golf and take so many long walks, before the monotony of having nothing to do becomes a burden in itself. Through my research on developing second careers after retirement, I had learned that it was wise to plan out one's retirement past the first couple of weeks. The story is told about the wife of General George Marshall (of Marshall Plan fame) who asked President Truman to give her husband a job after he had been retired for a bit saying, "I married him for better or worse, but not for lunch." My new friend told me how much he missed his wife who had passed away several years before. I told him how I was missing my very-much-alive wife myself. We chatted for several more minutes, and then it was time for me to get the Glide moving towards Quebec City.

Touring Quebec

It was a short hop and suddenly, I was there. Entering Quebec City I found Rte 17 and took Champlain Avenue down to the old port area. The sidewalks were packed with tourists from the many cruise ships that lined the dock area and the road was congested as I navigated the narrow and steep streets of the old city. I was told that motorcycles were not allowed in some parts of the city, but I saw many parked along the sidewalks while I was looking for a spot to park, so I thought it must not be that big of a deal. The steeply-angled streets and the extremely narrow parking spots gave me some real worries about parking. (Good brakes needed.) Besides, the Glide was fully loaded and I was concerned about leaving my gear unattended. Giving up, I headed back to the business area to search for a hotel, deciding to see the old part of the city later without the Glide.

There were several hotels on Rte 1 and eventually I found affordable digs at a place called the L'Abitation de Champlain on Boulevard Laurier. My decision was heavily influenced by a nearby internet café and a bank where I could exchange money. Learning from my previous stumbles with the language, I introduced myself to the desk clerk with a "how ya'll doing" and she immediately switched from French to English. I'm sure it did nothing to improve the image of Americans abroad but, on the other hand, it kept me from stumbling around hopelessly lost in a sea of syntax, yet again. After she kindly had pity on the poor yokel before her, it turned out that I was on a bus route that would take me to the "old quarters." She also told me that the exchange rate was par and there was no need to change out my U.S. dollars for Canadian dollars, which are called "Loonies." (I don't make this up.)

I took a bus ride into the "walled city" to play tourist. It was nice getting off the Glide without having to worry about traffic or finding a parking place. I was told that Quebec, an old city, would be celebrating her 400th birthday in 2008. The walled part of the city, the original fortified sector, was the oldest part of town. Small hotels, jostling with bistros and restaurants for space, made for a great people-watching place. One of the most impressive sights in town was the old Parliament building with its many tiers and turrets. I spent some time walking and gawking like any tourist, but, having already waved the white flag on the subject of language; it made no sense not to be what I so obviously was. Besides, I was quite happy in my tourist role.

After several hours of walking, I found an outdoor bistro for some dinner. Sitting next to me were two Canadian soldiers from a base nearby. They were heavily into their cup and trying to make some time with a couple of cute gals who were tourists from Washington State. After getting the brush-off from the girls, who apparently knew better than to go out with drunken soldiers, they turned their attention to me. One fellow, Jack, hailed from Newfoundland and said that it was a must-see on my trip. His buddy, Peter, rolled his eyes as Jack went on about Newfoundland being the friendliest province in Canada, as well as the most scenic. I started to tell them that Newfoundland was a bit off my route, but stopped once they started arguing about which were the most scenic spots in Canada. I decided to just let them go and see if civil war broke out in the Canadian army over the question. I wasn't really worried. They were obviously good buddies and though their exchange got loud, it stayed friendly. We sat and talked. I ate and they had a few more pints, then we parted ways. Jack insisted on giving me hotel and restaurant information for Newfoundland and I promised to one day make the trip over there. While I would have liked to see Newfoundland, it was a very long and expensive ferry ride to the island, and it just did not fit into my schedule. I would, however, if the chance ever rose, come back that way again, if only to revisit the charming city of Quebec and, perhaps, Newfoundland.

New Brunswick News

The next morning, after an excellent bowl of fruit and cereal at the local internet café, I bid farewell to Quebec City and promised her a return visit in the very near future. I knew Linda would love this charming city with its rich history and interesting people. When I started out on the road, it was surprisingly hot and humid but, with no rain or high winds forecast for several days, I was looking forward to the ride. Try as I might, I could not find the river road I wanted to take so I eventually decided to jump over to the Trans Canadian Hwy (TC 20), the Canadian version of our interstate system. The tarmac was in great shape as I traveled east, past farmlands with numerous lakes and streams, heading for my next destination, Riviera de Loup. Past that, I was not sure where I would end up for the night. Ste-Anne des Mon was my original stopping point but, with the fair weather, great scenery, and smooth roads, who knew! I thought that perhaps I would go past Rimouski and then head south towards New Brunswick, or go south out of Riviere du-Loup to Edmundston, New Brunswick. It was one of those days where I had not laid out a concrete plan and I was happy just to let the Glide take me down the road.

My northeast direction led me into hilly, forested lands and as the altitude increased, so did the beauty of the landscape. I had the St. Lawrence River on my left side and felt the chill rise from her as I climbed higher. The Glide purred along, grateful for the dryer and lighter air. After stopping at Riviere-du-Loup, only to find the tourist center closed, I decided to take CA 185/2 south towards Edmundston and look for lodging in Fredericton, New Brunswick. Sometimes when you change plans in mid-stream, you regret it. Happily, that was not the case. Soon after turning on CA 185, the land became more rugged and scenic. With a lake named Notre-Dame du-Lac shadowing the road to my left and dense forests to my right, I was experiencing sensory overload as I tried to take it all in.

Wanting to get some pictures, I pulled over at a rest stop where I met two riders from New Brunswick. Although they had heavy accents, (or was it me?) it was good to be speaking English as the default language once again. I had enjoyed the novelty of Quebec's predominantly French language but it had worn thin, especially when trying to understand news and weather reports. These two New Brunswick riders and I talked about biking, wetlands, and hurricanes, so I wasn't neglecting my duties. It was interesting to me just how many times on the trip this happened. I had come to realize that there are many more people who care about the environment than the media and the politicians would have us believe. If there was only some way to mobilize this great source of concern, it would be possible to take constructive action. It worried me for a time that I had no solution. Then it occurred to me that I was living in the solution. I was making this trip. Oh, I know RTR, by itself, wouldn't change things, but if everyone did his own RTR, in whatever fashion and whatever time, things could change.

It could happen. Wasn't that what wise men always said? "Be the thing you want to become; live the life you wish to have; Be the change you want to bring about." I felt a little better. My New Brunswick friends had helped teach me a lesson. Before we parted, I got them to pose for a picture and gave them each a RTR ride pin.

Traveling into New Brunswick, I noticed that the countryside was very similar to the northwestern U.S. The low, heavily-wooded mountains and the St. John River babbling on my left side were so like the Skagit River, still fresh in my memory, I could have just as easily have been on WA 20. In the distance, green-covered mountains formed a constant vista for me to gaze upon. After stopping for lunch in Edmundston, I decided that making Fredericton for the evening was too long of a haul. I had no pending media events for the next several days so, why push it? What a life. I could go at any pace I chose and put my head down wherever I wanted!

Near Woodstock, New Brunswick, I started to search for a motel and had the Zumo scan the area for a likely place to stop. A Best Western came up on the screen and I stopped to check it out. The desk clerks, Sharon and Amanda, gave me the royal treatment once they heard about RTR and I got a top-notch room with a good strong internet connection to boot. They suggested a local pub for dinner and, after taking a long hot shower, I headed into town. Woodstock is a quaint river town and I got a good history lesson from two ladies who were at the table next to mine. Once again, it was an early evening for me and it wasn't long after my head hit the pillow that I fell asleep.

After a leisurely Father's Day breakfast, I packed up to hit the road for Moncton. As I was getting the Glide ready, I met a group of actors who were filming a commercial for Best Western at the hotel. They noticed the Glide and my Louisiana license plate and, after chatting with them for a bit, I discovered that they were all Americans from Dallas, San Diego and Rice Lake, Wisconsin. They told me about their job, which takes them to locations all over the map to shoot commercials for the various hotels in the chain.

One of the women had recently visited New Orleans. She mentioned how surprised she had been that the city was in such good shape. Like so many people visiting the city for the first time since Katrina, she had expected to see nothing but devastation and ruin. I assured her that there were still parts of the city that had not changed since that fateful August day and that, given time, New Orleans would once again become whole. She asked my opinion as to whether some of the worst areas were worth reclaiming or whether they should be returned back to Mother Nature as green spaces. I shared my feelings with her that parts of the city should never have been developed in the first place and that, most likely, the footprint of New Orleans would indeed be smaller in the future. I was once again spreading the word and preaching my recovery gospel. If the teacher is willing the students will just show up. I remembered again my New Brunswick friends and the lesson I had taken from them. It was being played out again, just days later. We need that army to spread the word. Where are my fellow change agents? You're waiting, I know, for your moment to rise.

Back on Rte 2, with a sunny morning and a temperature around 20 C, I cruised out of Woodstock with a moderate breeze at my back. As the old saying goes; "May the sun shine on your face, and the wind be at your back". Driving east, the land gradually started to flatten out and there were small stands of spruce and pine trees. The St. John River continued as my companion, although she was hidden at times by the dense underbrush. A stop at Kings Landing, an old restored settlement on the river, provided me a much-needed rest. I contemplated paying the hefty fee to tour the restored village where character actors reenacted the history of the town, but decided to push on. I couldn't play tourist everywhere, not if I was going to do the job I set out to do.

At a gas stop farther down the road I met a couple, Bob and Theresa, from Halifax who were returning from Laconia. I told them about meeting the three riders from Quebec on the ferry to Burlington and they told me about the good time that they had at the rally. I had heard that the Laconia rally was one of the better ones to attend and Bob's comments confirmed it. As we were talking, Theresa told me about an encounter they had with elk and deer during an evening ride. They asked if I had ever had any critter encounters, and I told them about the bears in Washington State that I had detoured around and about some unfriendly cows in North Dakota. We laughed at each other's escapades and before parting they gave me some suggestions for sightseeing in Nova Scotia. You meet the nicest people on a Harley.

Moncton was an easy city to navigate and by 1500 I had found a little mom and pop motel with internet and glory be, there was a movie theater close by. I returned calls to Phil, Adam, and Jamie. I had messages from all of them. They had called to wish me a Happy Father's Day. I felt alone for a little bit after their voices faded, so I decided to celebrate Father's Day with a movie. The selection at the theater was not promising, but I went anyway. I would flip a coin and see what transpired. "The Silver Surfer" came up the winner and I give it about a 6 on a scale of 1-10. After the movie, it was off to Wal-Mart to shop for drinks and snacks, then back to the hotel. Everything closed at 1800 on Sundays there, so it was a quiet evening watching CNN and the Weather Channel.

The morning arrived with overcast skies and a brisk wind. After waiting for the weather to clear, I went north on NW Hwy 126 towards Campbellton, my destination for the night. The sun finally came out but was accompanied by my old nemesis, (All together now) The Wind! I was getting tired of battling the wind, especially when it consumed so much of my concentration and energy, but that is the life of a long distance rider. If it seems strange to call myself that, bear in mind, there I was almost two months out and with 10,000 miles of road behind me.

In Rogersville, I stopped at a charming roadside café that was also a general store, bakery, and florist shop. The aroma of fresh baked bread and cookies greeted me at the door and over a cup of coffee I started up a conversation with one of the locals named Eugene. He had lived in the U.S. for 20 years before returning to New Brunswick. While in the U.S. he had traveled extensively. One of the places he had visited was Lafayette, Louisiana. He told me of visiting New Orleans and how much he liked the city. The States, he said, were okay, but nothing compared to New Brunswick. My guess was that he was just a bit biased in his opinion, but then, aren't we all?

Highway 126 was unremarkable. I continued north to New Castle where I picked up Hwy 11. It was early afternoon by the time I reached Campbellton. I found a nice hotel in the center of town with a view of Chaleur Bay. With several hours of daylight remaining, I walked the town, found a grocery store, and also stopped in at the local newspaper to pitch RTR. The editor was out of town and, unfortunately, would not return before my departure on the morrow. I felt a little gloomy. It was always disappointing when I was not able to talk coastal erosion. It was the reason for my trip. I thoroughly enjoyed the sights and the ride, of course, but ever since Linda and I decided in our living room back in Mandeville that this was a message that had to get out, my trip was transformed. It wasn't just a ride. There was a terribly important purpose behind it. I wished the editor had been in so I could have told him that.

Happily, the staff at the hotel was friendly and asked questions about the trip, so I was able to spread the word on a smaller scale. They were a lively group, interested in both my trip and my bike. One of the staff told me about a former lover who had ridden her around on a motorcycle during their courtship. She liked his bike, but not him, and that was the end of that romance. I was not sure, but I thought that she might have been fishing for a nostalgic ride on the back of the Glide. Fortunately, I had my arms full of groceries, so I didn't have to turn down her request. There is only one motorcycle momma in my life and she was back in the good old US of A.

I had dinner at a local restaurant and my optimism of the morning was replaced again by a severe case of the "pity pot". I was not sure why I felt so down, but thought that a good night's sleep would cure my woes. Once again, I considered the possibility that I had been on the road too long. Perhaps I was just not up to the task of riding another 6,000 miles. That night I made this journal entry; "Oh stop your bitching, Terry, and just do it!"

Trekking the Gaspe Peninsula

The next day's ride was a makeup for the previous weekend when, due to weather conditions, I could not visit the Gaspe Peninsula. I had heard that the scenery there was rugged but beautiful and I wanted to visit the tip of the peninsula to gaze out on the Gulf of St. Lawrence. I calculated that if I left Campbellton by 0730, I could get to the peninsula, visit some of the areas that other riders had been telling me about and still make it back by the next day to Moncton to hook up with my friend Dwight. Although the town of Gaspe, which lies at the easternmost point of the peninsula, was only 200 miles from Campbellton, I was told to allow four hours to make the trip one-way. Then, of course, I needed to turn around and retrace the same route to get back to Miramichi, New Brunswick for the evening.

Once on Rte. 132, steep mountains hugged the road's north side. Chaleur Bay was on the southern side. Several small towns dotted the twisty road, providing both a very scenic but slow drive. The speed limit often dipped to 50 km/h (approximately 42 mph). This, combined with frequent picture-taking opportunities, ate up a lot of my travel time. I stopped in one very quaint village, Bonaventure, Quebec, to soak up some of the sea breeze and discovered a church, originally constructed in 1760, that was having its steeple repaired. It is good that people were preserving the past. I had seen such projects often on the trip. I wished, yet again, that same devotion could be shown for preserving the coast. (I know I have preached this sermon before but it can't be said enough; we all have the capacity to create change— now just go do it!)

I had originally wanted to make it to Gaspe by noon but, after 2.5 hours and only 100 miles, I knew that making it there was out of the question. The beauty of the entire peninsula would someday bring me back when I had more time to enjoy it. Now, I had to retrace my steps. Back I went over the same route but somehow got lost trying to find the bridge to cross Chaleur Bay. I eventually got myself going on the right road and made my way south of Campbellton. There's many a twist in the roads we take and the trick is not to go down the wrong one.

Leaving Quebec, and re-entering New Brunswick, I decided to take one of the scenic trails put together by the New Brunswick Tourism Office. Taking Hwy 11, I headed south on the Acadian Coastal Drive which follows the Chaleur Bay and the Gulf of St. Lawrence. It's a very rugged area but, again, the many small villages and the quaint setting make it a very enjoyable drive. The Zumo told me that there was a HD shop in Miramichi so I headed for it to pick up a pin and get some motorcycle chatter. At a gas station I met a Suzuki rider and, of course, our conversation turned to the weather. It was his contention that the moon predicts storms and, with some practice, one could determine fair or foul weather by simply studying the contour and phase of the moon. Maybe, perhaps, who knows? I was not going to challenge his science. What is that old saying, "contempt prior to investigation?"

Leaving Miramichi, I decided on a more scenic route back south and got on Rte 117, a continuation of the Acadian Coastal Highway (ACH) that I was on yesterday. My destination was Moncton where I was to meet up with my friend Dwight. The ACH proved to be a good choice and I hugged the rugged coast of the Gulf of St Lawrence. Stopping at Baie-Ste Anne, one of the many small villages that dot that road, I grabbed a cup of Joe in the Triple Decker Boy restaurant. I met the owner, Rosaline, a slight lady with a friendly smile which became even broader once she learned that I was a biker. She and her husband are riders and had a trip to Moncton planned for the weekend. They were going to the first annual Atlantacade, a rally fashioned after the very popular Americade in Lake George, New York. We chatted in a relaxed manner as if we were old friends. She proudly told me of her youngest daughter's upcoming high school graduation and plans for college. Her husband, like many of the men in Baie-Ste Anne, was out to sea lobster fishing. The area is known for lobster fishing and also for its extensive peat moss farms. It was peak fishing season, so things were quiet in town. I sensed that Rosaline was happy to have some conversation.

She inquired about my trip and I happily gave her the 15 minute RTR talk. I can be such an opportunist. Her eyes lit up when she found out that

I was from Louisiana and she talked about her distant relatives who live in Lafayette, Louisiana. Her ancestors were among those French Canadians who had migrated from the Acadian area to establish the Cajun culture of southeast Louisiana. I encouraged her to take a trip down to Louisiana to reconnect with her distant relatives and also to stop in New Orleans for a visit. I promised one of my famous tours if they made it to the city. Hopefully, she will one day take me up on my offer. I took her picture before I left and she sent me off with best wishes for my trip, as well as a complimentary cup of coffee.

I continued south and decided to take a route through the Kouchibouguac National Park, which proved to be a good choice. The roads were in excellent condition and I crossed several small streams. Of course, I took advantage of a few great photo opportunities that popped up. Continuing on towards Moncton, one scenic village after another greeted me. The area reminded me of Southeast Louisiana with its fishing trawlers, crab nets, and other maritime gear scattered around the weathered homes and storefronts. It made me, at the same time, homesick and determined that those picturesque Southeast Louisiana towns would not be swallowed up by the Gulf of Mexico again. I wondered briefly if the towns I was passing would not one day share the same danger. Of course, Why not? We are all subject to the same rules of nature. We need to realize that, while sometimes you're the pigeon, other times you're the statue.

A New Companion

As I approached Moncton the traffic picked up and I relied on Jill to get me to the local HD dealership to meet up with Dwight. It was early when I got there, so I grabbed lunch and returned just as Dwight was pulling up on his rented Electric Glide Classic. He had flown from New Orleans to New Jersey, where he rented the bike, then made the ride up to Moncton. Riding a touring bike was a new experience for him and he was enjoying the many features not found on the model he owned. After greeting each other, and getting a shop pin, (of course) we were ready to head out for Prince Edward Island (PEI) which was on my must see list.

I was somewhat anxious about crossing the Northumberland Strait, part of the Gulf of St Lawrence. The Confederate Bridge rises to a height of 200 ft and is 9 miles in length. Even with a moderate wind, I had been told that things could get tricky. I was assured by a local rider that we wouldn't have any problems with the wind that day. The locals had been right all along my route, so I put my faith is this one, too. I followed Dwight and we easily found CA 1 which took us to the approach to the bridge. We made a quick stop at the visitor's center to get a commemorative post card and a fridge magnet as gifts for some friends back home. The ride over the bridge was spectacular and soon we were on the other side, entering Prince Edward Island.

I saw a welcome sign and stopped to get an ABC picture. There we met a couple, John and Tanya, who were riding a very heavily loaded Yamaha Silver Star. They had been riding in the rain for the last several days and Tanya commented on their less than adequate rain gear. John blew off her comments and swore that what they had was adequate, and why spend good money for gear that you don't often use. I kept my opinions to myself but, as a seasoned rider, I believed in having good gear with me on a ride, regardless of how often I needed it. I had learned from experience. I supposed John would have to do the same. It (experience) is supposed to be the best teacher. My Katrina experience was, after all, what had brought me to this spot.

Dwight wanted to let Jill guide us to Charlottetown, our destination for the night. I saw by my map that Charlottetown was only 30 miles to the south, but Jill took us off the main road on a northerly course. It didn't feel right, but away we went taking a winding country road through lush farmlands. I had read that the dark red soil, which PEI is known for, gets its color from the volcanic activity which formed the island. While the sun started to sink in the western sky, we happily cruised through the countryside. Quite unexpectedly, the paved road ended and we were faced with a dirt road which Jill insisted that we take. Both Dwight and I decided that this was not a good idea. Our large touring bikes were heavily loaded with gear and we could easily get bogged down in the mud. Back we went to find an alternative route into Charlottetown. (Bad Jill, bad Jill.) On the other hand, as I thought about it, I should have followed my gut feeling. My instincts had been right and we were given instincts for a reason.

After several attempts to find a road that took us back to the main pike, we eventually arrived at our hotel. That night we celebrated with an excellent lobster and mussel dinner at an outside café. Charlottetown is a university town and the air was filled with scholarly discussions. Music from a jazz band played nearby. It was a little like home. Dwight and I listened to both the music and the talk around us in the quiet of the evening. It was very soothing. I realized that I was enjoying having a companion again. The new friends I had made along the road were nice, but, since Rob left (what seemed like a lifetime ago) I had been a lone ranger. Some things are better shared.

Both Dwight and I were in high spirits as we walked back to the hotel after a quick stop for ice cream. Our spirits were somewhat altered when we checked the weather forecast. The weather for the next day did not look good. We decided to press on anyway. While Dwight loaded our route into his Zumo, I set my alarm for an early start in the morning. We wanted to make the ferry by 0930 and I did not want to cut our time too close, especially if the weather turned wet. There was nothing to do but sleep and see what greeted us in the dawning of the day.

Touring Nova Scotia

It was stormy skies that greeted us in the morning. We had a light breakfast and got ready for the short ride to Woods Island where we would catch the ferry for Nova Scotia. After fueling up at the gas station, the attendant gave us some advice on getting to the ferry terminal. Unfortunately, we decided to take directions from Jill, forgetting her poor advice of the day before. This, in fact, turned out not to be the best choice. Also, as we left Charlottetown, the rain picked up and that further slowed us down. Dwight was having trouble with his rain goggles (He doesn't like a face shield) so we had to stop so he could clear them. He also needed to do a quick repair job so that they would stay on.

The route Jill had us take was off the main road and our schedule melted in the rain. We eventually found Woods Island just as the 0930 ferry was leaving. There was nothing to do but wait for the next run. We paid the toll and found a place to park our bikes next to a pavilion where we shed our rain gear. The next ferry would leave at 1300. As we sat, we were joined by several other riders who pulled up on a variety of bikes. Along with these other travelers, we made ourselves at home. The place was soon littered with luggage, gear and biker talk.

In a situation like this, bikers are a gregarious bunch. After some quick introductions, the discussion turned to the rain, our destinations, riding tips, and telling road stories. I met two riders going to Newfoundland and I learned more about the long ferry ride there. They confirmed what the young soldier in Quebec City had told me about the rugged scenery in Newfoundland. Knowing the ferry ride was long, they opted to reserve one of the small cabins to catch a nap and have some privacy. They told me that the locals in Newfoundland were very friendly and they definitely recommended that I make the trip over there on my next trip to the Maritimes.

John and Tanya, the couple we had met at the PEI welcome center, showed up in their less than adequate rain gear, and Tanya looked even less enthusiastic than she had been the previous day. As they shed several layers of wet clothes, she was obviously miserable and unhappy. She didn't make an issue of it with John, but he must have been reconsidering his decision not to get better weather gear.

Then, two Gold Wing riders joined our group and shared their story with us. These two friends, one from North Dakota and the other from Manitoba, went on a ride every summer. They each rode a Gold Wing trike and pulled pop-up campers. One of them buys a new bike each year and then has it converted to a trike by a company somewhere in Minnesota. They never know what their destination will be and have no set schedule most of the time. I thought I had it good!

Since I had been interested in buying a camper, these two experienced riders were a great resource for my many questions. I asked them about pulling the trailers, how well they worked, and their road- worthiness. They had used the campers for many years and said that one of their many benefits was the shelter they supplied during a strong rain storm. With a setup time of less than five minutes, they could pull off to the side of the road, pop open one of the campers, and wait out the storm in it. (I avoided looking at John and Tanya as they spoke.) One of the riders said that gas consumption does go up pulling the camper, but I didn't think that cost was a big deal for two retired guys who were both widowers. This wait at the pavilion, which would never have happened had it not been for our rain delay, was yet another example of something totally unplanned turning into a great opportunity.

It occurred to me that what had happened to us was probably the way it had been in the early days of travel. Groups of pilgrims would find themselves thrown into situations where there was no other option but to wait out a storm or, perhaps, the opening of a mountain pass. Having nothing more in common than the road, those travelers would come together to provide a sense of community for each other. Looking around at my companions for the day, I felt honored to be there at that pavilion, on that rainy day, at that exact moment in my life.

The ferry eventually came and we got our bikes strapped down on the lower deck. Most ferries require that you tether your bike as a precaution against rough water. After figuring out how to use the tie down system, we got the bikes secured and went topside for some hot coffee and lunch. The ride over was unremarkable and when we reached Caribou Island, Nova Scotia the weather had cleared to a grey sky, but happily, there was no rain. Our destination for the evening was Truro, Nova Scotia and we headed out, taking Hwy 104. It was a short ride and with (a now-behaving) Jill's help, we found a Best Western hotel that gave us a good rate, had an internet connection, and was close to an area with restaurants and shopping.

Dinner at a local pub was very good. Dwight wanted to get some lanolin to soften up his gloves, which had gotten soaked in the rain. We found a drug store that sold it in the form of a thick paste. Back at the hotel Dwight improvised using a hair dryer to soften up the ointment so it could be easily applied to his gloves. I put some on the back of my sheepskin seat cover, which had suffered a lot of abuse over the last two months. (So had my seat.) Dwight seemed satisfied with the results. Improvising instills a sense of self-sufficiency and is all part of a long ride.

Back during my preparation for the trip, (which seemed like a long time ago) I had made sure to pack the basic tools and supplies that would be needed should I encounter any minor mechanical issues on the road. As Dwight and I worked that evening on our gear (or as the Brits say, our "kit"), my thoughts went back to those brave travelers of the past that I had thought about while we waited for the ferry. In this case, I was thinking of the adventurers who had explored the western frontier of the U.S. Their only resources were what they had brought with them and whatever the land provided. They did as we had; they improvised, using their ingenuity to keep their gear in good repair. What Dwight and I were doing that evening was a continuation of a long tradition. Although times had changed, life hadn't. The old adage, "where there is the will there is a way," still holds true. As we worked we talked about the day's events; the drama of getting to the ferry; then meeting the other travelers at the ferry station. The time at the pavilion had been a highlight for both of us. In retrospect, we could have not planned it any better.

On the following day we were once again departing under the threat of rain. The sky was a dull grey and the cloud cover was heavy. We decided to put on our rain gear, leave Truro, and hoped to make it to Halifax, less than an hour's drive away, before the heavens opened up on us. With Jill's help I located the HD shop in Halifax. We wanted to purchase some goggles for Dwight and, naturally, a shop pin for me. While I was in the parking lot getting an ABC picture, I met Betty and her boyfriend Peter; a couple on their way west to ride the California's fabled Pacific Coast Highway. I told them I had fond memories of the old PCH. They asked me a lot of questions about Hwy 1 and I shared some of my favorite stops: Muir Woods; the upper portion of the PCH; and the "Big Tree." I could have gone on much longer, but why spoil it for them? Even though I knew a lot about the West Coast and even though I had been there before, there was something special about having the experience unroll before me. If you build up expectations, disappointment may follow. It is better to take it as it comes. I rejoiced at the pleasure they would take in the discoveries that I knew lay before them. We waved them on their way and went into the store to complete our errands. Inside, Dwight found his goggles and I spotted a restored 1985 Tour Glide that belonged to the owner of the shop, a real beauty. The Tour Glide was the great granddaddy of my Road Glide. It had been designed by the Motor Company as their premier touring bike in 1985. Although many changes had occurred since then, including a different name, I felt a kindred tie to this beauty. I drooled over it for a bit before we departed for our hotel.

The threatening storm clouds never materialized, so we shed our rain gear and headed for the hotel where Dwight had reservations. It was in the central part of Halifax and after checking in we put on our walking shoes to explore the city. Dwight enjoys history, as I do, and we learned a great deal. Halifax began as a major British port and military outpost. An old military complex, the Citadel, sits high above the harbor and we got a strenuous workout climbing up to see it. After exploring it for a bit, we headed back down to the harbor to seek out the condo where one of Dwight's relatives lived. The harbor area was alive with tourists, boats (tall ships, that is), and retail shops. A young guy dressed in a Scottish kilt was playing the bagpipes and I got a picture of him and Dwight together. There was a small shop where two guys were blowing glass vessels. I marveled at their dexterity in handling and shaping molten glass into such intricate shapes. To see a white hot glob of "stuff" assume form and shape, simply through blowing air through a tube while delicately manipulating and shaping the glowing mass with simple tools was an amazing experience. There was a festive air to the town. As we walked around the port, I was reminded of Pier 47 in San Francisco and the French Quarter in New Orleans.

Call from Home

On our way back to the hotel, we made friends with a guy connected to the local TV station, a CBC – PBS affiliate. I, of course, gave him the RTR pitch and he suggested that we drop by the station to make a play for some local media time. I asked him for an introduction, but he didn't want to get involved. He was somewhat critical of New Orleans, its mayor, Ray Nagin, the way Katrina had been handled, and scornful of our crime problem. It was disappointing. My critical reporter friend had a general grasp of the facts, but had been influenced by the media's "dump" on the city. Well, he had some points. I tried to explain the reality of the situation, taking them in reverse order.

There was no denying the crime problem was made worse in some ways by Katrina. The storm had wrecked the infrastructure and depleted the number of first responders. Many New Orleanians had quarrels at the government response to Katrina. The Mayor, though he had exhibited some feistiness in the initial days after the storm, had disappointed some of his constituents with his leadership since. I then tried to balance that with the fact that New Orleans was coming back. The response had been disappointingly diffuse, but the plucky citizens were, in many cases, doing for themselves what their leaders were failing to do. The city was not destroyed. The problems were being addressed. It was way too soon to write off a city as resilient as New Orleans had proven herself to be over the years. Unfortunately, as I spoke, I quickly saw that his mind was made up, so I thanked him for his time and we headed towards the station which happened to be on our way back to the hotel.

I could see that Dwight was a little taken aback by my boldness when I asked to see the news editor at the station, even though we had only had a short conversation with one of his reporters. Dwight told me that he was amazed at my skill at "getting my foot in door." I didn't bother to tell him that 11,000 miles of dealing with media types probably helped. When we left, I was hopeful that the reporter would call later for an interview, but I knew it was a long shot. I did get a promise that she would look at the web site. I had learned to be satisfied with whatever response I could get, so we left and made it back to our room.

It was laundry day, but there were no red beans and rice around (a New Orleans wash day tradition), so, while our duds were in the washer, we took a leisurely swim in the rooftop pool and worked on our tans. I had another good internet connection which gave me the opportunity to update the RTR site, catch up on correspondence, and pay some bills. What a difference in reception there was between here and the wilds of Montana and North Dakota. I had become very dependent on the internet to maintain contact with my family and friends. Without it, paying my bills, checking the weather, and updating the RTR site would have been impossible. It was for that reason I had my WiFi locator and I had used it frequently since that very stormy day in Malta, Montana when I purchased it. I had become accustomed to using it to find the strongest possible WiFi signal in hotels prior to checking in. Some desk clerks were surprised when I asked for a different room because of the internet connection. Though the clerks were sometimes skeptical of the WiFi finder, most were agreeable and went along with my request. Ah, technology.

After some discussion, Dwight decided to ride back towards Moncton with me. From there I would head south towards the U.S. border, crossing into Maine. He had dinner plans with his family and though he invited me along, I declined his invitation to join them. Instead, I would enjoy some quiet time. Even though we had only been traveling together for three days, I found that I was looking forward once again to the solitude of the road. That was not a reflection on Dwight. He had been an excellent traveling partner. I had enjoyed his company as I had Rob's, but the trip had changed me. I had been alone so much that it was now more comfortable. It had been fun with Dwight. I was just ready to be back in my old routine. I crave company and I crave solitude, sometimes both at the same time. Is that the human condition or what?

The company part was taken care of in the form of a highly-appreciated phone call. Linda called to tell me that she was going on a "girl's weekend" at the Lake of the Ozarks with her sister and cousin. I was glad she was getting out of St. Louis for some much-needed relaxation. Her work often takes her away from home for weeks at a time and frequently she is alone in her apartment after work. She loves her job, but her days can be very long and going back to an empty room for the evening can get old. Her sister has a place on the lake along with a nice boat. Linda grew up around the water and boating. She has told me of the many weekends that she and her family have spent there. I have never been that interested in owning a boat, even though I, too, grew up around the water. Our family had several friends who owned boats. Somehow, it seemed like more work than it was worth to get the boat ready, run it down to the launch, get it in the water, and then do the whole process in reverse. I had often heard, too, that owning a boat was a never-ending drain on the checkbook. Hmmmm. Sounds a lot like owning a motorcycle!

The last day with Dwight was one of my longest riding days of the trip. We were up at 0500 for a quick breakfast, and then off at 0630, as planned. Initially, there was some confusion about our route. Dwight was relying on

Jill to guide us and I was convinced that we should just follow the path that we took yesterday. I let him lead in and soon got frustrated with Dwight, and Jill, especially when we took several turns that eventually had us going over a toll bridge. Digging for the toll fare and trying to balance the Glide on a steep, grated incline was not easy. Eventually, we got out of town and I decided to let the bridge incident become past history. It just goes to show you that two Type A personalities will always have a hard time deciding who is going to be the leader.

Another Parting

An hour into our route the rain started. It was nothing serious, just a constant drizzle. We were both glad that we had on our rain gear. I had another quick thought about John and Tanya and wished them Godspeed in the weather. Dwight and I parted ways after going through the last toll booth on Hwy 102. With the usual male inability to express feelings and utterly unable to talk about the pleasure we had taken in each other's company for the last three days, we gave each other a big hug and he left without either of us saying much else. How else would two men part? Testosterone can be a real problem in this world.

It had been nice to have a riding companion, but it wasn't hard to part and it didn't take me long to get back into the groove of riding alone. I took NB Hwy1 West. I was excited about re-entering the U.S. After a quick stop at the HD dealership in Saint John, New Brunswick, I made my way to Saint Stephens and crossed the border without incident into Calais Ferry, Maine. There was a long line at the customs stop, but the officer barely looked at me. All he did was ask me about any purchases I had made and if I had any articles from Canada that I was bringing back into the U.S. This was going to be my last border crossing and after all my careful planning to have receipts and registrations for my electrical gear, not once had I ever had to produce them. Still, I was glad I had all the necessary documents, even if I never had to use them.

I was back in the U.S. It had been a wonderful time in Canada. I met some nice folks, saw some beautiful sights, and I spread the word about the wetlands to our friends to the north, but that was behind me. Ahead was the East Coast of the United States, a long ride to Key West, and the final ride along the Gulf of Mexico that would take me home. I was ready for all of it.

You never know who you will meet on the road.

Dwight and I on the ferry from Prince Edward Island to Nova Scotia.

To view additional pictures from the Maritimes go to www.ridingtherim.com

The Eastern Rim

Rim Day 59 Elapsed miles 11,111

Maine Meanderings

It was June 23rd and the Glide and I were headed south. I had decided in advance to take U.S. Hwy 1 down the eastern seaboard as far as I could. Theoretically, I would like to take it all the way to Key West, Florida. Theory is nice, but the road is all about being practical. It feels good to be back in the U.S and although I enjoyed my time in Canada, I was ready for regular cell phone service, U.S. currency, and the sense of security that comes from being near one's "home stone". After fueling up, I jumped on U.S. 1 and set out for my evening's destination. In less than 10 miles I encountered some heavy road construction and eight miles of road was announced by the dreaded sign "Payment Ends". Memories of Montana came back but, by now, I have learned to just take a slow deep breath and push onwards. The road was not all that bad and with some careful maneuvering I managed to pick my way around the potholes and broken up tarmac without too much of a problem. The scenery was great and I stopped for several picture opportunities before scouting out a place to stop for the evening.

It was my first time visiting the great state of Maine. As I rode parallel to the rugged coast, I understood why so many people went there on vacation. During the early planning phase for my route, I had wanted to cross over the top of Maine from Vermont but discovered that there were no roads leading from the western edge of Maine to the east side. That led me to venture into Canada and the Maritimes. I was glad that I took that route, even though it added several hundred miles to the trip. As I was meandering down the highway, I thought about all the wonderful people and places I had encountered in Canada. The memories would stay with me for a long time.

I passed several inns and motels but none felt quite right until I entered the small town of Machias, Maine, saw a sign for the Margaretta Motel, and noticed a restaurant with a gas station close by. No internet, but two out of three isn't bad. I was now back to my usual routine of getting myself cleaned up, giving the Glide a lick and promise followed by a little TV before heading out to dinner. There was an excellent show on the Weather Channel about global warming. It was so good that I called Linda and told her about the series. I knew she'd be interested.

With plenty of daylight left I walked into town. Less than a mile away, I found a very good diner called Helen's Restaurant where I had an excellent bowl of black bean chili. (Make this another food stop on your route should you ever pass through there.) Machias sits on a bay which was is fed by the Machias River and eventually empties into the Atlantic Ocean. I learned that from two town residents, Joey and Al, who were sitting on one of the many piers going out into the bay. Both were in their early 70s. They had known each other for over 60 years and were best friends. With them was Danny, Joey's dog, who promptly laid a ball at my feet to throw out in the bay for him fetch. I asked their permission to take a picture of the three of them and they agreed (Joey and Al did, Danny didn't say much). They gave me wide toothless grins (Joey and Al did, Danny didn't). The smell of rain was in the air and the sky was clouding up so I made a quick return to the Margaretta Motel. The parking lot was already filling up and I noticed two Harleys parked outside one of the rooms.

Later that evening I met the two couples who were riding the Harleys. They were from Kentucky and were trying to ride through all 48 states. Each summer they chose a route through a different part of the country. It seemed like an interesting way to plan several long trips and I hoped to one day try it. They wanted to know all about the Pacific Coast Highway in California. Was it as scenic as TV and movies made it out to be? How long did it take to go the entire distance? Would you go back again? What was your favorite part? To their first inquiry I said definitely "yes" and, for the last, told them the portion above San Francisco was my favorite. They asked about New Orleans and I offered to help them when they got down that way.

After a quick breakfast the next morning from the local gas station, (No continental breakfast from the Margaretta) my new friends from Kentucky came out to chat as I got the Glide ready for the day's journey. We were all going to Acadia National Park and made plans to meet at the park's welcome center later that day. I decided to stay on Hwy 1 and hugged the coast line down to Acadia National Park, which turned out not to be a good decision. The road was crowded with "Sunday" drivers and it took forever to make any real progress. The weather turned warm and after enjoying cool temperatures in the Maritimes, I was not ready for the heat and humidity. Also, I had grown accustomed to the openness of Canada and now had to deal with traffic, stoplights, and the tedium of a busy highway. What would I do when I reached New York City! I started to think that my heated gear would be making a UPS trip back to Louisiana in the very near future.

After struggling with the endless traffic, I finally made it into the park and got my National Park passport stamped at the information center. The riders from Kentucky were there as were a large group of riders from Quebec City. As we chatted I commented on my short but enjoyable stay in their city and instantly we all became friends. I took a group photo of them and made my plans to see the park. They offered to take a picture of me with the group but I declined. Later, I wished that I had taken them up on their offer because it would have made a great picture for the web site.

While the park was interesting, I expected something different. I was not sure what, but just not what was there. It was more mountainous than I had imagined and quite rugged in spots. I pulled off at a couple of spots and got some good pictures of the ocean and high cliffs. Stopping at a picnic area for a quick snack, I met a couple from Virginia with their three small girls. They were a young family and were trying to stretch their vacation dollar as far as they could. They told me of wanting their girls to experience the grandeur of the rugged Maine coastline. While they talked, memories of taking Adam and Phillip on trips came back to me and I told this young couple to cherish every moment they had with their children because some things can never be experienced twice. I told them of my trip and they politely listened to me as I gave them the five minute RTR talk. I cut it short because, though they listened attentively, I didn't think the girls would have stood for much more.

After leaving the park the traffic got more congested and by 1630 I was pulling into Brunswick, Maine looking for a hotel. I found a reasonable place close to a diner and unpacked my gear. I was ready for a quiet evening. While cleaning up the Glide, I noticed a loose screw on the power cord plug of the Zumo and nearly lost some of the parts as I was fiddling with it. I tried to piece the plug back together but, after several attempts, I decided to deal with it in the morning. Dinner was at an old-time diner made from a railroad car and it was quite good. The waitress, while friendly, was obviously bored as she took my order. Business was slow and I had the place mostly to myself which was good, because I was not in the mood to talk. The long day in the traffic and the problem with the Zumo had put me in an odd mood and I just needed to chill out in solitude.

Oh, what an ugly mood I was in the next morning! I was worried about things at home and the repairs needed to the Zumo. I told myself this was not the best way to start a day's ride. After a long talk with myself, I decided to let the day unfold on its own. I restarted the day with a positive attitude and a rare second cup of coffee. (You'd be amazed how well that works. Try it yourself sometime.)

I heard from Beth, my contact in Connecticut, that plans were in the works for a media event on Tuesday. I also touched base with Mary and caught her up on my schedule. We had fallen into a routine of setting up the week's events on Monday morning so she could send out press releases for the towns that I would be traveling through during the week. She is so damn good at this stuff! Don't know where I would be without her help.

Once again I tried U.S. Hwy 1, but, like yesterday, the traffic was tight. I couldn't blame it on Sunday drivers this time. After 10 miles, I gave up and found my way over to I-95. Getting back up to 70 mph does wonders for the soul. In no time at all the Glide and I were in high spirits as we sailed down the road. I found a Radio Shack and purchased two plugs for the Zumo; two because I was not sure which one would work and still be waterproof. I also got a phone charger for the bike because I was having problems keeping my phone charged during the day while I was riding. The Bluetooth connection on the Zumo was draining my battery quicker than I had anticipated. I couldn't chance that. The phone was my only contact with Mary and Linda. Having the Zumo alert me to incoming calls was absolutely necessary. With the Zumo running off of one plug and the cell phone off the other the Glide must have looked like a figure out of the "Transformer" movie or, at the very least, a high school electronics project gone sour.

Interstate 95 was a toll road, one of many I would experience on the East coast. Being unfamiliar with the whole toll process, I was concerned about having the correct change as well with the process of paying the attendant without tipping over the Glide. My attempts to do this in Canada had been gruesome failures. After a few toll stops I learned to recognize the lanes for those who, like me, did not have a toll pass. I also learned to be cautious of the slick oil spots in front of the toll booths as I stopped to pay the fare. I got in the habit of just taking my time at each toll booth, lowering the Glide down on her kick stand while paying my fare. I am sure this irritated some of the drivers behind me, but it was the best I could do.

Touching just a small part of New Hampshire, I got an ABC picture and then made it around the outer loop of Boston on I-95 without incident, thanks to Jill. She was on such good behavior that day; she alerted me to road construction and an accident; and recalculated a route to get me around the delay. The Zumo paid for itself many times over on the trip and this was one of those times I was glad to have Jill along for the ride. Linda always teases me that I am having an affair with a computer-generated voice, kind of like the feminine computer voice on "Star Trek." I must admit that I sometimes caught myself talking back to Jill as if she were a real person who could hear me.

Sometimes the Zumo would route me in a different direction than the one I wanted to take. If I ignored the route, Jill's voice would come up and patiently suggest that I turn around, go right or left to get back on track. I let Jill know who was in charge and told her in no uncertain words to let me do the driving. As I look back at it now, I can imagine what other drivers must have thought as they saw me talking back to the screen of the Zumo. One time I remembered feeling like Tom Hanks' character in the movie "Castaway." He carried on a relationship with a soccer ball called "Wilson," even to the point of painting him with a nose and mouth. I never did that. Maybe thought of it, but never did it.

Connecticut Connections

Clearing Boston I pointed the Glide towards Rhode Island and searched for a welcome sign so I could get an ABC picture. I couldn't locate one and decided to find a local HD shop and use it as a point picture. Again, Jill guided me to the shop. As I pulled up, I noticed a group of riders hanging out on the front porch. After parking the Glide, they informed me that the shop was closed on Monday's but that they, like me, hadn't known about it until they got there. Two riders, one on a Sporty and the other on a 750 Honda Shadow, were checking out the Glide's decals and RTR flag. Inquiring about the ride, they were amazed that I had already ridden 12,000 miles and still had many more to go.

What really impressed them was that had I ridden in all types of weather including rain which they avoided at all costs. One of the guys, Jim, told me he didn't even own a rain suit and, even if he did, he would never carry it with him. According to him, packing rain gear is bad Karma. I wondered what they did if they got caught out in an unexpected rain shower, but didn't pursue that line of thinking with them. I understood and could sympathize with them because, in my earlier riding days, I would avoid going out when there was a small threat of rain. Mostly it was because I was not confident in my riding skills on wet pavement, which I am certain is the case for most beginning riders. I also did not want to get my bike dirty and have to polish all of the chrome accessories.

When I purchased the Glide I decided not to add any accessories that were not functional and to avoid any extra chrome parts. I put my money into items that would make my ride more comfortable. These included a Tour Pak to increase my luggage capacity, a custom seat to ease the aches of riding all day, a beefier motor, and several other items that, while not necessarily adding to the Glides appearance, did make her a "dream touring machine". To some riders the omission of chrome accessories may seem like a mortal sin, but I had no regrets, especially after a long day in saddle or, worse yet, a long day of riding in the rain. When I purchased her in the fall of 2004, I had no idea that one day I would be sharing road stories with two guys in Rhode Island. I chatted with them for awhile and then turned towards the road and into Connecticut.

Beth had found me a Days Inn hotel in Old Saybrook, Connecticut at a good rate. Things here on the East Coast were more expensive than I was accustomed to and I was ever mindful of keeping the cost down for America's WETLAND Foundation and the Coast Guardians. They were paying for me to plant the seeds about coastal restoration, not to live it up on their dime. The hotel while simply furnished was clean and, best of all, had a strong internet signal. I looked over my schedule for the next several days and decided I could stay for two nights to explore the area. I inquired about a place for dinner and the owner's wife, Mrs. Patel, directed me to a seafood restaurant not far away.

Dinner was at Nancy's Rosemary and Sage in Old Saybrook. The waitress suggested I try the clams, one of the restaurant's specialties, because they were just coming into season. They call them "steamers" and they were served piping hot in a metal bucket. I was given a cup of the broth they were steamed in and was instructed to dip the clams into the broth. It was similar to dipping boiled shrimp in hot sauce. These early season clams are considered to have a soft shell but it felt pretty hard to me. The clam's foot protruded out of the shell which was a trait for this particular species of bivalves. I was not sure if the foot was to be consumed but the waitress told me not to be shy about it. I didn't take the time to tell her that I was a dedicated crawfish eater who "sucked the heads" and had downed far worse looking things than this. She suggested a pitcher of beer to wash down the clams but I opted for some iced tea which I was sure was against the local custom, but then again I was neither a local nor a beer drinker. I did take the waitress up on her suggestion to try the special dessert which was some sort of strawberry and ice cream concoction. Very delicious!

It was great not having to get up, pack and hit the road the next morning. After a leisurely breakfast provided by the motel, I sorted through my kit and decided to ship back my heated gear along with some items I had picked up on the road. Close by was a West Marine outlet that I noticed the night before on my way to dinner. (Damn but those clams were good.) I was able to exchange the cigarette lighter plug that I had purchased in Mandeville for a new one at no cost. Now that I no longer needed the plugs from Radio Shack, I exchanged them and got a small set of Phillips screw drivers for any future work needed on the Zumo. I also got a refund of ten bucks! Life is good.

I was scheduled for a media event at the Hammonasset State Park. I found the park's entrance and was waved through the gate as had been prearranged by Beth. The park sat on the Atlantic shoreline and was very scenic. At the far end there was a center for education and special events. Inside were live exhibits of the wildlife that inhabited the area. They were donated to the exhibit during the summer months and then reclaimed by their owners in the fall. What a wonderfully symbiotic way to share what you have with others and still enjoy them as your own. Beth had done a good job of contacting the local media about the event. The media and several members of her group, Friends of Hammonasset, greeted me as I rode into the pavilion area. They listened as I went through my Katrina story and wetland destruction talk and then I had a chance to learn about their wetland issues. In that area, rapid housing development was encroaching on the sensitive wetland areas just off of the shoreline. Freshwater runoff from the newly developed areas was slowly destroying the saltwater grass and foliage that sustained the wetland areas. We talked about how their problems were similar to those of Louisiana, but unique in that they had a fresh water intrusion problem while Louisiana's wetlands had saltwater intrusion issues. We decided that it made little difference as to the exact nature of the problem because, in the end, it was a lack of understanding of how nature works. Human beings were the real problem.

The group wanted to hear about my travels and I spoke to them about the winds across the Mojave, the beautiful mountains on WA 20, and the great, flat plains in Montana. As I was speaking, it occurred to me just how far I had come and how many different places I had seen. A couple of local newspaper reporters wanted pictures of me on the Glide and following a question and answer session, we did a photo shoot. I thought the event went very well.

The sun was starting to set as I made my way back to the motel to freshen up for dinner. Beth had invited me out and we went to a wonderful restaurant on an inland bay where the seafood was great. I had never been quite sure how Beth had found out about me and, at one time, thought she might be associated with a local H.O.G. chapter. Boy was I off base. It turned out that she had been in Lafayette, Louisiana visiting a friend and had read about the trip in a local newspaper. I guess I was not the only one planting seeds.

Beth had thought that the trip was a great idea, so she then contacted me about hosting a media event in her area. She was quite the organizer and I was very grateful for all of her help. It was a pleasant dinner. We talked about traveling, friends and relationships, and becoming involved in issues that speak to our passion. I mentioned my concern about getting around New York City and she suggested an alternative route to Westchester. She gave me great directions to avoid the traffic, if that is possible, when traveling around NYC.

Back at the motel I studied my maps and decided that the plans for New York City and Washington, D.C. were not going to work. I had originally planned to meet Linda on Long Island and we would stay with friends in New Jersey. Mary had been trying to line up a media event in the city, but so far we had not gotten any bites. I had only one H.O.G chapter interested in a ride which would have been on a Sunday. Doing it would put me behind for an event in D.C. To follow our original plan would mean crisscrossing between Washington, D.C. and NYC and I was not ready to battle that much traffic. I called Linda that night and we decided to ditch the NYC part of the trip and have her fly into Baltimore where we could spend some quality time together. So, the decision was made and I was off to bed feeling good about the next several days, especially about seeing Linda.

Following the directions from Beth, I went south through Connecticut and into New York, eventually ending up on the Garden State Parkway which took me south into New Jersey. Although the traffic was heavy at times, I encountered no major problems navigating around New York City. The Garden State Parkway took me south of New York City where I hooked up with the New Jersey Turnpike which eventually put me on the Pennsylvania Turnpike. Turnpikes are very different from the interstate roads that I was used to. In addition to the toll areas, there were service areas in the middle of the turnpike. These large areas offered gas, food, and shopping, and were quite easy to access. At one stop I got a sandwich and noticed that a pack of smokes was $8.00. Thank God I don't have the habit any more.

Once into Pennsylvania, the traffic started to ease up and I found my hotel in Westchester. I was cooling off in the pool by 1500 hours. I had done a lot of traveling through some very pretty scenery and I had made it through what I had thought would be the most hectic traffic of the entire trip, other than Los Angeles. Once again, my apprehensions had proven unfounded and I congratulated myself on a job well done.

At the hotel, I met some riders from Ohio and Kentucky who were on Honda Gold Wings. One guy told me how he had quit his job at Home Depot to become a motivational speaker. He had met a kindred soul, for that is one of several things that I do. We shared experiences about our mutual love for speaking and I wished him well in his new career. At dinner over a tasty bowl of clam chowder I met another guy whose name was Peter. He had the quintessential Jersey accent and was in town for a training session for a new job he was starting. He told me this was a new opportunity for him and a chance to improve his skills. Seems the universe is trying to send me a message about career options and goals in my life.

Riding Into the Past

I was off to York, Pennsylvania the next morning and although it was only 0730, the day was already starting to heat up. The country side was delightful with neatly trimmed farms and quaint houses. It was Amish country, so it was not unusual to see horse-drawn buggies out on the roads.

In Lancaster, I passed Revolutionary War era buildings. Some had historic plaques detailing who had lived there or what significant event had occurred in that area. It was in Lancaster that the framers of the Declaration of Independence had found refuge after fleeing Philadelphia. Unfortunately, the area was full of British sympathizers so they continued on to York which was where I was going. I looked around, trying to picture the scene. It was the area that the Founding Fathers rode through as they fled the British army when they escaped from Philadelphia. While it would take me a little over one hour to make the trip, it took them several days on horseback. I tried to imagine their sense of urgency as they rode towards York, knowing that the fate of the new county lay in their hands. Or perhaps they did not realize that they were on a path of destiny. Perhaps they were unaware that they were midwifing the birth of what would become the greatest nation on the planet. All of that lay in their hands as they fled for their lives. Everyone should see those sights. We all need an awareness of how we came to be what we are. If we could do that, perhaps it would be easier for us to work toward what we want to be.

My first stop in York was the Harley Davidson plant and I managed to get there just as a tour was starting. Unfortunately, it was the change-over period for the 2008 models and, we were told, much of the plant would be off limits to visitors. Even with limited access, the tour was interesting and I was glad that I decided to take it. I had previously toured HD plants in Milwaukee and in Kansas City, but I had looked forward to the York facility because it was where my Road Glide came to life. At the gift shop I picked up some goodies, got my ABC of Touring picture, and with much of the day left, I went searching for a motel.

I was starting to feel the drain of being on the road for over two months. It was exhilarating. It was educational. But at times, it was tiring, and the opportunity for getting off the bike early was very appealing. Moving to a new location nearly every day, eating out, and just navigating through traffic was more tiring than I had anticipated. This combined with the weather and event-planning left me quite drained at times. It gave me even more respect for the Founding Fathers who had endured even more and for much longer.

The motel I selected was next door to Laugerman's Harley Davidson dealership which had a wonderful motorcycle museum. There were several early model bikes, memorabilia, and lots of interesting Harley Davidson displays. I got a pin and chatted with several patrons who were either having their bikes serviced or just hanging out. One fellow, George, a security guard, had just returned from a trip out west and we traded road stories about the sites that we both had visited. He was envious of my trip and swore to one day to chuck his day job and go for it all.

That was a common theme with many of the riders I met. While many were envious, most could not see the possibility of doing a ride like RTR unless they quit their jobs and became kings of the road. I was frequently asked if I was retired, and if I wasn't how I managed to take on this project without a job waiting for me when I returned. Although my employer and I had agreed that, when I returned, I would have a job at least for the short tem, nothing was etched in stone for the long haul. I have always had a lot of faith in my ability to find meaningful work and I was not especially worried about the part of my future waiting when the ride ended. I tried to share my optimism with those I met and I hoped that some of it stuck with them.

With the sky still dark (but no rain); I made it over to a local mall within walking distance. I was trying to get some exercise in each day to ward off the ever-growing thickness around my waist. After some window shopping, I went looking for a barber shop but could only find a beauty salon. There were no other customers and the attendant looked like she wanted some company, so I decided to go in for a trim. I was getting quite shaggy by this time. I had kept my promise to Linda not to cut my hair for the entire trip. However, as I had in Superior Wisconsin, I got my beard trimmed. That wasn't really cheating. The stylist turned out to be very friendly and also a rider. Her boyfriend owned a Softtail and she wanted one of her own. She gave me the low down on a local mall that had a cinema and offered some suggestions for dinner. The cost of the trim was $8.00. I threw her a sawbuck and walked out feeling like a new man. Just as I got back to the motel, the sky opened up with a long hard rain. The owners of the motel, members of the extended Patel family, were very nice but they had no explanation as to why the internet was not working. They suggested that I link on to an open WiFi connection from a nearby business that just happened to be another hotel. One does what one has to; it's the way of the road.

Looking at my calendar, I realized it was June 29th and that I had approximately 23 day to go from New Jersey to Slidell, Louisiana. Even allowing for several rain delays and a couple of days off the road, there would be plenty of time to make the Road Home event that we were already planning. I decided to take it easy and, if necessary, have shorter riding days. (Later in Florida, I would ride during the coolest part of the day to avoid the mid-day heat and humidity.) As the rain pounded the windows of my second story room, I started to think about what the future held for me. Hopefully, Linda and I could start to plan a different direction for our lives. Where and what I was not sure, but my gut told me that a change was in our future.

Environmental Solidarity

The overnight rain continued into the morning and I woke up to a steady, and at times intense, downpour. With the luxury of not having to pack up the Glide and ride off to my next destination, I felt like a rich man. I peeked out my window to check on the Glide. I wanted to make sure that her cover was in place and that everything was okay. The weather forecast predicted clearing skies for the afternoon, so I went about researching the history of York. I decided I would play tourist when the sun came out.

I made another trip over to the HD shop to pass the time and met a rider who planned to ride all the scenic roads west of the Mississippi River mentioned in the *Readers Digest Scenic Road* book. He had a very ambitious schedule and I suggested he allow extra time to slow down and smell the roses along the way. I shared with him my regrets about having to pass up some sites in order to make a scheduled event or just because I thought I had to keep moving. Next time around, I would plan to take twice as much time as I thought was needed just to make sure I stopped to smell the roses.

York's historical area was easy to find and I got a great parking spot for the Glide. It was close to everything. I signed up for guided tours of several old homes, given by young guides in period dress. It was very informative. I learned that York hosted the Continental Congress during the Revolutionary War and I also got a glimpse of everyday life in mid 1700 America. The homes seemed so small and I wondered how so many people could have lived in such cramped quarters. After several hours of walking through the historic area, I found a restaurant close to the Susquehanna River which runs through the downtown area.

Sitting out on the patio were a group of friends engaged in a discussion on the health of the local rivers and the environment. They must have sensed my interest because they invited me to their table. There I met Michael Helfrich, a "River Keeper" for the Susquehanna River. I learned that River Keepers are members of a national organization. Their purpose is to monitor the health of rivers to prevent pollution and to check on other intrusions into what should be the natural course of the major rivers. After finding about RTR, Michael told me about a media event they had participated in earlier that day that had been well attended by the local press. He insisted on calling his media contacts to arrange an interview with me. As we chatted, I learned that he and his friends had just come back from Louisiana where they participated in an event to raise public awareness about cypress trees being destroyed to make garden mulch. The event was staged in Baton Rouge and Robert Kennedy, Jr. had attended. Michael went out to his car and brought back a "Save Our Cypress' tee shirt for me. (I still have it to this day and wearing it brings backs fond memories of meeting Michael) What a great guy. After declining several offers to show me the night life of York, we parted. He promised to mention me on the

Susquehanna River Keepers web site and also to promote RTR to his fellow river keepers down the Atlantic seaboard. He turned out to be as good at his word and did both.

Later, on my return to Louisiana, I did research the cypress mulch controversy that Michael had told me about. I discovered that, while Louisiana forbids the destruction of cypress trees to make mulch, neither Florida nor Texas had similar laws. I learned that cypress mulch, other than looking nice, has very little nutritional value as mulch and that there are several more sustainable alternatives that could be used. Though I hardly needed another cause to become involved in, Linda and I became active in our local Save Our Cypress organization. We tried to educate our friends and local merchants about the harm that comes from buying cypress mulch. (This was much to the chagrin of my children who just rolled their eyes saying, "There go our parents trying to save the planet again." Well, I have had worst said about me and I gladly wore the mantle of a green earth warrior.)

As I lay in bed in York that night, all of that was still in the future. My thoughts, as I headed for sleep, were about getting back on the road, hooking up with Linda, and how sweet life is, if only you will let it be so. I knew that activism in a cause I believed in, is a part of the sweetness of my life. If the unexamined life is not worth living (was that Socrates?), a life devoid of action was also of little use. I don't mean mindless action. Mindless action, for me, would have been taking the trip only for my own pleasure. I would have enjoyed it, but it would have had no purpose beyond that. Adding purpose to your life enriches you. Lying in that bed, I knew I was a rich man, and I had a lot to look forward to.

The Road That Leads to Linda

The next day, I was off to Gettysburg and Baltimore. As I was getting the Glide packed, I discovered I must have thrown away or lost my National Parks Passport. Although I was not sure how much I would be using it, I wanted to keep it as apart of the RTR memorabilia that I had been collecting. After stewing a bit, I decided not to get too upset about it. After all, that was only the third major thing that I had lost on the trip. (As it turned out, when I arrived home, I discovered that I had unintentionally put the park passport along with some other items in a package that I had shipped back to Mandeville. So, the good news was that I had not lost the passport, and the even better news was that I hadn't obsessed over misplacing it, which I could have easily done. Oh, Terry! You are getting a new perspective on life.)

Taking the advice of an employee from Laugerman's HD shop, I took Pennsylvania Rte 243 from just outside York to Gettysburg. It was an excellent road that lazily wound through the rolling countryside. Small towns were scattered around lush farmlands planted with corn and hay. I set myself a leisurely speed of 45 MPH. With the dry air and moderate temperature, my spirits were high. At Gettysburg, I located the local HD shop to get directions to the battlefield (and also, of course, for a shop pin). It was Saturday and there were lots of riders at the dealership, several of whom were H.O.G. members. I enjoyed sharing a lunch of dogs and burgers with them that the dealership had provided. A couple of riders asked about the trip and were rewarded with my 15 minute RTR talk. The discussion, as it often did, turned to New Orleans— What was left to salvage in the "destroyed city?" and, was it really worth it to rebuild a town that was destined to flood again? I reassured them, as I had done with so many other groups, that the city was not "destroyed" and that with the restoration of the wetlands and coastline, much of the damage from another Katrina type storm could be avoided. I was not sure if they believed, or could even grasp, what I was saying but the important thing was that they were listening.

Finding the battlefield was easy, although it was not what I had expected. Spread out over several hundred acres, you view the battlefield by driving on one-way roads lined with monuments commemorating a particular battle or regiment. (It was very similar to the battlefield at Vicksburg, Mississippi. I wonder if all Civil War memorials are the same. On the other hand, what else could you do?) Parking the Glide, and getting on and off at each monument, got a bit tedious. After about an hour, I had enough. I realized that it would have been better to go on the guided tour rather than to attempt it on my own. I debated about it, but decided that the tour was for another trip. Certainly, the battlefield was worth seeing. Someone once said that the blood shed at Gettysburg and the soil it was spilled into made the mortar that built our country. I think they meant that without the Union victory on those bloody days, the fate of the nation could well have been different.

Leaving Gettysburg with Jill's help, I continued on some wonderful country roads and then accessed the interstate in Maryland. I had made a reservation at a Holiday Inn close to the airport. As I was checking in, I explained to the desk clerk that I had been on a motorcycle ride for over two months and had not seen my wife for many weeks. I got an upgrade to their best suite and some complimentary fruit. Once again, Holiday Inn bent over backwards to accommodate me. Of course, being a Platinum level member in their rewards program didn't hurt either. Linda called from one of her connecting cities and was somewhat stressed. It had been a hectic summer for her and I hoped that the downtime in Baltimore and D.C. would help to recharge her batteries. Linda's flight would arrive at Baltimore International in the late afternoon.

With some time to kill, I headed out to the local HD shop to pick up the requisite pin and get an ABC picture. Stopping by HD shops was always a mixed bag. Some were very accommodating when they heard about my trip and provided helpful suggestions about the area. With others, usually the larger dealerships, it was all business. While I never expected any special treatment, it was nice to get a little lagniappe (That's Louisiana speak for a "little something extra") every once in a while. I had wanted to visit as many dealerships as possible on the trip and my collection of pins was growing. I vowed that, after this trip, I would avoid going into a motorcycle shop without a specific reason— well, maybe, sometimes, just to browse! After getting a picture, I found a small grocery and then headed back to the hotel to clean up and wait for Linda.

Linda's flight got in later than expected, but we had a great reunion and both of us enjoyed sleeping in. I managed to do a load of laundry while Linda spent the morning hanging out. We decided to explore the Inner Harbor area of Baltimore that afternoon, a place I had once visited back in late 1980s. The transit system on the east coast is great and the hotel shuttle bus dropped us off at a station where we caught a train into the city. The cost was nominal and payment seemed to be on the honor system. The Inner Harbor area was alive with people and we enjoyed playing tourist as we walked under a sunny blue sky. There were restaurants and shops to explore and, best of all, a Barnes & Noble where I savored a fine cup of Joe. It was the first B&N I had visited since Flagstaff, Arizona back in late April. That seemed like such a long time ago. Looking around, I could also see that it had been a place very far removed from this busy metropolitan city. It reminded me of the diversity of our country and the wisdom of the Founders in choosing as our motto "E Pluribus Unum"— Out of many, One. That night we dined at a place close by the hotel and just kicked back. It was great being with Linda and off the road. We didn't talk about the trip or about events back home. It was nice just being together and doing nothing.

The next morning Linda took a shuttle to the train station for her short ride over to D.C. The Glide was ready and waiting for me and I finished loading her up for my own short ride to DC. I took the Baltimore–Washington Parkway, which provided some nice scenery and easily made it into D.C. I was pulling into the Holiday Inn, which ironically, was next to the national headquarters for FEMA. For many storm victims FEMA came to symbolize the inadequate and mismanaged response to Hurricanes Katrina and Rita. Another time, I might have given the building a raspberry as I passed, but being with Linda had a mellowing effect on me.

The hotel was very close to the Mall and, once Linda arrived, we headed out to explore the sights. Although I had been to D.C. on several business trips, I, unlike Linda, had never visited the Capitol and the many monuments in the area. I let her plan our day's activities. She knew just where to go and what to see. On one of her previous trips there, she and a friend had roller-bladed around the mall area. That seemed like a great way to not only see the sights, but also, get some exercise. We mingled with the crowds and, once again, played the tourist role to the hilt. Dinner that night was at a local place and we packed it in early because the morrow would be another full day of taking in the sights.

We put on our walking shoes and got an early start the next morning. First, it was off to the Smithsonian's Main Building which is called the "Castle". We then tried to get tickets to the Holocaust Museum, but they were already filled until 1400 hours. I had always been interested in the Holocaust and put the museum on my "must see" list. Linda was not all that excited about seeing it with me but, being the good trouper that she is, she agreed to go. Her disappointment at not getting early morning tickets paled next to mine, but she made a good show of it anyway. I had not realized you needed to get advance tickets for many of the exhibits and naively thought one could just walk up to the front door and get in.

The Washington Monument and Reflecting Pool were exactly as I had pictured them to be and I couldn't help but think about the scene from the movie *Forrest Gump* where he and Jenny meet in the middle of the Reflecting Pool during an anti-war rally. I got some great pictures of the whole area as we walked the entire Mall. I never realized how close the White House was to the Mall, but we didn't even attempt to get in on a tour of it. The 4th of July weekend was no time to visit D.C. if you were on a tight schedule, which we were. Even with the close proximity of everything, we probably walked over eight miles in the two days we were there. It felt great just walking and I certainly needed the exercise.

We made plans to meet Mary Lousteau, my project manager, for lunch. The America's WETLAND Foundation office was a short train ride away in another part of D.C. I enjoyed the electrifying energy of the crowds as we made it over to Mary's office. Over the past several months, Mary had not only planned our media events, but also became a friend who, on many occasions, sympathetically listened to my whining when things were not going well on the road. She was always upbeat and her calm reassuring voice kept me grounded on several occasions. We spoke almost daily but had never met, so finally seeing her in person was great. She treated us to a great lunch and I also got to meet the rest of AWF staff.

Back at the hotel, our friend Patty, who worked in the area, picked up Linda. I followed them to her house in Virginia on the Glide. Patty set a fast pace and, with holiday traffic, we got separated. I followed what I thought was her car, but ended up tailing some strangers who gave me some odd looks as they pulled up in front of their house with me behind them. Fortunately, I had Patty's address and after plugging it into the Zumo, Jill got me back on track. Patty's husband Michael rides a Harley Davidson Fat Boy while she has a Low Rider, both of which were heavily customized and loaded with chrome accessories. I noticed the look on Michael's face as I pulled the Glide into his neatly organized and very clean garage. The Glide had taken a beating over the last several months and looked a little tattered. Michael tactfully asked if I wanted to wash her down, using his special soap and treated water, but I declined saying I was tired from the ride and would just give her a lick and a promise until the next day. My thoughts went back to the motel in Flagstaff, Arizona where some riders had displayed similar disapproving looks on their faces as I cleaned up the Glide with another lick and a promise. Others might not understand, but the Glide knew. We were soul mates.

The morning brought clear skies and we looked forward to a day-long ride that Mike had planned. Linda borrowed some riding gear and a helmet from Patty and we set out for the Blue Ridge Parkway. Mike took us over some great back roads. The Virginia countryside spread out around us as we coursed through quaint small towns full of Independence Day bunting and banners. Many of the fields had low stone walls that, no doubt, had been laid down in the 1700s. It had been a long time since Linda and I rode two-up and having her hugging my sides brought back many sweet memories.

We ended up on U.S. Hwy 40, known also as the National Road. The National Road was the first highway built entirely with federal funds. The road was authorized by Congress in 1806 and construction began in Cumberland, Maryland in 1811. I had read that this was one of the first cross country roads developed in the U.S. from American Indian trails. When the settlers came, these paths were eventually used by their horses and wagons. You could still find old way-stations and rest stops on parts of the road. Supposedly, you could take it all the way to St Louis, but that was the wrong direction for me.

Our route took us very close to Skyline Drive which is the northern terminus of the Blue Ridge Parkway. I first rode the Blue Ridge on my Road King Classic in 2002 while attending the National H.O.G. rally in Richmond, Virginia. That had been my first long motorcycle trip since 1975. The beauty of the magnificent mountains along with the quiet stillness of the forest had left a lasting impression on me. That trip also rekindled my love for the road. It was the catalyst that made me become a long distance rider once again.

Mike knew of a place that was open for lunch but, as we entered the steep driveway going to the restaurant, Patty's bike stalled in neutral and went down with her still on it. Although her speed could not have been more than 5 mph, the bike fell on her ankle and she received a bad sprain. Fortunately, that was the extent of her injuries and she was able to ride back home after taking a couple of Tylenol. She is one tough lady who typified the grit and determination of a road warrior. By late afternoon, the skies darkened and a line of storms rolled in. We elected to stay high and dry and enjoy the fireworks on TV rather than to venture out to a local park. Besides, it was the last night of my visit with Linda and I wanted to wrap the memory of her about me like a warming scarf for when I went back on the road.

Back to Business

I let Jill guide me through the heavy traffic over to New Jersey the next day. Once again, trusting Jill turned out not to be a good idea. It was one small town after another with endless traffic and stop lights and I was traveling at a snail's pace. It was only because I had made an early departure that I made it on time to my media stop in Absecon, New Jersey which was being hosted by Atlantic Harley Davidson. My contact there, Bob Enter, had set up a luncheon meeting with the H.O.G. chapter and the local press. The owner, Ben Petrovic, met me as I rode up. After learning that I needed a new rear tire, he offered to get me fixed up while I was meeting with the group.

The H.O.G. chapter was curious about the state of affairs in New Orleans and asked a lot of questions about my route and travels. After a photo session and an interview with Bob, who writes a column for a local newspaper, I picked up the Glide. In addition to a much needed new rear tire, I got her an oil change and wash. Ben gave me a very nice discount and I, once again, felt the close camaraderie between riders and realized again the benefits of being in the brotherhood of Harley owners. This was not to say that the same relationship does not exist with other riding groups. I was sure that the Honda Gold Wing Road Riders Association and the Yamaha Star riders had the same relationship with their dealerships, but Harley was my brotherhood and I was grateful for it.

I set off with a dealership pin and tee shirt, compliments of Ben, and found a hotel just down the street. Once again, I found myself staring at a menu without much of an appetite, but knowing I needed to eat something before retiring for the evening. I asked my waitress to recommend something. I got the same bored expression and the standard answer "Everything is good" that I had received so many times before. I tried again by saying "If you were going to order something what would it be?" This time her response was a little more pointed and I ordered some type of local sandwich which was just okay. Eating my meals out every night was taking its toll on me, both in my attitude and in the girth of my waistline. I once again reminded myself that I would need to change my diet once I got off the road. However, convenience reigned over discipline and greasy spoons prevailed for a little while longer. I am sure that with some effort I could have found healthier venues to dine at but, by the end of each day, the last thing I wanted to do was don my riding gear and saddle up for a ride to find a place to eat. If a restaurant was within walking distance, that was good enough for me.

That night in the hotel, I started to make room reservations for the next few days. I had started to notice the limited availability of reasonably priced rooms on this leg of the ride and thought it best to make advance reservations that could be cancelled without penalty should my plans change. I knew I would be making good time over the next several days because I had only a couple of media events planned. Besides, I was going to meet up with my son Adam in Vero Beach, Florida and did not want to miss seeing him.

The folks at Atlantic HD gave me directions to the New Jersey Garden Parkway and I found the entrance that would take me south. The Parkway is a beautiful road lined with trees and rolling countryside and the toll was only $2.00. It was a pleasant change from the last several days of riding congested Interstate systems and other major thoroughfares in the area. After a short hop, I arrived at the ferry terminal and paid $24.00 for my passage over to Delaware. I was now a pro at getting the Glide on and off ferries and, as usual, bikes and pedestrians were allowed on first.

As I was tying down the Glide, I met a family of riders who were going to the Delaware-Maryland H.O.G. rally. Their group consisted of a mother-father-daughter team. Bryon and his adult daughter Julie were on one bike and Byron's wife Kim on the other. The rally was in Dover and they invited me to ride with them. I had the time (and besides I could get an ABC picture at the rally to add to my point count). On the ferry, I learned that Byron and his wife were seasoned riders who had taken several trips to Florida and the West Coast.

Byron's next planned trip was a ride on U.S. 50, the Lincoln Highway. He was going with three of his friends and we debated the merits and drawbacks of riding with a group on a long trip. On the one hand, the camaraderie was great and safety in numbers was always a plus. However, when you ride in a group, different ride personalities and preferences often result in conflict. Some riders like to stay on the road till dusk and others are looking for a motel by mid-afternoon. I had ridden with guys who liked to party each night and then sleep in the next morning. My preference was to find lodging by mid-afternoon, perhaps earlier, depending on the weather. My night life usually consisted of dinner, back to the hotel to clean up the Glide, journal, and catch up on the news.

Preferences as to riding pace and routine are a very individual thing and no one way is really better than another. I preferred to take a leisurely pace whenever possible, but didn't mind hitting the throttle to get past heavy traffic and congestion. A comfortable day in the saddle for me was 300 to 400 miles; less if there were interesting sights to see. I am lucky that I have several good friends who like to ride as I do. It makes for a good group on a road trip. To wind up, my considered opinion on the topic is, "it's a toss up when it comes to solo and group riding." I enjoy both but seem to favor solo rides, especially when they are for extended periods like this one.

The ferry ride was a little rough and I went down to check on the Glide's tie down straps. I noticed that Byron's bike, which was not secured, was in danger of tipping over from the rocking of the ferry. Fortunately, he was right behind me and we managed to secure both of his bikes before an accident occurred. Once we landed I followed Byron and Kim over to Dover for my ABC picture and to check out the rally. They wanted me to stay, and even offered to help me with a motel room, but I wanted to get back on the rim.

Chesapeake Bay

The going was slow as I followed U.S. 13. There was construction and lots of traffic lights. After finally reaching the end of U.S. 13 which goes the entire length of Delaware, I took the Chesapeake Bay Bridge Tunnel over to the eastern shore of Virginia. It would be the second time in two days that I would enter, leave, and re-enter the same state. The Chesapeake Bay Bridge Tunnel is approximately 20 miles in length. It consists of several bridges between small islands, with tunnels underneath the shipping channels. The bay was busy with commercial activity and I enjoyed watching the many fishing boats and ships as they went about their business.

As I was riding, my thoughts roamed to James Michener's book *Chesapeake*. He is one of my favorite authors and, although much of what he writes is fiction, the historical background that he brings to the reader makes for a very good read. In *Chesapeake*, he described in rich detail the heavily wooded forest and the abundant wildlife that had inhabited the area prior to the time of the English settlements. He tells of the water shimmering from the backs of fish as they swam in pools so vast that it seemed as if the entire bay was alive. Sadly, the English colonists destroyed much of the beauty, undoing what took nature many thousands for years to create. The parallel to what was happening with our coast was not lost on me.

Now, the bay is home to large ocean-going vessels and bears heavy marine traffic. I had heard that, through a concerted effort, the pollution problems which had plagued the bay area were finally being addressed. Slowly, the marine life that Michener had written about was returning. A similar thing had happened to Lake Pontchartrain in Louisiana. For years, agricultural run-off and shell dredging had slowly polluted the lake, making it uninhabitable for marine life or human use. Finally, after enough concerned citizens gathered as one to protest the loss of this great lake, the dredging for shells was stopped and agricultural run-off was controlled. At first, there was not a noticeable change in the fish, shrimp and crab population. However, by the end of the third or fourth year, schools of drum and redfish started to appear on a regular basis. Now, after some 20 odd years, the lake teems with wildlife and is a source for the seafood that southeast Louisiana is so well known for. There is a lesson in both of these examples for us humans. If we honor our environment by not filling it with the pollution caused by our excessive lifestyles, nature has a way of sustaining itself. If we do our part, nature can provide an abundance of riches beyond our imagination.

Back in Virginia, I had Jill guide me around Norfolk and onto U.S. 17 which would be my route for the next several days. I had always wanted to ride that highway and had planned to do so when I was in Richmond,

Virginia in 2002. Unfortunately, a series of tropical storms that had popped up off the East coast persuaded me to take an inland route and I never made it back. No threat of tropical weather was evident as I approached my night's destination, Elizabeth City, North Carolina. It was approaching 1600 hours and the road was wearing thin as I searched for a room on the Zumo.

I located a Days Inn in Elizabeth City and, as I pulled into the parking lot, I discovered that the shifter linkage on the Glide was broken. With no way to shift up or down, I rolled into a parking spot in front of the office, hoping it would be close to my room. The clerk at the front desk was nice and gave me a room a few spots down from where I was parked. After unloading the Glide, I inspected the shifter problem and discovered that the coupling on the shifter rod had broken. Using a plastic tie, I managed to make a temporary repair that would get to me the nearest HD shop, wherever that was. The desk clerk, who was a Harley rider, gave me directions to a HD shop that was five miles down the road. It was too late to call for an appointment, so I cleaned up the Glide, took a much needed shower, and headed over to a gas station for a Diet Dr Pepper. (Haven't heard that for a while, huh?)

After dinner and back at the hotel, I chatted with two riders who were on a long cruise to the Outer Banks. They were both in their 60's and we hit it off well. One fellow was riding a very tricked-out 1800 Honda and the other one was on a 1300 Honda. I told them that I had owned several Hondas in the past and hearing me praise Hondas put me in good graces with these guys. All too often Harley riders take on a condescending attitude towards non-Harley riders, a sort of, "if you're not riding a Harley you're not riding a motorcycle" attitude. I had never bought into that mindset and believed that what counted was that you were on two wheels and enjoying the road. The Honda guys invited me to ride with them to the Outer Banks, but getting the Glide whole was my top priority. The Outer Banks could wait.

I got an early start out of the hotel after a barebones continental breakfast and headed straight towards the HD Dealership. Just as I was arriving, their H.O.G. chapter was leaving for a group ride, so, unfortunately, I didn't get a chance to talk with them. The service writer was very nice and found a "used" replacement part that was exactly what I needed. Someone who previously purchased a new bike wanted the chromed version of the linkage coupling, so the shop had kept the old one in their spare parts bin. They sold it to me for 25 cents and charged me $29.00 for labor. What a deal! While I was waiting for the part to be installed, I spoke with a local rider about going to the Outer Banks. As it was Saturday, he warned me that the traffic would be very tight and the going slow. He suggested I wait until

Monday and get an early start. Waiting until Monday was not an option, so I decided to make it a short day and ride as far as Williamston, North Carolina to get out of the heat.

A Fellow Rim Traveler

In Williamston, I located a motel and got a room but found that it would not be ready until later in the afternoon. I decided to try my luck with the Outer Banks. I thought I might get on from the southern end. Taking Rte 64, I headed east and passed through low, and sometimes swampy, farmlands that were sparsely populated. Cotton, tobacco and corn seemed to be the major crops and, while the countryside was pretty, it was rather unremarkable. By 1330, I was in Columbia and grabbed a quick burger at Mickey D's. Afterwards, I found a local tourist/nature center. The center was situated at the end of a lake and had several exhibits on the local flora and wildlife. The thermometer was now spiking at 90 degrees and my guess was that the heat index was in the triple digits. I really had wanted to see the Outer Banks, but decided to head back to Williamston taking the same route that got me to Columbia. I had planned on going south and then cutting back north, but a local told me there was nothing to see but farmlands and there weren't many places to stop for water or fuel.

A local steakhouse provided dinner that night and, for the first time since leaving Louisiana, I was offered collard greens as my side dish. I was nearing home! The steakhouse was one of those family-owned "dinner clubs" and the food was delicious. Linda called to surprise me with the news that she would be joining me in Charleston and Savannah next week. Although it had only been a few days since we parted, we were both looking forward to rendezvous in Charleston. I checked myself out in the mirror, trying to see me as she would see me. Hmmm, my hair was getting long but I kind of liked it. I wondered how long it would be before the novelty of long hair would start to wear thin?

The next morning I was greeted with cloudy skies that threatened rain, but the temperature was cool and the riding was great. Staying on U.S. 17, I passed through numerous small towns, all asleep on a Sunday morning. Just outside of New Bern, North Carolina at a gas stop, I met a fellow who was jogging in the thick humid air that hung so heavy that morning. I asked him where he was going and he replied, "south". I then inquired where he had come from and his response was, "north". That sounded all too familiar because, on several occasions, I had given the same responses.

Once, in the southwest, a motorist asked me the same questions and I responded by telling her that I was headed west and I was coming from the east. I felt like a characters in a John Wayne movie. The Duke would indicate that he was riding west into the sunset, a lonely pilgrim on the road to the magical place destination called"No Particular Place". Well, this fellow, like me, did have a destination. Ironically, we were both heading in the same direction. While I was "Riding the Rim", he was "Running the Rim". His name was Reza Baluchi and he had started out on June 17th from Central Park in New York City and was running the entire perimeter of the lower 48 states. We marveled at meeting each other on that quiet Sunday morning. We exchanged contact information, promising to keep in touch. He was raising money for a hospital in Denver, Colorado and I made a donation to his project. (Months later, in January of 2008, I received a call from Reza telling me that he had finished his run. We talked about the challenges and rewards of what we had each accomplished.)

Entering South Carolina, I stopped at a rest area for an ABC picture and got some good advice on how to avoid the beach traffic in Myrtle Beach. Just as I was approaching my hotel, the skies opened up. Holiday Inn once again came through with a great room upgrade, a suite this time, and I dried off the Glide before tucking her in for the night. The internet connection was strong and I made reservations for rooms in Charleston and Savannah. Now that my reservations were set for the next several days, I decided to get some exercise and walked over to a nearby shopping mall to do some window shopping.

While not the best place for impulse buyers, mall-walking always provided me with an opportunity to stretch my legs and to interact with people other than convenience store clerks and the occasional traveler that I met on the road. I enjoyed watching families with young children as the parents struggled to keep them in check. I thought about all the times the boys and I would hit the mall on a Sunday afternoon as a low-cost way to have an outing. The mall this day was filled with teenagers, ears glued to their cell phones, strolling about in large groups, trying to look cool and hip. It's an American rite of passage and it was kind of comforting.

Antebellum Adventures

The next day, early morning showers gave way to a cloudy and humid sky which made for a cooler day on the road. U.S. 17 continued to live up to its reputation as a fine road. The section between Myrtle Beach and Charleston was similar to many of the parkways I had ridden. The road went through scenic farmlands with a nice section intersecting the Marion National Forest. However, the closer I got to Charleston, the less scenic the road became. After a quick stop at Low Country HD in Charleston, I headed for the night's lodging. Once again the skies opened up with a strong thunderstorm just as I was pulling into my hotel.

During the short ride over to Charleston, I had been preoccupied with thoughts about the last several days. In memory, I played back the presentations from the Live Earth concert that I had watched not long ago. I could not get the words of Al Gore out of my mind. He had emphasized that each of us can make a difference, in our own way, toward saving the planet. His words were inspiring and the concert was very uplifting. I could sense Gore's humility as he appeared on stage with the band U2 to talk about global warming. Like RTR, where I was using my skills to make a difference, the musicians and Al were using what they did best to create a change. I got chills thinking about it. I began to imagine how I could tie that theme into a lecture series, and perhaps a book. (I eventually did develop a presentation titled, "You Are the Difference: Creating Change in and Around Your Life." As of this writing I have spoken on change to hundreds of individuals who were/are looking for a way to make a difference in their lives.)

Once again, I enjoyed the luxury of not having to plan the day's route and navigate the Glide. When Linda arrived, we set out in her car to explore the historic sections of Charleston. It is an old city made famous in many stories, the most noteworthy being *Gone with the Wind.* The atmosphere of the Civil War Era was everywhere. While we walked through neighborhoods lined with antebellum homes, both of us wondered who had lived there, and what it must have been like living through that difficult period in our country's history. We also saw homes which reflected the Colonial period of this area. Many had historic plaques dating back to the early 1720's. The streets were narrow and the homes fronted right up to the street, much like the French Quarter in New Orleans.

Looking for a place to eat lunch, we stumbled on a street that wound its way up to an old church. The church was lit by dark stained glass windows and had heavy wooden pews which had, no doubt, been filled by many prominent parishioners over the years. As we sat in the dark cool recesses of the church, I wondered about the lives of those who had occupied the pew that I was now sitting in. What crisis in the tremulous history of Charleston had they endured? I wondered if the church provided them relief from those hectic times. My stomach and Linda reminded me it was time for lunch so I left those thoughts, for others to contemplate, feeling a little more connected to this wonderful city. After lunch, we shopped at an open-air market and I bought Linda a sundress that looked great on her. The clerk was a young gal who had moved to the area from the North to attend college at one of the many universities in Charleston. She suggested that we visit James Island and Folly Beach where she lived. She also suggested we get there in time to enjoy the sunset. We decided to take her suggestion and after a light dinner, headed for James Island.

The original Port of Charleston was built on a peninsula protruding into the bay. The Ashley River flowed by one side and the Cooper River on the other. Fort Sumter, which was built to protect the city, sits at the mouth of the bay before it opens to the Atlantic Ocean. James Island is southwest of the city and we easily found the road to it. The island had a laid back atmosphere, and many of the homes looked like those on the Gulf Coast. As we rode out to Foley Beach, the sun was just starting to set. I took several pictures of the wetlands or what is commonly referred to as "low lands" in this area. It was nice having Linda drive. It allowed me to take in the scenery. It was very different from being on the Glide, navigating traffic, looking for a suitable and safe parking space … Hey; I could get use to this real easy.

The next morning, after a leisurely breakfast, Linda followed me in her car for the short ride to Savannah, our next stop. Once again, Holiday Inn was our host. I must really be racking up the points by now! After settling in, we headed over to Hilton Head Island, a short drive from Savannah.

The island is divided into areas called "Plantations," each with its own golf course and/or marina. Hilton Head has several gated neighborhoods. In fact, many of them charge you just to drive through them. As we rode into one of the communities I felt a sense of uneasiness as I viewed the manicured lawns that led up to stately homes. My thoughts took me back to the rugged coastal towns in northern California with their throw-back-to-the-60's energy, the small community of Kenmore, North Dakota where I had been treated so kindly by the Chinese restaurant owners, and Rosaline, the owner of the small of café in Baie-Ste Anne, New Brunswick who shared with me her desire to some day visit Lafayette, Louisiana to find long-lost relatives. Somehow I had felt more comfortable in these places than in the well to do communities I was visiting. A justifiable, self-righteous indignation welled up in me as I stared at the opulence around me. I could have easily stopped the car and got out to deliver a great egalitarian rant in that bastion of moneyed privilege that would have warmed the soul of my old college bull session buddies. Fortunately Linda was driving and I knew she would have none of it. She would have been right, too. I reminded myself that I knew little of the people who lived here. They had as much right to their lifestyle as did the rugged folk in Kettle Falls, Washington. The phrase "contempt prior to investigation" kept echoing in my mind. Wasn't that what I was doing now! I was prejudging a lifestyle that I knew little about and discounting it because it did not fit my vision of the American dream. I thought about the many people I had met over the last two months who had prejudged post- Katrina New Orleans. With only a superficial understanding of the situation they had decided that she was not worthy of being rebuilt. How was my prejudging the good folks of Hilton Head any different that that of the naysayers of my beloved New Orleans? The answer was obvious; there is no justification for contempt prior to investigation.

And then, too, it may have been the hot humid air on a warm South Carolina afternoon that was putting me in such a cantankerous mood. Whatever it was, I decided to let sleeping dogs lie and get on with the day. I shared none of this with Linda who is far more tolerant than I in these situations, and I was glad that she was there to temper my mood.

The next morning after breakfast we headed down to the old part of Savannah. On the drive to the historic part of the city I started to feel a certain affinity for the place. It is old, southern, and full of history. Like good tourists, we purchased a "trolley tour" of the city. The tour was a great idea and we saw several old homes as we passed through some of the more famous "squares." (James Oglethorpe designed the city as a symmetric grid of perfectly aligned streets, interspersed with park areas that are called squares.) Most have a fountain or statue and offer a quiet place to sit, rest, read, or just chill out.

One of my favorites was Chippewa Square where the park bench scene from *Forrest Gump* was filmed. I got to sit in the same general area that Tom Hanks did as he narrated the story of Forrest's life while waiting for the bus to take him to his beloved Jenny. We also saw the home where the movie *Midnight in the Garden of Good and Evil* was filmed and the home that was in the movie *Cape Fear*. The town was one big movie set! That wasn't true of course. There are places, like my own New Orleans, that serve as movie locations. I think the reason is that these are cities where the lives of the people have shaped the place, imbuing stone and pavement with the hopes and fears and loves of all the people who had passed that way. This is what comes off the screen into the minds of the viewers. Soaking the city up, I kept thinking about what a nice place it was and how I could easily live there. Finally, the trolley dropped us off in the old business area on the

Savannah River where we had a great lunch. The heat index was well into the low 100s as we started to head back to our car.

After cooling off in the room and catching a much needed nap, we headed into old Savannah to do some exploring on our own. Linda and I found a great coffee house facing Chippewa Square and over a cup of strong chicory coffee we talked about moving to Savannah. We wondered about housing costs, employment opportunities, and the cost of living. It may never happen, but, after so many lonely evenings on the road it was a nice, warm, domestic, and very loving, thing to do. What a pleasant evening.

The next day, all too soon, it was goodbye again to Linda as I headed south towards Key West, Florida. This would be the last time we would see each other until I arrived back home. The parting was not as wrenching as it might have been because our days apart were drawing to a close.

The Riding Fraternity

The trip to Brunswick, Georgia was quick and I found the HD dealership with the help of Jill. The HD shop was the prearranged meeting place for me to hook up with my hosts, Jamie and Adam Sanders. Jamie and I had been corresponding about an event with their H.O.G. chapter over the last several months. Adam met me at the shop. He and two other riders were my tour guides for the day. After a short ride, we arrived at a local restaurant which was situated on an inlet of the Atlantic Ocean. Joining us for lunch were some more riders along with Adam and Jamie's daughter. I learned about the fishing and shipping history of the area, both of which are still major economic forces.

Following a very filling lunch, my hosts took me on a gentle ride through the numerous wetland areas which dotted the coastline. At one point we stopped on the top of a recently constructed bridge which spanned a marshy area. The bridge was 200 ft high and Adam informed me it was one of the highest bridges in the southeast. Looking from the structure's precarious height, I was reminded of a scene in "Saturday Night Fever" where Tony (John Travolta) and his friends clown around in front of some girls on the Brooklyn Bridge by pretending to fall off but actually land on a catwalk just a few feet below the deck of the bridge. (I guess you can see that movies are a constant point of reference for me.)

Adam invited me to peer over the railing but, with my vertigo, I decided just to get a couple of pictures and retreat to the safety of the Glide's seat while the rest of the group peered over the edge. Watching them, I was glad that Glide was steady and secure on her side stand. Later, as we rode back to my hotel, Adam invited to me join he and Jamie for dinner and a night on the town. We made plans to meet later that evening and I enjoyed a nice hot shower and short nap before they picked me up. We had dinner at a waterfront restaurant on Simon Island. The Sanders' daughter was our waitress and so we got the special deluxe service. A few of their friends joined us. Some were riders, though not all were Harley owners. We had a full table and as the evening wore on, I was struck at how nice it was to sit there and soak up the conversations between these long time friends.

After dinner we walked over to a long public fishing pier where I saw several small sharks being tagged and then thrown back in the water. It was a volunteer program to help track the migration and growth of the species. Several folks were grilling fish right out on the pier and the aroma was unbelievable. Adam told me about nearby Jekyll Island and the exclusive homes there. Close by was privately-owned Sea Island, which had been the site of the G-8 conference in 2004.

The events of the day were what I had envisioned when first planning RTR. I was meeting up with other riders who not only shared my passion for riding, but also were concerned stewards of the environment. I truly enjoyed meeting and sharing that special evening with all of them. One of the unexpected pleasures, as well as learning experiences, of the trip was these meetings with just such folk. I had known they were out there, of course, but meeting them, looking in their eyes, hearing their voices as they spoke their concerns made a great impact. Communication, even in our technologic world, is a one to one affair. That's how the world is changed, one to one. I really felt a surge of pride that I had made the RTR effort. That may be what is needed on the part of all of us. I don't mean everyone should get a Harley and ride the rim, (it'd clutter up the road) but I do think that if folks in different parts of the country could share that kind of communion, the interdependence of us all on each other and on the land would take on new meaning. Well, a lot of thoughts to end a nice evening.

Looping Florida

The next day, an early start without breakfast had me on the road by 0730 with hopes of beating the impending heat. I made it through Jacksonville by 0900 and had breakfast at a Waffle House, probably not as nutritious as my usual bowl of cereal, but it was the Waffle House! It was already starting to heat up as I pushed towards Vero Beach, Florida on I-95.

It was one of the rare instances that I elected to use the interstate system rather than the state or U.S. highways. I did veer off at one point to ride a supposedly "scenic route" called A-1-A. It followed the coast and was lined with beach houses, however there very few opportunities to actually see the Atlantic Ocean. The area reminded me of Gulf Shores, Alabama with its rows of condos and beach houses. It was a depressing reminder of the impact of people on the environment. It brought back memories of the couple I met in Oregon who were on an outing on Mother's Day and could not find a public spot to try their hand as some fishing. Growth is necessary; it's even good, if done with forethought and prudence.

At the first opportunity I got back on I-95 and headed towards Daytona Beach, where I stopped at the worlds "largest Harley Davidson dealership". The HD shop in Daytona Beach is actually a large complex complete with hotel, barbershop, restaurants, and a travel agency. As I browsed through the wide selection of accessories, I noticed several items not usually found in your run of the mill dealership. Their inventory of bikes was impressive and they also had a "fly and buy" program. You fly in, buy your bike, and they make all arrangements to get you on the road home driving your brand new HD. Impressive. And smart business.

Along with purchasing the pre-requisite dealership pin, I got a new cargo net to accommodate my rain gear on the top of the tour pack. The net that I had purchased back in California was too big. The new one allowed for a more secure tie-down for my often-used rain gear. One thing about traveling in the south during the summer months, you can count on an afternoon rainstorm each day. I usually don't mind getting a little wet because it cools me down, but, in Florida a rain shower could turn into a torrential downpour at a moment's notice. It was wise to have one's rain gear close at hand.

Then it was onward to Vero Beach and, as predicted, the sky started to cloud up with some distant thunder claps to announce the coming rain. The Zumo was giving me weather warnings, but I made it to the hotel by 1330 without getting wet. Once out of the weather, I got a little surly. (Grumble, No laundry at the hotel and the WiFi signal was weak.) Well, I'm an experienced traveler so there was little reason for surliness. For several years, I had been using micro-fiber clothing when I toured. Not only did they do a great job of wicking moisture away from the skin, but they are also easy to clean and dry quickly. So, once again, the famous (to me) RTR laundry came to the rescue as I washed out a couple of shirts and some underwear in the sink and hung them up to dry with the help of a hair dryer, Then, after some clever experimentation on my part I discovered a WiFi signal in the bathroom so I set up office in there to catch up on my email and update the website. The things a guy will do to stay connected!

Checking my route for the next day, I decided to take the Florida Turnpike around Miami towards the Keys. I had been warned to be careful about going through Miami on I-95 due to both traffic and the driving habits of the local population. Even though I would be traveling on a Sunday, the turnpike seemed like the best bet. Several local riders had also suggested I go that way.

My plan for the evening was to meet Adam for dinner. I hadn't seen him since May when I attended his graduation from Louisiana Tech in Ruston, Louisiana. He was staying in the area and getting some more hours aloft at a local flight school. He reasoned that the extra flight time could help him land a job with a major airline and I thought he had made a wise choice in opting to go that route. Florida had several flight schools. (Think, unfortunately, of the 9-11 terrorists who used them for training purposes.) The one in Vero Beach accommodated pilots by allowing them to fly at night after the regular students were finished. As it turned out, though, the weather that had caught me had also forced Adam to detour to another field so he would not make it back to Vero Beach until late that night. Still, we had a nice chat on the phone. It was good to hear his voice and get an update on his employment situation. He felt confident that the time in Vero Beach was well spent and he was excited about a job offer that he thought was coming from a major airline. I would have liked to hook up with him but, like most things in life, you can't control the weather.

The Rims End: Key West

Up for an early start, I was anxious for two things to happen: I wanted to get around Miami without incident and I wanted to experience the Keys. Getting around Miami proved to be less difficult than I had expected (surprise, surprise!) and I easily found the connection to Homestead, Florida, the jumping off point for entering the Keys. Reuniting with Hwy 1, (and also the rain) I had a real sense of excitement as I passed through Key Largo and then down through the many small islands to Key West. The weather continued to be wet, but refreshing, and I enjoyed riding through several small towns. The going was slow due to traffic but, fortunately, most of it was headed north as vacationers traveled back home. As I rode further south through lush vegetation surrounded by emerald green water, the Gulf, at times, was lapping at the edge of the road.

The day was still young as I pulled into Key West but I started to scope out a hotel for the night. I usually avoided tourist information places that advertise "reasonable motel rates" but this time I decided to try one that was near the harbor area in Key West. It proved to be a good choice. The agent there got me connected with the Spindrift Motel at a very reasonable rate for two nights. The motel was close to Duval Street which is the "happening place" in Key West. The owner of the Spindrift was biker-friendly and he allowed me to pull the Glide into the motel's courtyard where I was able to park within spitting distance of my room. While the motel was a no frills type of place, it was clean and the air conditioning gave out a frigid stream of air. There was a small pool and a laundromat which I badly needed to use. While there was no internet hook up, I scanned the area and found a connection at a nearby Best Western. I invited myself over there to use the internet. I had used their chain enough in the past that I thought we had developed a relationship. Given the opportunity I can rationalize anything.

A short walk from the Spindrift found me at a local Cuban bodega where I ordered a mouth-watering sandwich and stocked up on snacks for the room. I once again had that "rich as a king" feeling that my friend Rob and I had experienced in northern California. Wow, Rob, California; A continent and a lifetime away. It was too bad Rob couldn't have come the whole way. He would have loved it. On the other hand, I had cherished my time alone. What a contradictory creature I was! Well, I would share it with Rob when I got back and he would be happy for me. That was all in the future, anyhow. For the moment, I was in Key West, with reasonable accommodations, almost two days to wander about and not a worry in the world.

Key West seemed to be a delightful place. It is an unusual place, touristy, but not crowded, with a real local/alternative spin in the air. It is also very hot and humid. It almost felt like home. The island dimensions are a mere two miles by four miles so everything is very accessible. Motor scooters were everywhere and appeared to be the preferred mode of transportation. Needing the exercise, and not wanting to offend the Glide, I decided to see the area by foot. When the evening air started to cool down, I put on my walking shoes to stroll out and see the sights.

Duval Street, the main drag, was a cleaner, tamer version of the famed

Bourbon Street in New Orleans. It had the usual bars and tee shirt shops, but fewer strip clubs. I went to the Floridita, the famous watering hole that Ernest Hemmingway frequented while living there. I passed on the Papa Doble, a vicious margarita drink he invented, and instead ducked into a local shop for an ice cream. I may be a macho biker, but having heard what was in the drink, I knew it wasn't for me. By 2200 hours, I was walking back to the Spindrift. The sky rumbled with thunder and lightning. After a quick check on the Glide, I retired to my room, set the AC to "hanging meat", and drifted off to a very restful sleep.

I spent the next day touring Key West. My first stop was a buoy which marks the most southern spot in the United States. With a little maneuvering, I got the Glide lined up and took an ABC picture. I visited the harbor area and an older residential area which again reminded me of New Orleans both in architecture and in the slow pace of life. In one of the residential areas I saw my first wild chickens walking around. I would later learn they are part of the Key West culture. The houses in this mostly residential area were small cottages and raised "West Bahamas" homes. The vegetation was very lush with palms and banana trees growing everywhere. I liked the area and compared it to the back end of the French Quarter in New Orleans, which is mostly residential and somewhat off the beaten track from tour busses and sightseers. I went back to the motel for a nap. I wasn't tired of course, but the Glide needed the rest.

Later, taking off on foot, I went over to the Ernest Hemingway Home and Museum for a tour. The guide was very informative and I learned about this major American author, so well known for his many novels and stories. The house was completely restored and is much the same as Hemingway left it. He was eccentric in many ways. For instance, he was a lover of cats and allowed them complete access to the entire house. Their descendents still roam the property and are very friendly. I enjoyed the visit. Of course, during the tour, it rained.

While our tour group waited out the storm, I tried to strike up a conversation with a couple from West Virginia. I must have been getting desperate for conversation or just lonely, but after several unsuccessful attempts to get them to buy into my rambling monologue, I finally gave up and waited out the storm in silence. Leaving Hemingway's home I found the first office of Pan American Airlines and also the "Little White House" which is, actually, a group of buildings used by several presidents as a summer retreat.

After returning to the motel, it was over to the Best Western to get online. Linda had sent a message with news that her job opportunities in Louisiana were looking good and that she was sure she could find full-time employment in the Mandeville area. This was very good news! I knew her job was important to her and we had accepted that we would sometimes be apart, but during the enforced separation of the ride, my joy in our occasional reunions was ample indication that a stretch of time together would be welcome. For us both, I hoped.

It was laundry time and while my "duds were being suds", I took a quick dip in the pool. Even though the water was tepid, it felt great. I was soon joined by a couple of other guests who were also on a motorcycle trip. They were from central Florida and had come down to the Keys for a brief vacation. Eventually, our discussion got around to the reason for my trip and I made up for the lack of conversation with the West Virginians at the Hemingway house by giving them the 15 minute RTR spiel. Had they known of the reason for my need to talk, I am sure they would probably have cursed the couple from West Virginia long before the time I was finished. On the other hand, they might have cursed in any event.

On my way to dinner I stopped by the marker buoy to take some pictures of the beautiful sunset and met a family from Calgary Alberta. They were on a family vacation and rented an RV to drive all the way down to Key West. The father's name was Terry (another one, but I couldn't call him "Montana" like the other and to call him "Alberta" might have caused an international incident.). We chatted about riding and their trip. It turned out he was originally from Moncton, New Brunswick and he was delighted when he found out I had been there earlier in the month. His son and daughter, both teenagers, and very Goth, looked bored with the whole vacation thing. I could see this was probably going to be their last "family" vacation. I remembered the wonderful time that Adam, Phil, and I had in Las Vegas just this past year. I had enjoyed being with my boys and it had been great kicking back while they went out and did the town at night. Nothing was forced and we all enjoyed each other's company. I hoped it would work out that way for this Terry and his family.

Meeting up with Terry's family caused me to do some remembering. I thought about being with Rob on the Pacific Rim. Then, I thought about leaving Seattle to fly to Adam's graduation. There had been the phone call from Linda about working in Mandeville. Now, again, I thought of my boys. Since that time, family had come to mean even more to me. After one last stroll down Duval Street for ice cream I headed back to the motel. I was going to leave in the morning. This time, I was going home.

Joey, Al and their four legged friend Danny in Machias Maine.

Reza Baluchi "Running the Rim" – New Bern, NC.

Wetlands in Brunswick, GA.

The end of the Eastern Rim.

To view additional pictures of the Easter Rim go to www.ridingtherim.com

The Gulf Coast

Rim Day 83 Elapsed Mileage 14,962

Coasting Home

To my left were the waters of the Atlantic. To my right, the Gulf Stream was arcing across those waters to warm the shores of Britain. I was at the southernmost point of the United States and was getting ready to depart. This was it, the last leg, the final "rim" I would follow on my way home to Louisiana. Was I ready for the trip to end? What challenges would I face, on these final miles? What were the challenges I would face once I got back home? Would I, could I, see the event through to its end? Would my luck hold out with the weather, the Glide, and, most importantly with my attitude? These were questions to be pondered as I set out on the last 1,500 miles.

Leaving Key West, I had to put on my rain jacket and drive through moderate showers all the way to Key Largo. At Key Largo there was heavy construction and an accident that had traffic stopped both ways. Several cars were turning around and going back south into Key Largo and I decided to follow suit. Once again, Jill came to the rescue and I found Card Sound Road that got me around the traffic problems. Card Sound Road must have been constructed as an alternative to U.S. 1. Except for one river crossing where they collected a toll, the traffic kept moving at a good pace. Near Homestead, I picked up Rte 997 instead of taking the Florida Turnpike. This turned out to be a poor choice due to heavy traffic and an endless number of stoplights. After eventually reaching U.S. 41, I stopped for gas and water. The temperature was in the mid 90's and I was sure the heat index was well into the 100's.

Meeting three riders from St. Louis who were on their way to Key West, I shared the traffic information with them and showed them how to get to Card Sound Road. I suggested the Spindrift Motel, but it seemed they had other lodging plans. While I was getting fuel, a woman rider pulled up on a Gold Wing and was met by several other riders. They were going to a Christian Motorcycle Association (CMA) rally in Tennessee. As we talked, I told them how the Slidell CMA chapter had been a strong supporter of RTR and that several of my fellow H.O.G. brethren were also CMA members. Just as I was leaving, a guy rode in on a Sportster with this girlfriend on the back end. They were really loaded down with gear, but no rain suits. I could see that the girl wanted to get off the bike for a while, but her old man would have nothing to do with that and off they went without even a water break. Not my idea of a fun time, but then, I wasn't calling the shots. It was interesting to note how different each of these groups had been. The world of motorcycling is more varied than the average Joe thinks.

Highway 41 cuts right through the Florida Everglades with only a couple of places to stop for fuel and, more importantly, water. In a pinch, I guess one could always wring out his shirt, which would no doubt be saturated from the high humidity. One stop on the route was the National Park Center where I got some great pictures of several alligators lounging in a nearby ditch. The day was really turning into a steam bath, but I pushed on towards Fort Meyers which was my destination for the night. I took an ABC picture at the Ochopee Post Office, supposedly the smallest Post Office in the country. I tried to compare it in my mind's eye to the tiny one in Luckenbach, Texas, but, maybe, that one wasn't there any more. I wondered if Willie might know.

The sky started to darken with impending afternoon rain showers and I just missed getting caught in them before I found an EconoLodge motel in Fort Meyers. I asked the desk clerk for a room with a good WiFi connection and she assured me the one I was getting had a strong signal. Unfortunately, she apparently did not know much about the hotel's WiFi system and I had trouble getting on line. Later that evening as I was outside watching the streaks of lightning flash across the sky, I met the owner of the motel who, interestingly enough was also named Mr. Patel. (I didn't inquire if they were related to my East Indian hosts at the motel in Old Saybrook, Connecticut, but I thought about it. Perhaps the Patels were going to be like the Hiltons one day. Then I shook my head to get the road-spanned fantasies out of it and went on about the business of an internet connection.) After I explained the WiFi situation, he said he would move me to another room the following day. I thought that was very nice of him considering the motel was booked up.

Journaling that night it came to me, once again, that I was beginning the final leg of the trip. I became reflective about the past months of riding. I started to realize this grand adventure would soon be at its end. Though there were several thousand miles of road still in front of me, I couldn't help but be a little regretful. I threw off the thought and didn't dwell on it. I had another talk with myself. I was not leaving anything. I was returning to Linda. I had pictures. I had a journal. I had a huge fund of memories and experiences which would take a long time to digest. I began to feel better about it all. Then, of course, I thought about what was lacking. For instance, it was a shame that the plans to film and record the trip hadn't worked out. I wanted to share what I had found. You can guess what that turned into. I had to remind myself again to look at the cup as half full. Finally, I got to sleep.

Thom Edison and Me

I spent most of the next day touring the Ford/Edison Museum. What a treat to revisit this historic place! My first visit had been sometime in the late 1970's. Even though it had not changed much, to a Thomas Edison fan like me, it was like seeing everything for the first time. Edison was one of my childhood heroes and I was fascinated with his life. Growing up, I wanted to be a chemist and inventor like old Thom, but could never quite cut the mustard when it came to the course work in school.

I was awash in history. Thomas Edison built a laboratory and several homes on 14 acres he had purchased in Fort Meyers back in the very early 1900's. It was here that Edison, Ford, and Firestone had developed a life-long friendship while they fished and enjoyed the lovely beaches of the surrounding area. Although best known for his work with electricity; the first commercial light bulb, the phonograph, the motion picture camera, and the movie studio, Edison was also interested in botanicals and natural science. While at the Fort Meyer location Edison experimented with several kinds of plants, looking for a more efficient way to produce latex for manufacturing rubber.

His laboratory, left untouched since he last used it in the 1930s, included the cot that Edison would use for his frequent catnaps during the his long work day. He had been known for working round the clock and was one of those individuals who could recharge his batteries with a 20 minute "power nap", although I don't think Mr. Edison would have used that exact term.

Motoring Florida, Thinking of Home

After touring the grounds for nearly three hours I headed out towards the local HD dealership to get my requisite pin. By now I had amassed quite a collection and actually had been forced to send some home in one of my shipments. At the dealership, I met Randy who was retired and originally from St Louis, Missouri. He was dropping off his bike for service before flying back to Missouri to visit his family. We talked about his retirement and how much he enjoyed having free time to pursue his many interests. I told him he was probably in the minority when it came to men enjoying their retirement. It has been my experience that too many guys found themselves with too much time on their hands. He understood what I was saying and he told me a couple of his friends went back to work part-time for that very reason.

It was now mid afternoon and once again the sky was bubbling up with dark clouds. The sound of thunder accompanied me on my way back to the hotel. As promised, the innkeeper moved me to a room with a better internet connection and I caught up on some much needed correspondence. Dinner was at a local mall where I planned on taking in a movie, but nothing caught my fancy. My funds were getting low anyway and I couldn't justify going to movie just to do something. So, as the old saying goes: "When the going gets tough the tough go shopping". My shopping was, of necessity, limited to window shopping, but I got some much needed exercise walking around the mall. I could sense that I was getting bored or perhaps burned out from the road. Even with short riding days and two night stops, my stamina was fading. Although my day at the Edison complex was a treat, I wondered how many more really interesting days lay ahead for me. Regardless of how I now felt, I was still on the rim and committed to seeing the project through to its end.

After an early start it was off to St Petersburg. Once on the road, I let my mind wander to a "spoofing" problem with my RTR email. Evidently someone was sending emails with my address and spamming other folks with lots of trash messages. My hosting company told me there was nothing they could do about it. If that was really the case, why was I paying them for a "secure" hosting spot on their server? I groused about it to myself as I rode. While there was nothing I could do about it at that particular moment, the diversion was a welcome as the scenery on U.S. 41 offered little to look at.

Riding at a leisurely pace, I once again reviewed the events of the past months and how enjoyable they had been. Those thoughts were coupled with the anticipation of getting back home and off the road. I knew it was a good sign when I could appreciate where I had been but was looking forward to where I was going. If it were not for the media event planned in Sarasota and the "Ride Home" event planned with my H.O.G. chapter, I could easily be back in Mandeville in two or three days. The weight of staying in hotels, eating restaurant meals, and the heat seemed to intensify with each day. I found myself losing focus and not appreciating the adventure that each day brought. I had another talk with myself. Six months down the road, I did not want to look back with regret because I had not been fully aware and engaged in the last part of the trip. Terry! Wake up! Get involved! "The time is now; the place is here. There are no ordinary moments" (Those are not my words they come from a wonderful book by Dan Millman titled *Way of the Peaceful Warrior*. A good read should you ever come across it.)

The ride through Sarasota and then St Petersburg was unremarkable. On my way to Tampa I saw a sign for the Ringling Brothers Circus Museum in Sarasota and decided to visit it the next day. Other than that, there was only road, except for a rather crucial milestone. The Gulf of Mexico was on my left all the time. Now I really was on the Gulf Coast and I would stay on the Coast all the way home. I followed I-75 across the Tampa Bay Bridge which was a very impressive structure. Out of the flat plains of the Florida landscape, this monster rose above the bay and arched its way over to Tampa. I made a mental note to get a picture on my way back to Sarasota the next day. I had bypassed Sarasota because I was ahead of schedule and had decided to spend the night in Tampa. There was nothing in particular I wanted to see; it just seemed like a good place to lay my head down. To be able to do something just because I wanted to, what a luxury! And moments before, I was complaining about being on the road. Although it was still early afternoon, I found a reasonably-priced motel in Tampa. I had started to get off the road earlier and earlier each day to avoid the heat and my requirements for lodging now included a pool. In this case, my quick dip in the pool to cool off from the day's ride was cut short by the usual afternoon storms, so there was time for a leisurely nap before heading out for dinner at a local diner.

It would be a short trip back to Sarasota so I made time for a stop at Jim's HD shop in St Petersburg the next morning. There, I met several riders who were out for an early morning putt. We exchanged road information and I got some good advice on finding the Ringling Museum in Sarasota.

Stopping on the south end of the Tampa Bay Bridge, I took several pictures of the bridge shrouded in haze from the early morning humidity.

Circus Time

The Ringling Museum is actually three venues: the Ringling Mansion, the Ringling Art Museum, and the Ringling Brothers Circus Museum. Sarasota had been the winter headquarters for the Ringling Brothers Circus for many years. Here, John Ringling had built an elaborate winter mansion for his wife Mabel and their family. In their travels to Europe seeking new acts for the circus, they purchased antiques and pieces of art to decorate their Venetian-style mansion. The mansion was decorated in rare Italian marble with rich tapestries hanging from the high walls of the main room. We were told the mansion looked today much as it had when the Ringling family lived in it. We learned about the heydays of the big top, as well as its demise. With the advent of modern day arenas, the days were numbered for the "big top" tent that was so closely identified with the traveling circus. Today very few shows actually have a tent-style circus.

The art museum had several exhibits on loan as well as permanent exhibits from the collections amassed by John and his wife. The museum was mostly graced with art from Europe and, while I don't know much about art, I could still appreciate the beauty of the paintings and sculptures. I followed a guided tour through one of the exhibits titled "Saints and Sinners" and learned some interesting trivia about early Christianity and its artwork. Also on the grounds of the mansion, which is now owned by the city of Sarasota, there are several buildings containing circus artifacts, from the early circus days up to the present time. The experience was very impressive and well worth the visit, should your travels ever take you to Sarasota.

I had always been fascinated with the circus, as most young boys are. Baraboo, Wisconsin was at one time the summer home to the Ringling Brother Barnum Bailey Circus. It had been many years since I last visited there, but memories of it flooded back to me as I walked through the exhibits in Sarasota. I had actually worked at a circus, selling toys and souvenirs, when it came to Madison, Wisconsin where I grew up. On one of these occasions, the boss man refused to pay me until the show closed on Sunday night and then only after I helped take down some of the high wire rigging. My fear of heights kicked in and I promptly called my dad who drove over to the arena and chewed the guy out for taking advantage of me. Although my employment under the big top was short lived, I fell under the trance of circus life, which ultimately led to traveling with a carnival as a barker. But, that is a story for another day.

Milestones

With some time to kill before meeting up with my host Jan who was my Sarasota contact, I looked for a mall and perhaps a Barnes and Noble. With Jill's help, I located a mall near my meeting point with Jan, but found no coffee shop. Pushing Jill to her limits, I located a BAM (Books – A – Million) not far away and, after a few wrong turns, found myself pulling into their parking lot as the skies looked ready to open up with the predictable afternoon rain shower. Seeing an overhang by the front door, I eased the Glide onto the sidewalk and parked her there like I owned the place. Unknown to me, the release of the new Harry Potter novel was scheduled for that evening and the store was getting ready with some special attractions. Several of the clerks were dressed up as characters from the book and one guy in particular looked very much like Harry himself. Enjoying my cup of Joe, I noticed a guy setting up a massage chair. He motioned me over and told me he was giving free massages as a way to drum up future business. I am usually not one for getting a massage, even though I once dated a very good massage therapist. However this fellow was insistent and gave me one heck of a good neck rub. He noted how tense the muscles were in my back and asked about motorcycle riding. I didn't go into the 15,000 plus miles I had ridden over the last three months but I briefed him on the ride and its rigors. I left feeling pretty loose and relaxed.

I met up with Jan and he guided me to his condo which he and his wife had graciously offered to me for the next couple of nights. I contacted their H.O.G. chapter early in the planning phase of the project and they were very enthusiastic about setting up an event. This was still another example of fellow H.O.G. members extending a helping hand to a rider out on the road. After settling in at the condo, I spoke with my son Adam and learned his time in Vero Beach had been productive. Job opportunities were looking good with a couple of airlines.

He was going to Europe the following week to travel with three of his high school friends for three weeks. What a way to end your college years and begin a new job! He and I talked about the trip before I left. He had been concerned about taking a vacation when he didn't have a job. I strongly encouraged him to take the trip and worry about work later. Ironically, this was similar to advice my mother had given me which, of course, I had not taken. Many of my early years were spent working and I missed out on some great experiences. I was happy that Adam was not following in my footstep in this particular instance.

Dinner with members of the H.O.G chapter was at a nondescript restaurant which served up some good local seafood. After a lengthy meal, they were all set to go bar-hopping, but I politely begged off, claiming a long day in the saddle. Interestingly enough, my abstention from alcohol had never been an issue with the many riders I had met nor with those who had been my hosts; so much for the hard drinking-biker image. Back at the condo, I relaxed and caught up on my personal journal. I worked on coordinating the Ride Home event with AWF and the Northshore H.O.G. chapter. I tried to think things through because it was an event that could get tricky, considering all the players involved. Linda had a good suggestion: Why not make it to Bay St. Louis, Mississippi over the next few days to attend the TriState Respiratory Conference. I could hang out there until Friday and make the ride into Slidell for the event. Once again, the voice in my head told me to take it easy, enjoy the ride, and worry about the destination later. It sounded like a plan to me, though I thought I should check this out with Mary and Lisa.

The next day marked three months on the road for me. My hosts in Sarasota arranged for an event at Rossiter's HD and when I arrived at the dealership they were having an open house and barbeque. I was warmly greeted by several of the H.O.G. chapter members and we sat around eating delicious burgers while sharing road stories. They wanted to know all the details about the ride, including how it was to live on the road for three months; what was the best part and worst experience, and was I looking forward to getting back home. My answers, now rehearsed from similar conversations came easily. Living on the road had its moments, but, at times, the loneliness of a hotel room and the empty seat next to you in a diner got old. My best experiences were those that were not planned but the ones that just happened, like meeting Mike, the violin player in San Francisco, or Rosalie in the small New Brunswick fishing village. The worst experience, hands down, was the wind on the Mojave Desert. Was I anxious to get home? Yes, of course, but I was trying to take the road one mile at time and not dwell on the end of the trip. As I talked, I saw several appreciative nods in the audience and I knew I was among my brethren. Sharing road stories with other riders had become one of the most enjoyable parts of the trip. The discussion often was more braggadocio than actual fact, but it was usually entertaining. For the most part however, riders were eager to share stories of their favorite ride, the worst road, and where to get a good meal. Food always played a part in any ride. I especially enjoyed hearing how other riders handled problems on the road, what gear they traveled with, and who they had met.

The chapter planned a ride to Myakka State Park which has one of the largest inland wetland areas in Florida. Myakka Park was a part of a plantation at one time, and the land was later donated to the state. A reporter and film crew showed up from SNN Channel 6, the local Comcast affiliate. The reporter interviewed me and a couple of the chapter members and then we did a shoot with her signing off the broadcast while riding on the back of the Glide. She had never ridden on a motorcycle, but she did a great job. Our group of about 20 took off towards the park, with a film crew member riding with one of the chapter members. As we entered the park, the skies started to open up in a typical Florida thunderstorm. The poor camera man was only wearing a tee shirt and I am sure he felt the sting of rain drops as we rode into the park. It was Florida and rain was to be expected. The rain finally let up and he got some great film of us riding in formation. Even with the torrential downpour, everyone's spirits were high as we pulled into the nature center. Although we were good and soaked, it was a beautiful place. The road was lined with lush tropical foliage and teeming with brightly colored birds. I gave a short presentation on the wetlands and the reasons behind RTR. Of course, everyone present, including the camera man, got an RTR ride pin. Eventually the group started to saddle up for the ride back into town.

A couple on a Fat Boy volunteered to get me back to my condo. Halfway there, the sky once again opened up and we had to pull off and take refuge under the overhang of a church. The rain was coming down in sheets and the wind started to pick up. We were soaked to the skin and with the wind, actually started to feel a chill. While waiting for the rain to subside, I learned that Danny and his wife, my guides, met in Sarasota when he had come down from Michigan to find work. Neither were bikers before they met, but now motorcycling was an important part of their social life and were active in the Sarasota H.O.G. chapter.

Finally, the rain let up enough for us to get back on the road and after a short ride I was back at the condo, drying off and doing laundry. I planned on meeting friends for dinner that night, but decided to cancel on them in order to watch for the RTR piece on TV. Sure enough, at 2000, the Channel 6 piece came on and was repeated every hour. They did a great job on the editing, although I wished they could have dropped a couple of inches off my waistline. I was glad that this event had been scheduled. The publicity we had gotten for RTR was worth dragging my feet for a couple of days to keep the date. Once again, I reminded myself that it was all about faith, about getting out of the way to let things unfold as they are meant to be.

I had a restless night with very little sleep and woke up with a sour stomach. Do I sound like an old man or what! The plan was to meet up with the Rossiters H.O.G. Chapter and accompany them on their annual breakfast ride to a restaurant in St. Petersburg. There was a small, but enthusiastic group at the dealership and we were led by Matt, a rider who looked like he had many miles under his belt. I decided I would forgo the breakfast and split off from the group once we crossed the Sunshine Skyway Bridge in Tampa. Matt did a good job of keeping us together and, it being Sunday, the traffic was light. The clouds from the day before persisted and we rode in a light mist, but most of us did not put on any rain gear. After saying my goodbyes to the group, I continued north. There, the light rain gave way to a beautiful blue sky with floating, white, puffy clouds that, somehow, reminded me of the opening credits from the Simpson's TV show. Matt and the group told me to take Veterans Expressway, a toll road, and although it cost $7.00, it was well worth it considering the minimal stops I would encounter. There was no place to stop for fuel, but the guys from Rossiters had forewarned me to top off before I got to the toll gate. The expressway ended at U.S. 98 and I headed west towards the Gulf to pick up FL 19 at Bayonet Point. Hwy 19 was a great road with four lanes. It coursed through small towns that were separated by stretches of smooth payment lined with long leaf pine trees. I passed through Crystal River, Otter Creek and Fanning Springs before reaching my night's destination at Perry.

A Day's Inn offered a good room rate but horrible internet service. However, just down the street was a Hampton Inn where I was able to log on after explaining my situation to the desk clerk. I received a call from Rob who was checking up on me and wondering about my plans for the final leg of the trip. It was really great hearing from him and catching up on things back in Mandeville. After dinner I took a stroll down to the local Wal-Mart just to do some window shopping. Forgetting that it was Sunday, I caught them just as they were closing, but the walk was still nice and it felt good to stretch my legs. I finally felt like I had settled into a comfortable routine for the last few miles: Up early to get on the road and into a motel by 1400 or 1500 in the afternoon. Kick back, journal, grab some dinner and go for a walk. Hey, this wasn't so bad, but how was I ever going to adjust to a regular work schedule again?

The next day, July 23rd, I passed the 16,000 mile mark and with the cool morning air in my face, I continued on my route west. The ride was great. The road was canopied by hardwood trees that replaced the long leaf pines of the day before. I had the road to myself, with the exception of a few fast moving lumber trucks. At Hwy 267, I entered the Apalachicola National Forest which took me on a more northerly course that cut out a lot of small town traffic. The temperature stayed cool and it was a real treat riding without sweating through my gear. After exiting the forest, I once again got on a more westerly course using Hwy 20, which roughly parallels I -10. Going first through Freeport and Valparaiso, and then staying north of Destin, I avoided the beach traffic. It was the peak of summer vacation time and that would have meant a lot of tourist traffic. My destination for the evening was a Holiday Inn in Crestview, Florida which was just off of I-10. Swinging north on FL 85, I reached the hotel by early afternoon and got settled in.

After several conferences with Lisa and Mary, we finalized the plans for the Ride Home event. We decided to combine our event with another one at Mike Bruno's Northshore Harley Davidson in Slidell, Louisiana, hoping to dovetail with their publicity. Mary was contacted by a New Orleans radio station that wanted me to come in for an interview when I returned. The RTR team was still pushing hard for all the media attention that we could garner. I can't say enough about their hard work and dedication to the project.

That evening, I noticed how frayed my riding gloves had gotten. Was this some sort of sign that it was time for the ride to end? Was it time for me to try on, not only a new pair of gloves, but also a new outlook on life. Was it time to get off this road and onto a new, but not necessarily better, path? Oh! So many questions, with so few answers. A line from Sam Keene's *Fire in the Belly: On Being a Man* came to mind, "Seek not the answer but live in the question…"

The next morning, I woke up to the sound of thunder accompanied by an intense display of lightning. It felt wonderful to just hunker down under the covers and wait the storm out. My thoughts went immediately to Linda and how nice it would have been for her to be here with me. We both loved the rain, especially during one of Louisiana's infamous hot summer nights. You could smell the storm even before the sheets of hard rain started to fall. For a brief time the hot, heavy air turned cool as the thunder and bolts of lightning sparked up the skies. We would often put on a pot of Community coffee and sit on our front porch, taking in the light show that Mother Nature was providing. It was the equivalent of going to a drive-in theater where you could enjoy a great show without the confines of being in a building.

The rain continued through breakfast but, by 0900, it had slowed to a light drizzle. As I was packing the Glide, I met a couple from Illinois who were traveling with their son in a very tightly packed Shelby Cobra Mustang. For those of you who have never heard of this marvelous piece of machinery, it is the epitome of the classic muscle car. My friend Dick often spoke of the one he had owned. As I chatted with the couple, I could imagine Dick tucked behind the steering wheel, revving up the ponies under the hood and looking for another "cool cat" to race against. Both of them were riders and he had an Ultra Classic. Like me, he enjoyed long distance riding and his son told me about a couple of trips he has taken with his parents on their bikes. I never had the opportunity to take my boys on a road trip when they were this lad's age, and I wondered if they would have become as enamored with motorcycling as this young man was.

The short ride to Mobile on the now familiar roads made me realize the end of the ride was right around the next bend. Nearing Mobile I decided to visit the small community of Bayou La Batre which is south of Mobile on Rte 188. This small fishing village was the location of the Bubba Gump Shrimp Company portrayed in the movie *Forrest Gump*. Mobile Bay and the surrounding waters are a rich source for shrimp, crab and commercial fishing as Forrest and his old friend Lieutenant Dan discovered. (Hollywood must have liked what they saw in this quaint town because it was later used in the movie *Pirates of the Caribbean: Curse of the Black Pearl* starring Johnny Depp.) On this particular day, most of the fishing boats were out to sea and with nothing much else to look at, I turned the Glide around and headed towards Mobile. Pulling out I could almost hear Forrest telling me, "Life is like a box of chocolates, because you never know what you are going to get." You go, Forrest.

I headed up to Saraland and got a room at a Days Inn. A Ruby Tuesday's restaurant within walking distance provided dinner that evening. My cell phone's battery was starting to wear out and was no longer holding a charge, so I investigated several of the new models at an AT&T store nearby. After a good cup of dark rich southern coffee, not my Community chicory blend, but then after three months of drinking the thin, dark water that Yankees call coffee, I wasn't going to complain. As I sat savoring my coffee, I drifted back to my earlier thoughts about my friend Dick and his Shelby Cobra Mustang.

It might have been that, down deep inside of me, there was a hidden "muscle car" guy crying out for a new experience. Perish the thought! What would all my tree-hugging, global-warming friends say if I pulled up at a DNC meeting with that ride? Snapping back to reality (or sanity) I went over the previous day's discussion with Mary. The Ride Home event was getting firmed up, but I was not sure how many bikes and riders would show up. Media coverage was another unknown, but I would be coming home, that's what was important!

The Brim of the Rim

Later that evening, I got a call from Mary. She had me scheduled on the WRNO Jim Brown radio show for Friday and an appearance on WWL-TV on the following Tuesday in New Orleans. She was somewhat apprehensive about scheduling events that would follow the conclusion of the ride so closely, but I assured her that, although the ride was drawing to an end, my commitment to AWF, the Coast Guardians, and restoring our wetlands would continue. I told her to set up any media opportunities that came up and not to worry about my schedule.

I was in a reflective mood that evening as I made a journal entry. I had no regrets about the trip or that it was nearly at its end. I had ridden and seen more than I could have ever imagined. Other than not interviewing people about their passions in life, I believed I had experienced, at some level, everything I set out to do and more. Even with fewer media events than I had hoped for, I believed that we made a difference in wetland awareness; a difference for the coastline; a difference in my attitude about life; and a difference in my approach to the future and my perceptions about the past. I planned to continue to journal after the ride, perhaps daily, because it had become one of the most welcome parts of my day.

While packing up the Glide the next morning, I received a call from Mary about an interview with the local Fox affiliate, Channel 10, in Mobile. Her timing was great, as usual, and the station was on my way out of Mobile. We did the piece out in the parking lot and the cameraman got some great shots of the Glide as I answered the reporter's questions. I could tell she enjoyed being in the morning sun and we had a rather long, in depth, discussion. By now, you could probably guess what she asked and how I responded. As we were wrapping things up, her camera man wanted to get some shots of me riding the Glide as I pulled out their parking lot. We did three takes and they waved me off as I headed towards the highway.

On the short ride to Bay St. Louis, Mississippi, the traffic was heavy, but I kept up a good pace at 70 mph and only hit a little congestion around the casino exits as I entered Mississippi. That part of the Gulf Coast had several casinos, most of which were rebuilt after Katrina. Not being a big gambler, I usually only went there when I was working a show or on a speaking gig. At the Mississippi border, I got an ABC picture and really felt like the trip was coming to its end. Home was really just one state line away.

I remembered there was a B&N at the Gulfport, MS exit and, with the morning still young, a strong cup of Joe seemed in order. Enjoying my coffee, I flipped through a couple of car buying guides. I had promised Linda that I would get rid of my gas-guzzling pickup truck and buy something that was gentler on the environment and on our fuel budget. She had been driving a hybrid for the last several years and was pushing me in that direction. A hybrid seemed like a good choice and it would certainly be more acceptable to my tree hugger friends than the Mustang I had been fantasizing about, and, of course, I would stay on Linda's good side, too.

I landed in Bay St. Louis and found a room in a strip motel on U.S. 90. While not the ritziest of accommodations, it was clean and safe. It seemed like a fitting way to spend my last night on the "rim". My accommodations had run the gambit from the Hummingbird Motel in Aberdeen, Washington to the Sportsman in Malta, Montana, the luxury of a Crown Plaza in Washington, D.C., and, now, the motel in Bay St. Louis. My room would not be ready until mid-afternoon, so I set off for the TriState Respiratory Care meeting which was being held at one of the local casinos. I was greeted warmly by my coworkers and several of the conference attendees who had been following my travels on the RTR web site. It felt good to be hanging out with them, but I was not used to being around a "business crowd" so I slipped out when the opportunity arose. I tried to figure out my uneasiness. I was still dressed in my riding gear, so I felt a little conspicuous. Also, the day's heat and humidity had taken its toll on me and I was bit rank! To be honest, I thought there might be another reason for my "antsy-ness." The next day, I would be off to Hutchinson Street.

Journey's End

The trip home was short sweet and uneventful, which was just fine with me after 92 days and 16,000 plus miles of riding. As I rode into Louisiana on I-10, I spotted the "Welcome to Louisiana" sign and, attached to it, an

America's WETLAND sign! My thoughts once again, as they had over the last several days, shifted to thinking about the conclusion of the trip. Was this the end or just the beginning? Was there really an end point for the "Rim" or would the RTR project perpetuate itself? What will the next phase of the RTR look like— workshops, books, who knew? Was this only a brief pause in my life, a rest stop on the perpetual highway of self discovery? What was it that I would choose to become? Oh, so many questions and still so few answers. In the coming days, I had several events already scheduled and then, of course, there was the Ride Home event so it was best to stay current and get out of the future until a later time.

Turning off I-12 onto the familiar U.S. 190, I took in all the subtle changes that had occurred to Mandeville during my absence. Time had not stood still for three months. The post-Katrina construction boom was still strong on the Northshore where so many had fled from New Orleans. It seemed there were new businesses and more people. There weren't actually major changes, just a sense that the place had changed in my time away. Or perhaps I had changed and was seeing the familiar with new eyes. That was a good thought. Wasn't that what I had set out for? I wanted the people of the United States to view the danger to the wetlands and the coast differently, and I wanted to get a new viewpoint on life for myself. Here was proof that RTR had been a success. Whether it was or was not may or may not be debatable, but one thing was certain, I had changed. By 1030 I was in my driveway putting the kick stand down on the Glide, saying farewell to the Rim, and saying hello to my next experience.

The next day, I had a late morning phone interview with a local radio station host who had been an early supporter of the project. Later that day, I got a few minutes of air time with another show. Both of these went well. By now, I was a seasoned pro at getting the most information squeezed into the smallest amount of air time. Sitting in my home office being interviewed was a bit strange. I kept on thinking it was time to pack up my gear and get the Glide ready to role to the next destination. My little lap top that had served me so well on the rim was now replaced by a 19" monitor and I was sitting at a real desk. What had been so unique during the early days of the trip became the norm, the standard that I judged everything else by. Getting back into life off the rim was going to take more of an adjustment than I had imagined.

I was alone in the house for most of day and I busied myself with going through the stacks of mail that had accumulated for three months. I ventured out to the local B&N and, for the first time in over three months, was driving something other than the Glide. In addition to the size difference, I was driving a truck; the deafening roar of silence as I rode with the windows up and the air conditioning on was a startling contrast to the deep rumble from the Glide that I had become accustomed to. The next day would be the "Ride Home" and the official ending of my trip.

The weather forecast for the next day called for storms in the evening, but I was determined to make the Ride Home a true "ride home", even if it meant a wet ride home. The rain fizzled out by late afternoon and I, once again, put on my riding gear for the trip over to the rendezvous spot for the night's event. The group that met me at the 1-10 Welcome Center was small, but I was grateful to those who did show up. We rode as a group, Harley, Honda, and BMW riders, to the HD dealership. With the Northshore H.O.G. Chapter's flag flapping in the wind on one of the member's bike, we rode into the parking area which was filled with people attending the bike night event. Linda and several of our friends were there and I was overwhelmed by the support that everyone had given me, not only by coming out that evening, but also over the previous three months and the long months of planning. A rider and his young son came over to talk with me. The young man had several questions and I could see the look of a future long distance rider in his eyes. America's WETLAND Foundation sent a media person to interview me and we all had a great time.

Suddenly, it was time for my last media event. The spot on WWL TV's morning show went very well. The show's producer, a biker, had requested that I bring the Glide with me this time and I was happy to accommodate her. I rolled the Glide right into their studio and the deep rumble of her pipes got the attention of the show's hosts. With the ride over, I turned my thoughts to my life in the days ahead. Later that day, Duke called and we set up a meeting to discuss employment issues the following week. The post-ride planning had started. I looked at my journal and read words that were very dear to me:

"This is my last entry"

Smallest U.S. Post Office – Ochopee, FL.

H.O.G. chapter at Rossiter's HD – Sarasota, FL

The road home.

To view additional pictures of the Gulf Coast go to www.ridingtherim.com

Part III:
After the Ride

Home Again

*I*t had been a busy week and, after four days, I was somewhat getting used to not being on the road. The quietness of riding in a car was still a novelty to me and, of course, Linda and I were getting re-acquainted and accustomed to living together again. We talked about how we had been apart for almost three years and that each of us had become more independent and set in our ways. We both knew that there was a happy medium and that it was just a matter of time before we found it. For now it was off to Gulf Shores, Alabama, in a car, for some R&R at the beach.

Lessons from the Rim

Afterward, not long after, but when my back didn't ache, and the windburn faded from my face, and the tension of riding left my body, I looked back at the last few entries in my journal. As I re-read them, I felt a mixture of pleasure and sadness. I had felt such a sense of excitement and fulfillment. I had completed the ride. Linda was going to be working from home. The news was filled with much talk about re-building New Orleans. That was then. A lot has happened in the two years since then. It's time to do a summing up.

Adam was hired by a major airline and is happily flying as I write. I am happy to report that my other children are also doing well in their various careers and endeavors. We are truly blessed as a family and have much to say grace over around the table.

Linda found employment, albeit for a short time, in our area, and we were finally able to mesh our lives together. As of this writing, unfortunately, she is traveling again for work, a symptom of the economy. We again, for now and only for now, I hope, have a relationship punctuated by separations. It's a little different, though. I think that, during my RTR ride, recognizing how much we missed each other and how very much our brief reunions during the ride had meant to us, brought home to us both how very much we need each other and how much we value each other. Not a bad outcome of a springtime ride.

The Glide and I are still together. Although a bit worn, a little more frayed at the edges, and maybe with a little less spark in the old engine, I still manage to swing a leg over her saddle on a regular basis. Oh, SHE, the Glide, has not aged, other than the normal wear and tear that one would expect after 75,000 miles of road adventures. I am the one feeling the miles. All the same, she is one of the great loves of my life. We have been through a lot together and that is always the cement that binds love together. I have been asked whether I will ever trade her in for a new ride and my answer always has been and will always be– NEVER. Her rumble is strong, unlike mine (except when I eat something disagreeable) and besides, who other than I, can see the beauty under the faded paint and scratches? The memories of RTR flood back to me each time we hit the road. Leaving her behind to ride off on a new, flashier, bike would be like leaving a good friend stranded on the side of road. Sometimes, I am asked if there is another adventure waiting for me and the Glide, and what that adventure would be. Well, yes, but I am not sure. There are so many interesting places to see in this great land of ours that is hard to pick which one to visit first and, besides, I still need to bring home some bacon occasionally.

Linda and I are still involved in local and national events related to the wetlands. My good friends at America's WETLAND Foundation are still working hard at getting the message out there and I help whenever I can. I kept the promise I made when meeting Michael, the River Keeper from York, Pennsylvania. Linda and I have become involved in educating the public about the destruction of cypress trees for the production of mulch. After researching the topic, I was astounded by the methods used to obtain cypress mulch, so astounded that I need to share some of my research.

Briefly, cypress trees, "supposedly dead," are pulled out of the swamps. These "supposedly dead" trees are loaded on large vessels that, in themselves, destroy the natural state of the swamps and wetlands. The trees are sent to mills where they are turned into garden mulch. Supposedly, the cypress mulch is "good for the plants." Nonsense! While cypress mulch is highly sought by those who fancy its color and texture, it has little nutritional value for garden plants or shrubs. Further, there are very suitable alternatives, from both an aesthetic and environmental viewpoint, which are readily available and that do no ecological damage.

Linda and I do our best to bring this information to our neighbors, friends and local businesses who use or supply cypress mulch. I'm not sure they understand the science, but I hope they understand the passion with which I communicate the facts to them. And I am doing my part, too. After some "gentle" prodding from Linda, I traded my old gas-guzzling pick-up truck for a hybrid car. Both of us are concerned about the nation's dependence on fossil fuels and the carbon foot print we are leaving for our grandchildren. A few of my friends inquired about my motives for giving up my truck, wanting to know if it was more a matter of acquiescing to Linda's wishes, or from a real concern for the environment? To those who ask I refer to an old biker quote: "If you gotta ask, you just wouldn't understand".

The Recovery Continues

On the larger scene the economy is in a deep recession, we have a new President, brave men and women in our military are still dying on foreign soil, the New Orleans Saints may have a chance at the Super Bowl this year[*] (how many times have we heard that), and New Orleans politics is still making headlines in the national media (unfortunately we have heard this way too often).

What has this got to do with the RTR? Not much really other than that the recitation of these events illustrates the natural ebb and flow of life, the movement of the cosmic curtain that envelops us all, and the mystical aspects of life that no one can predict with any certainty. So it is with my life post-RTR. I resumed my position as a clinical specialist; returned to teaching; and continue to make the rounds as a professional speaker. As an outgrowth of the trip, I have developed a series of workshops and presentations using my experiences from RTR. I'd like to think my ride is continuing through these appearances, for there is still so much to be done.

There has been some progress on the wetland's front. The Army Corps of Engineers finally agreed to close off the Mississippi River Gulf Outlet (MRGO) which many felt was responsible for the loss of wetlands just south of New Orleans. Federal monies which were allocated in 2006 are just now starting to show up for smart levee construction and wetland restoration. Diversion projects which move silt and fresh water from the Mississippi River into the marsh are to be built and river bottom soil that is annually

---

[*] The Saints won the 2010 Super Bowl. Miracles do happen.

dredged from the river is to be used as fill to create a foothold for new wetland foliage. We'll see.

All of this is good but unfortunately we are still losing the battle against the Gulf. For each precious mile of wetlands restored several more get gobbled each year by salt water intrusion.** The most important step has yet to be taken. The restoration of the barrier islands south of the Mississippi River's mouth has been largely ignored. They are the first line of defense in preventing a tidal surge from coming across the marsh and through our rivers, lakes and bayous. Unfortunately, these barrier islands, little more than spits of sand, are all but gone, victims of the ever-present erosion by the Gulf abetted by the apathy from Washington. Compounding the problem is the rising sea level which many, including myself, attribute to global climate change. Whether you believe in this phenomenon or not, you cannot ignore the clear evidence that sea levels are rising everywhere on the planet. Whatever finger of blame you choose to point, it is no longer possible to ignore the obvious.

It sounds rather bleak, but not all has been lost. The wakeup call from Mother Nature has not gone unheeded and there is a renewed sense of urgency that something must be done. There has been a heightened level of awareness across the country that time may be running out. The time for studies and conferences is past. Many citizens are clamoring for action rather than words. Many are now aware there will be a point where wetland and coastal loss surpasses man's ability to restore them.

What of New Orleans? New Orleans, my beloved city, the jewel of the South; what of her? The news again is mixed. Rebuilding continues, albeit on a slower track than most would like to see, but there has been progress. There are parts of the city that still look as they did immediately after Katrina. Perhaps they will never be rebuilt; perhaps they should never have been built in the first place. But the bright light of hope burns in more homes at the time of this writing than it did when I left New Orleans on that sunny day in April of 2007.

One example is the rebuilding of the Lower Ninth Ward in New Orleans. This area was destroyed during Katrina when the levees failed, allowing tidal surge from the MRGO to destroy almost 90% of the homes. Through the tireless efforts of Brad Pitt and his organization *Make It Right*, new housing has been built for those long-time residents who wanted to return. More importantly, because a catastrophic event such as Katrina

---

** As this book goes to print, the Deepwater Horizon oil disaster continues to destroy the fragile wetlands still recovering from Hurricanes Katrina and Rita.

is often the catalyst for new technology, these homes are being built using the latest "green technology" including solar power, renewable building materials, and ecologically sound construction methods. No one is so naive as to believe that a major storm will never threaten New Orleans again, and so these homes are designed to resist the destructive elements of a hurricane rather than bow to its wrath. Thank you Brad, and thanks to all those who are working to *Make It Right* once again in New Orleans.

In fact, the greatest news out of New Orleans has been the activism of those young people who have been moving into our city. New Orleans had been an aging city. Since the storm, there has been an influx of these young people who came to help rebuild and have stayed to make it their homes. I have a lot of hope for them. Many others, including some celebrities, have come, made an appearance and left with the promise to return. They may return. I hope they come back. Time will tell. This new generation, however, isn't going anywhere. They have come, they have sunk their roots, and they will not settle for the vague promises of the past. With every day that passes they are "making it right" by their very presence. "Like a tree that's planted by the water, they shall not be moved." It delights my heart. They too, have answered the call that set me on my journey. The response of these young re-builders may even be better than mine. My journey is ended. Theirs is ongoing.

So, where are we? Change has happened, change is happening, and I am grateful to be part of it. I would like to think that Riding The Rim was the catalyst for change that I hoped it would be. I found my voice somewhere during those 16,500 miles and I hope that I have helped those I met to find theirs. My last hope, my greatest hope is that, if you the reader have followed me on my journey to this point, you will now set out on a journey of your own. I once heard that the measure of a teacher is not how many students he has but rather the number of teachers he creates. The real success of RTR would be if it inspired the efforts of others. To anyone who may wonder how they can be part of change, whatever change it is that would move you to find your voice, I offer this advice from Mahatma Gandhi; "Be the change you want to see in the world".

Safe riding and keep the rubber side down.

Appendices

Appendix A: Route

Rim Day	Destination	Mileage between destinations	Cumulative mileage
Southwest Rim			
April 21	Jennings, LA	286	286
April 22	Clute, TX	238	524
April 23	McAllen, TX	379	903
April 24	Eagle Pass, TX	274	1177
April 25	Marathon, TX	237	1414
April 26	Marfa, TX	333	1747
April 27- 28	El Paso, TX	208	1955
April 29	Tucson, TX	378	2333
April 30	Flagstaff, AZ	287	2620
May 1	Kingman, AZ	195	2815
Pacific Rim			
May 2-3	San Diego, CA	386	3201
May 4	Ventura, CA	261	3462
May 5	San Louis Obispo, CA	138	3600
May 6	Half Moon Bay, CA	257	3857
May 7-8	Sausalito, CA	51	3908
May 9	Fort Bragg, CA	172	4080
May 10	Eureka, CA	149	4229
May 11	Crescent City, CA	88	4317
May 12	Florence, OR	190	4507
May 13	Eugene, OR	93	4600
May 14	Portland, OR	133	4733
May 15	Aberdeen, WA	204	4937
May 16-17	Seattle, WA	147	5084
May 18-20	Off the Rim to Ruston, LA		

Rim Day	Destination	Mileage between destinations	Cumulative mileage
Northern Rim			
May 21	Burlington, WA	81	5156
May 22	Kettle Falls, WA	301	5466
May 23	Kalispell, MT	302	5768
May 24-25	Malta, MT	362	6130
May 26	Kenmare, ND	401	6531
May 27	Roseau, MN	367	6898
May 28	Thunder Bay, ON	359	7257
May 29	Duluth, MN	211	7468
May 30	Houghton, MI	270	7738
May 31	Green Bay, WI	280	8018
June 1-5	Madison, WI	149	8167
June 6-7	Grand Rapids, MI	145	8312
June 8	Ann Arbor, MI	174	8486
June 9	Clyde, OH	220	8706
June 10	Toledo, OH	39	8745
June 11	Irving, NY	310	9055
June 12	Watertown, NY	293	9348
June 13	Burlington, VT	176	9524
Maritimes			
June 14	Saint-Hyacinthe, QB	112	9636
June 15	Quebec City, QB	192	9828
June 16	Woodstock, NB	337	10,165
June 17	Moncton, NB	183	10,348
June 18	Campbellton, NB	206	10,554
June 19	Miramichi, NB	365	10,919
June 20	Charlottetown, PIE	255	11,174
June 21	Truro, NS via Ferry	93	11,267
June 22	Halifax, NS	68	11,335

Rim Day	Destination	Mileage between destinations	Cumulative mileage
Eastern Rim			
June 23	Machias, ME	407	11,742
June 24	Brunswick, ME	261	12,003
June 25-26	Old Saybrook, CT	293	12,296
June 27	West Chester, PA	283	12,579
June 28-29	York, PA	70	12,649
June 30-July 1	Baltimore, MD	140	12,789
July 2-3	Washington, DC	70	12,859
July 4	Leesburg, VA	139	12,998
July 5	Absecon, NJ	228	13,226
July 6	Elizabeth City, NJ	337	13,563
July 7	Williamston, NC	170	13,733
July 8	Myrtle Beach, SC	251	13,984
July 9-10	Charleston, SC	98	14,082
July 11-12	Savannah, GA	113	14,195
July 13	Brunswick, GA	113	14,308
July 14	Vero Beach, FL	290	14,598
July 15-16	Key West, FL	307	14,905
Gulf Coast			
July 17-18	Fort Myers, FL	308	15,213
July 19	St. Petersburg, FL	161	15,374
July 20	Sarasota, FL	112	15,486
July 21	Myakka State Park, FL	59	15,545
July 22	Perry, FL	255	15,800
July 23	Marianna, FL	235	16,035
July 24	Mobile, AL	99	16,134
July 25	Bay St. Louis, MS	121	16,255
July 26	Mandeville, LA	56	16,311

Appendix B: Equipment

The Glide:
2005 Harley Davidson: HLRTI Road Glide. Color: Black Cherry.
Engine modifications: Big Bore -2 kit with 230 cam and Screaming Eagle exhaust.
Additional equipment: HD King Tour Pak, subtle longhorns handle bars Mustang One Piece touring seat with rider and passenger back rest, Alaskan Leathers sheepskin seat cover, Kuryakyn Switch Blade foot pegs

Luggage:
Nelson Riggs King touring bag, tank bag and trunk bag, Harley Davidson King Tour Pak and saddle bag liners

Tools and Emergency Supplies:
Pocket Plugger tire repair kit, tire pump, assorted American standard and metric wrenches and sockets, slotted and Phillips head screwdrivers. Vice grips, pliers, duck tape, electric and heat resistant tape, plastic ties, Quick Weld compound, trouble light, heat resistant glove, extra fuses and light bulbs, chemical glow sticks, security cables, first-aid kit, eye wash,

Riding Apparel and Clothing:
FXRG touring pants and boots, HD Switch Back jacket and 2-Piece rain suit, GOR-TEX rain gloves, Aerostich wind block fleece jacket and Roper gloves, Gerbing heated gloves and jacket Liner, Seal Skin waterproof socks, Fast Company Draggin jeans, Nolan N102 helmet, fleece balaclavas, safety vest, Blue Blocker sunglasses, Duofold wicking underwear and Performance SS tee shirts, Veritherm expedition weight thermal bottoms, cotton socks, AWF polo shirt and cap.

Maps and Navigation:
AAA Regional Maps: Southwestern States, Western States/Provinces, Central States/Provinces, Atlantic Provinces/Quebec, Northeastern States/Provinces, Southeastern States, Map compass and calipers, Microsoft Street and Trips mapping software

Electronics:
Panasonic digital camera and digital tape recorder, lap top computer and accessories
Garmin Zumo 550 GPS with XM Radio, WiFi finder, Nokia cell phone, assorted charging units and connections cables

Mobile Office Supplies:
Listing of business accounts, credit card number and on-line access information, 2 blank journals, calculator, pens, pencils, highlighters, stapler, paper clips, rubber bands, website account information, blank CD, USB drive, RTR business cards

Documents:
Motorcycle registration and inspection validation, HD extended warranty, motorcycle repair manual, living will, power of attorney and medical directive, proof of U.S. and Canadian insurance, U.S. Customs certification for proof of purchase: computer, GPS, tape recorder, camera, emergency contact cards, U.S. Passport, National Parks passport
Louisiana driver's license, VISA and Master credit cards, and bank cards

Etcetera:
Laundry detergent, fabric softener sheets, sun screen, insect repellant, Boudreaux's Butt Paste, assorted toiletries and personal care items

Appendix C: Websites of Interest

Riding The Rim: www.ridingtherim.com
America's WETLAND Foundation: www.americaswetlands.com
Environmental Defense Fund: www.edf.org
Ducks Unlimited: www.ducks.org
Make It Right: www.makeitrightnola.org
National Wetlands Inventory: www.fws.gov/wetlands
National Wetlands Research Center: www.nwrc.usgs.gov
Save Our Cypress: www.saveourcypress.org
Save Our Lake: www.saveourlake.org
Save Our Wetlands: www.saveourwetlands.org
Smart Growth America: www.smartgrowthamerica.org
Wetlands International: www.wetlands.org

LaVergne, TN USA
04 February 2011
215206LV00002B/58/P